When the State Speaks, What Should It Say?

When the State Speaks, What Should It Say?

· ·

How Democracies Can Protect Expression and Promote Equality

Corey Brettschneider

PRINCETON UNIVERSITY PRESS

Princeton and Oxford

Copyright © 2012 by Princeton University Press
Published by Princeton University Press, 41 William Street
Princeton, New Jersey 08540
In the United Kingdom: Princeton University Press, 6 Oxford Street
Woodstock, Oxfordshire OX20 1TW

press.princeton.edu

All Rights Reserved
Library of Congress Cataloging-in-Publication Data

Brettschneider, Corey Lang.
When the state speaks, what should it say? : how democracies can protect expression
and promote equality / Corey Brettschneider.
p. cm.
Includes bibliographical references and index.
ISBN 978-0-691-14762-8 (hardcover : alk. paper)   1. Freedom of speech.
2. Democracy.   I. Title.
JC591.B75 2012
323.44'3—dc23
2011047406

British Library Cataloging-in-Publication Data is available

This book has been composed in Bauer Bodoni

Printed on acid-free paper. ∞

Printed in the United States of America

1 3 5 7 9 10 8 6 4 2

For my mother, Susan Brettschneider

Contents

· · · · · · · · · ·

Acknowledgments

• •

I BEGAN THIS BOOK DURING A FACULTY FELLOWSHIP at the Edmond J. Safra
Center for Ethics at Harvard University. The Center was a wonderful place
to develop the ideas presented in this text. I am grateful to the director
of the Center, Dennis Thompson, for granting me the fellowship and for
leading our sessions. I learned a great deal from the fellows and faculty
associates, especially during two talks, when I presented drafts that were
later incorporated into the book. I found their own work and company to
be nothing short of inspiring. In particular I would like to thank Philip
Pettit, Archon Fung, Sarah Conly, Arthur Applbaum, and Jed Purdy for
their illuminating conversation. Nancy Rosenblum and Frank Michelman
in particular made several early suggestions that were very helpful. More
recently, I was invited back by my law school mentor, Lawrence Lessig,
who took over as director. I gained a great deal of insight during my
presentation to the Center's outstanding faculty and fellows, including
Larry, Eric Beerbohm, Tommie Shelby, Frances Kamm, Nir Eyal, Daniel
Viehoff, Moshe Cohen-Eliya, and Frank Michelman.

At Brown, I am lucky to have a group of political theorists who are
both brilliant and generous friends. John Tomasi, Sharon Krause, David
Estlund, and Charles Larmore are everything one could hope for in colleagues. I presented early versions of the book both in my Constitutional
Day Lecture, organized by John, and in our Political Philosophy Workshop. The sessions provided a chance to develop many of the ideas here,
especially those in chapter 3. Steven Calabresi provided helpful suggestions and good comments throughout my work on this project. I have
also benefited from our wonderful undergraduate and graduate students,
especially Huss Banai and Minh Ly, both of whom I expect will make their
own mark on our field soon. Minh in particular provided amazing research assistance and help in editing the book at all stages, for which I am
deeply grateful. His excellent, insightful, and substantive comments also
improved the argument of the book at many points. David McNamee and
Isaac Belfer talked over many of the ideas here and helped me to shape
them. Matt Hodgetts and Kevin McGravey gave great comments and, with
Jonathan Topaz and Risa Stein, helped to edit the page proofs.

Although I wrote this book years after I finished my PhD, in many ways
it grew out of discussions I had as a graduate student with my mentors
at Princeton University, especially Amy Gutmann, George Kateb, Stephen
Macedo, and Gilbert Harman. The faculty fellows at the time, especially

Joan Tronto, Simone Chambers, and Leif Wenar, also discussed ideas that influenced the book.

I had the privilege of presenting drafts of chapters before several workshops across the country. Jeff Spinner-Halev and his colleagues hosted me at the University of North Carolina, Chapel Hill, with Colin Bird joining us. The session ultimately resulted in an exchange between Jeff and me that was published in the journal Political Theory, and that shaped chapter 5 of this book. During that same trip, I also gained insight from a helpful discussion with Jack Knight.

I presented much of the material here on religion to the faculty workshop at Harvard Law School. I thank the participants for their comments, in particular Richard Fallon, Cora True-Frost, John Goldberg, and Benjamin Zipursky. At the University of Pennsylvania, I received terrific comments from Jeffrey Green, Rogers Smith, Ellen Kennedy, Samuel Freeman, and Nancy Hirschmann. At Columbia, I benefited from the insights of Melissa Schwartzberg and Mitchell Cohen. For a helpful session at the Yale Political Theory workshop, I thank Bryan Garsten, Steven Smith, Andrew March, and Paulina Ochoa.

I presented various parts of the manuscript twice at Princeton, once in the Program in Ethics and Public Affairs (PEPA) seminar and a second time during my fellowship at the University Center for Human Values. I am grateful for the fellowship and the earlier invitation. I thank the Center's director, Charles Beitz, for these opportunities and for his perceptive comments on the manuscript and enlightening conversation during the year. I remembered Princeton as providing an intense and satisfying intellectual experience when I was a graduate student, and I was thrilled to find it as vibrant as ever. For wonderful hospitality, collegiality, and comments on this project I thank Melissa Lane, Stephen Macedo, George Kateb, Alan Patten, Alan Ryan, Kim Scheppele, Tom Christiano, Jonathan Quong, Gerry Mackie, Anna Stilz, Tim Mulgan, Janet McClain, Nan Keohane, Bob Keohane, Jan-Werner Mueller, Erika Kiss, Jeff Stout, Eric Gregory, Elizabeth Harman, Leif Wenar, Brookes Brown, Colleen Murphy, Adrienne Martin, John Seery, and Alex Guerrero. Kristi Olson provided comments during my presentation at the Center and when the manuscript was nearing completion.

At the University of Colorado, I received astute comments from David Mapel and Steven Vanderheiden. In Australia, I had the pleasure of presenting both at the Australia National University and the University of Melbourne. I thank my hosts Bob Goodin and Adrienne Stone, as well as Christian Barry, Geoffrey Brennan, and John Dryzek.

I presented some of the material from this book at various meetings of the American Political Science Association and other regional meetings. I thank my fellow panelists from those meetings, especially Rob Reich,

Nancy Rosenblum, Steve Shiffrin, Anna Marie Smith, Eric Beerbohm, Tommie Shelby, Sarah Conly, Elizabeth Beaumont, and Brookes Brown.

Rob Reich and Austin Sarat reviewed the manuscript and provided extremely careful and helpful commentary that I used in my revisions. For insightful comments I also thank Eamonn Callan and John McCormick. Lucas Swaine offered valuable comments on a near final copy of the manuscript.

Some of this material and related ideas were previously published. An earlier version of chapter 2 was previously published as "The Politics of the Personal: A Liberal Approach," American Political Science Review 101 (February 2007): 19–31. An article version of chapter 4 appeared as "A Transformative Theory of Religious Freedom: Promoting the Reasons for Rights," Political Theory 38 (April 2010): 187–213. An article version of chapter 3 was published as "When the State Speaks, What Should It Say?" Perspectives on Politics 8 (December 2010): 1005–19. I would also like to thank my terrific editor, Rob Tempio, for his support of this project.

Finally, I thank my wonderful family, Alli Brettschneider, Sophie Brettschneider, Kim Brettschneider, Pat Heppell, Eric Brettschneider, Jeanne Rostaing, Robert Klopfer, John Weisz, and Jenny Weisz, for their support of me and my work. For a particularly helpful conversation about the book, I thank my friends John Leibovitz and Monica Lesmerises Leibovitz. I dedicate this book to my mother, Susan Brettschneider, who taught me from a young age that the personal is political.

When the State Speaks,
What Should It Say?

INTRODUCTION

· · · · · · · · · · · · · ·

Averting Two Dystopias

AN INTRODUCTION TO VALUE DEMOCRACY

A RECENT REPORT FROM the Southern Poverty Law Center suggests that hate groups advocating racist ideologies have been on the rise in the United States since the election of the first African American president.[1] In the advanced democracies of Europe, studies of public opinion show that anti-Muslim hostility is a growing problem.[2] As evidence mounts of increasing bigotry on both sides of the Atlantic, questions of how to respond to hate speech have become more pressing.

Traditionally, political and legal theorists have proposed two types of responses to hate speech. Some thinkers have stressed the need for a neutral approach to rights protection.[3] This group broadly defends the United States Supreme Court's current free speech jurisprudence, which does not protect threats or "fighting words," but does protect what I call "hateful viewpoints." Hateful viewpoints are opinions that are openly hostile to the core ideals of liberal democracy. In defining hateful viewpoints, it is important to emphasize that there is a distinction between the emotion of hate and the content of hateful viewpoints. Hateful viewpoints are defined not necessarily by their emotion, but by their expressing an idea or ideology that opposes free and equal citizenship. Those who hold hateful viewpoints seek to bring about laws and policies that would deny the free and equal citizenship of racial, ethnic, or religious minorities, women, or groups defined by their sexual orientation. The neutralist approach upholds free speech and protects hateful viewpoints from coercive sanction, despite their discriminatory content, because neutralism claims that the state should not endorse any values.[4]

In contrast to the neutralists, other thinkers have argued that free speech rights should not protect viewpoints that are hostile to the values of a liberal democratic society. Thinkers in this second group, the "prohibitionists," broadly endorse the kind of legal limits on hate speech that are found in most liberal democracies outside of the United States.[5] Although there are free speech protections in these countries, there is no legal doctrine of "viewpoint neutrality" that would extend the right of free speech to all viewpoints, including hateful ones. Some viewpoints are deemed too extreme to be tolerated, and they are prohibited, often by criminal law. For example, many liberal democracies believe that they cannot risk tolerating the fascist ideology that ultimately gave rise to the Nazi regime. They ban Holocaust denial and other viewpoints that are associated with the fascist ideology.

Most liberal democracies outside of the United States prohibit not only the fascist ideology, but the expression of hateful or discriminatory viewpoints more generally. These prohibitionist laws go beyond banning threats against specific individuals, and outlaw speech that displays hatred or animus toward ethnic, racial, or religious groups. For instance, section 319(2) of the Canadian Criminal Code bans public communication that "willfully promotes hatred against any identifiable group."[6] In the influential *Keegstra* case, the Supreme Court of Canada upheld the conviction under the Criminal Code of a teacher who had expressed and taught anti-semitic views.[7] The teacher had hatefully described Jews as "subversive" and "sadistic" "child killers" who had "created the Holocaust to gain sympathy."[8] Like the Canadian government, Australia has adopted national and regional human rights laws forbidding racist speech. The country's Racial Discrimination Act of 1975 prohibits public acts that "offend, insult, humiliate or intimidate people on the basis of their race, colour or national or ethnic origin."[9] The Federal Court of Australia ruled in 2002 that the Racial Discrimination Act banned Holocaust denial, and it ordered a defendant to remove material denying the Holocaust from an Internet site. In France, the former actress Brigitte Bardot has been convicted five times for violating hate speech laws, and fined up to 15,000 euros (equal to $23,000), for her anti-Muslim remarks. Bardot had referred to Muslims as "this population that is destroying us, destroying our country by imposing its acts."[10] Besides Canada, Australia, and France, other countries that ban hate speech include Britain, Germany, India, the Netherlands, and South Africa.[11]

Perhaps the most prominent case of prosecuting a particular ideology was found in the Netherlands. Dutch prosecutors in 2010 announced that they would try Geert Wilders for the crime of inciting hatred against Muslims. A sitting member of the Dutch parliament, Wilders had produced a film and had made repeated statements claiming that Islam was an inherently evil religion with no place in Dutch society. Although he was ultimately acquitted, Wilders would have faced two years in prison and the equivalent of more than $25,000 in fines if he had been convicted. According to prosecutors, Wilders' hate speech was incompatible with the egalitarian ideal at the heart of Dutch democracy.

The Dutch controversy regarding Wilders is striking in its differences from American political discourse. If a similar case occurred in the United States, the Supreme Court would most likely strike down any laws prohibiting a political viewpoint, no matter how heinous. An indictment like Geert Wilders' would be met by a chorus of criticism claiming that the government was attacking freedom of expression. Free speech advocates would be quick to argue that citizens, especially elected officials, have the right under the First Amendment to express their political viewpoints, even when those viewpoints are hateful or discriminatory. On this issue, the Dutch and American approaches to hate speech seem to be worlds apart. In the Netherlands, a focus on the ideal of equality makes it possible for the state to seek to defend equal citizenship by banning hateful speech. In the United States, an emphasis on rights of free expression makes such a proposal almost beyond consideration.

I find both of these approaches problematic. The neutralism popular in the United States fails to answer the challenge that hateful viewpoints pose to the values of freedom and equality—values that are essential to the legitimacy of the democratic state. As Simone Chambers and Jeffrey Kopstein point out, the viewpoints of hate groups such as the Ku Klux Klan and American Nazi Party constitute "bad civil society," in that they seek to undermine freedom and equality and thus oppose the core values of liberal democracy.[12] The problem for the neutralists is that hateful viewpoints threaten not simply any political ideal, but the very freedom and equality that justify protecting the rights of free speech for hate groups in the first place. In other words, hate groups attack the most basic ideal of public equality that underlies liberal democracy, an ideal I refer to as free and equal citizenship.

Although the neutralist approach to hate groups is problematic, the alternative approach, favored by the "prohibitionists," has its own drawbacks. The prohibitionist strategy of having the state coercively ban hate speech overlooks the fact that the core democratic values of freedom and equality require the state to allow citizens to develop and affirm their own political views. The prohibitionists fail to heed the importance of Meiklejohn's argument that free citizens need to be able to debate arguments, even those that challenge the foundations of liberal democracy. Without this freedom, citizens cannot endorse democracy itself.

I aim in this book to develop and defend a third position that resolves these problems. I suggest that we distinguish between a state's coercive power, or its ability to place legal limits on hate speech, and its expressive power, or its ability to influence beliefs and behavior by "speaking" to hate groups and the larger society. On my view, the state should simultaneously protect hateful viewpoints in its coercive capacity and criticize them in its expressive capacity. The state should respect the rights of these groups, but it should also use its expressive capacities to criticize their hateful views. In this way the state can protect the right to express all viewpoints and, at the same time, it can defend the values of freedom and equality against discriminatory and racist challenges. I use the term "discriminatory viewpoints" to refer to views that oppose or are inconsistent with the ideal of free and equal citizenship. "Hateful viewpoints" are extreme instances of discriminatory views. While individuals and groups are entitled to have their rights respected, they have no right to have their discriminatory or hateful views left unquestioned. I refer to the process of defending the values of free and equal citizenship as "democratic persuasion."

Part of this book will focus on how liberal democracy should respond to hateful viewpoints. But my broader ambition is to propose a liberal democratic theory, called "value democracy," that accomplishes two purposes: first, it should defend robust rights of free speech, religion, and association. This requires the state to refrain from coercively banning political viewpoints, religious groups, or civil associations, though the state should be allowed to coercively stop violence or threats against particular persons. Second, value democracy should articulate the reasons that justify why rights should be respected in the first place, and it should attempt to convince citizens to adopt the democratic values of freedom and equality as their own. These reasons for rights explain why the state and its citizens should uphold the rights of free speech, association, and religion for all persons who are subject to the coercive power of the government. In contrast to other democratic theories that are value neutral, my account bases democracy on the affirmative values of free and equal citizenship. These democratic values should be adopted by citizens and promoted by the state, because they ground the legitimacy of the government and justify protecting rights.

According to value democracy, all viewpoints should be protected by rights of free speech from coercive bans or punishment. But the state also has an obligation in value democracy that extends beyond protecting freedom of speech. It should engage in democratic persuasion, actively defending the democratic values of freedom and equality for all citizens when it "speaks." The notion of state speech is common in First Amendment jurisprudence. It often refers to the various non-coercive functions of the state, ranging from pure expression, such as speeches, to issues of funding. My wider theory of democratic persuasion draws on that doctrine to defend the active promotion of democratic values. But I want to clarify that the title of the book is not about the factual question of what the state does say. Rather, it refers to the normative question of what the state should say. The ideal of democratic persuasion is meant to answer that normative question. It provides a guide to identify when state speech is appropriate, to elaborate its content, and to define its proper limits. I thus emphasize that not all state speech qualifies as democratic persuasion. State speech only qualifies as democratic persuasion when it promotes the democratic values of free and equal citizenship, and is consistent with what I call the "substance-based" and "means-based" limits on what the state can express. The means-based limit bars the state from punishing or coercing citizens who express viewpoints that dissent from the fundamental values of democracy. The substance-based limit requires state speech to be compatible with free and equal citizenship and prohibits the government from promoting a particular sectarian view or comprehensive doctrine.

I also want to clarify that the notion of state speech should not be confused with the claim that there is only one state actor that speaks on behalf of democratic values. As the book argues, no single part of the state has a monopoly on interpreting the core values that are central to democratic legitimacy. Rather, a variety of state actors, as well as democratic citizens, should engage in democratic persuasion. It is common to the president, Supreme Court justices, legislators, local officials, and ordinary citizens protesting unjust state action that they can invoke, and attempt to articulate, the ideal of free and equal citizenship. In this book, an important example of a citizen who pursues democratic persuasion on behalf of the ideals of freedom and equality is Martin Luther King Jr. The state can support the efforts of citizens like King to engage in democratic persuasion not only by protecting their right of free speech, but also by actively affirming the values of freedom and equality. For example, the state can recognize King's defense of democratic values by dedicating an official holiday and public monuments to him, and by teaching the lessons of the civil rights movement in public schools. Both citizens and state officials can therefore engage in democratic persuasion.

By using democratic persuasion to articulate the reasons for rights, value democracy aims to answer the critics who contend that liberalism cannot defend its most basic values or counter the threat to equality that might come from hate groups in civil society. In particular, I reply to the common criticism that liberalism is plagued by an alleged "paradox of rights."[13] According to this paradox, the neutrality implicit in liberal defenses of free speech, association, and religion leads liberalism to be complicit in its own demise. These rights are said to commit liberal democrats to a form of neutrality that protects the opponents of liberalism.

One worry, expressed by "militant democrats," is that liberalism can do nothing about the rise of groups that advocate the dismantling of liberal democracy. Militant democrats, like Karl Loewenstein, argue that the only way to ensure the stability of liberal democracies is to limit the rights of hate groups that threaten the foundational values of these regimes.[14] Militant democracy differs from liberalism in advocating not only limits on hate speech, but also restrictions on rights of hate groups to associate freely and to participate in the democratic process. Another kind of criticism suggests that even if liberal regimes do not literally fail, they are flawed in that they can offer no response to the critics who attack them.

This concern is often expressed by the worry that "a liberal is a person who cannot take his own side in an argument." On some accounts, liberalism's silence about hateful and illiberal views constitutes a kind of tacit complicity with the enemies of free and equal citizenship.

These two concerns motivate the accusation embodied in the paradox of rights: that liberalism's commitment to free and equal citizenship in the public sphere is potentially undermined by its protection of inegalitarian beliefs in the private sphere of civil society and the family.[15] A variant of this criticism is made by communitarians, who worry that liberalism's neutrality and its protection of rights prevent the public values of free and equal citizenship from being affirmed and defended in public.[16]

Value democracy answers the paradox of rights by introducing the idea of democratic persuasion as a fundamental commitment of liberal society. Democratic persuasion extends the familiar principle that law, to be legitimate, must be widely publicized. It adds the further obligation that the state should publicize the justification for those rights protected by law—namely, their basis in the values of free and equal citizenship. When these values are attacked, the state should attempt to defend free and equal citizenship against the criticism of hate groups. The state's defense of democratic values should be "persuasive" in that it should aim to be convincing. This means that democratic persuasion should not merely recite the values that underlie rights; it should argue for them. The aim of democratic persuasion is to change the minds of the opponents of liberal democracy, and, more broadly, to persuade the public of the merits of democratic values. By engaging in democratic persuasion, liberal democracy can avoid the paradox of rights: it offers a way for the legitimate state, without coercively violating rights, to respond clearly to its harshest critics and to challenge the hate groups that oppose the values of free and equal citizenship.

I will suggest in chapter 1 why the ideal of free and equal citizenship requires civil rights protection in the areas of race, gender, and gay rights. These protections use the force of law and coercion to protect racial minorities, women, and gays. Value democracy regards civil rights protections as fundamental. But in upholding the democratic values of free and equal citizenship, value democracy does not limit itself to protecting civil rights. The values of freedom and equality for all citizens should also be articulated and defended through democratic persuasion. Although citizens should retain rights to disagree with anti-discrimination laws, the state has the obligation to use its expressive capacities to defend the values of free and equal citizenship against criticism from hateful or discriminatory groups and individuals.

My theory of value democracy is thus "expressive" in two senses: it protects the entitlement of citizens to express any political viewpoint, and it emphasizes a role for the state in explaining and defending the ideals that underlie free speech protections. I will extend the argument from freedom of expression to freedom of religion in chapter 5: value democracy protects the expression and practice of any religious view, but it is also committed to persuading citizens of the values that justify protecting religious freedom in the first place. In this persuasive role, the state appropriately employs its expressive powers—as an educator, speaker, and spender—to convince citizens to adopt the values that underlie legitimate law. When it uses these powers, the state does not regulate expression; rather, it expresses itself to defend the very values that underlie rights, including freedom of expression and religion.

One objection to democratic persuasion might come from critics who are concerned about excessive state power. In their view, more power for the state might imply less liberty. However, these critics overlook that the state already engages in expression and persuasion. State officials express the values that are fundamental to our society by building public monuments to civil rights leaders like Martin Luther King, by celebrating official holidays that honor democratic ideals, and by funding efforts to advance freedom and equality for all citizens.[17] In short, an expressive role in promoting democratic values already characterizes many practices of contemporary governments.

My account of democratic persuasion and value democracy offers a coherent justification for these expressive practices. But when the practices of states and political actors oppose free and equal citizenship, my theory also offers a way of criticizing them. Throughout this book, I will suggest the proper aims, scope, and limits of the expressive capacities of the state. I will defend a role for the state in defending and promoting democratic values among the citizenry, as well as a duty for citizens to adopt democratic values as their own.

Another reply to the critics of democratic persuasion comes from a deeper examination of the challenge that the paradox of rights poses to liberal democracy. Specifically, I want to suggest why two attempts simply to define away the paradox will not work. Although I believe that the paradox is resolvable, I also think those who have appealed to it raise an important problem that accompanies robust rights protections in liberal democracies.

According to the paradox of rights, liberalism justifies rights protections based on an ideal of equality, but the liberal state cannot respond to critics of equality who are protected by rights. Some thinkers might try to argue that the paradox of rights does not exist, because there are simply different kinds of equality that, in the end, do not conflict with each other. These thinkers might contend that while some rights-protected viewpoints challenge unequal conditions such as inequality of income, they do not necessarily challenge the kind of equality that is the basis for rights and equal citizenship. Since these viewpoints do not challenge free and equal citizenship, it is said that they do not lead to a paradox of rights.

I acknowledge that some kinds of inegalitarian beliefs do not violate the ideal of free and equal citizenship. As I will suggest in chapter 1, some views might be inegalitarian in their metaphysical or theological conception without opposing the ideal of free and equal citizenship. Similarly, individuals might have an account of the distribution of wealth in society without challenging the basic ideals that underlie liberal democracy. Such viewpoints should not be subject to democratic persuasion. However, the thinkers who dismiss the paradox of rights ignore how other inegalitarian beliefs do oppose the ideal of free and equal citizenship. For instance, the American Nazi Party, the Ku Klux Klan, and other hate groups advocate a conception of inequality that is at odds with the very ideal that all citizens should be treated as free and equal. They oppose the ideal of freedom and equality in at least one of the following senses relevant to citizenship: they deny that all citizens possess equal rights, they oppose recognizing the equal citizenship of minorities or women, or they defend discrimination in education or employment. It is the expression and endorsement of these kinds of inegalitarian beliefs that give rise to the paradox of rights. This conflict between the ideals of liberal democracy and hateful viewpoints that deny free and equal citizenship cannot simply be defined away.

Another attempt to dismiss the paradox of rights comes from the prohibitionists who deny the political nature of inegalitarian beliefs. Perhaps the most famous prohibitionist view of this form is "militant democracy." As Karl Loewenstein argues, democracies should limit the right to express fascist viewpoints. Loewenstein tries to evade the problem of violating the right of free speech by claiming that fascism is not an ideology or a set of viewpoints, but rather a type of "tactic." Similarly, some defenders of prohibiting hateful viewpoints contend that such views are not speech but actions. On this view, there is no loss that comes from prohibiting hate speech, because prohibition does not limit ideas or valuable expression, but is similar to stopping violence.

The problem with this second attempt to dismiss the paradox of rights is that, while fascists and other hate groups have engaged in violent action, they express political views in their books and speeches. While the state may certainly prohibit violent action, the paradox of rights still emerges when these political viewpoints are expressed. Even views that oppose the core values of liberal democracy can still be political viewpoints. Therefore, we cannot ignore the paradox of rights by denying that some hateful viewpoints are held at the level of ideas, distinct from unlawful action. Although I will suggest how democratic persuasion can respond to the paradox of rights, prohibitionists such as Loewenstein are wrong to think that we can merely solve this dilemma by banning hateful viewpoints. As I will argue in chapter 3, because hateful viewpoints express political ideas, however vile, they are entitled to protection, as required by rights of free speech. But while it would be a mistake to pursue prohibition, Loewenstein and others are correct to argue that these hateful viewpoints cannot merely be protected and left unchallenged.

My emphasis on seeking to change hateful and discriminatory viewpoints through a process of democratic persuasion may provoke a strong defensive reaction from the neutralists. The neutralists will argue that I am wrong to distinguish hateful or discriminatory speech from other viewpoints. They will resist my claim that discriminatory speech should be criticized by the state and not treated as strictly private or ignored. In response to the neutralists, it is important to remember that value democracy respects the right of free speech, and rejects the coercive bans on hateful viewpoints that are endorsed by many of the world's liberal democracies.[18] My aim is to preserve the doctrine of viewpoint neutrality in the protection of free speech rights, while rejecting viewpoint neutrality in state speech. The state should be viewpoint neutral in protecting all speech, regardless of its content, from coercive bans or punishment. But it should not be viewpoint neutral in its own speech. Instead, it should engage in democratic persuasion, supporting the ideal of freedom and equality for all citizens while criticizing hateful or discriminatory viewpoints. If viewpoint neutrality is to be preserved in the protection of free speech rights, however, it must answer important and widely held concerns about hateful viewpoints. These concerns are reflected in the bans on hate speech that have been enacted in almost every other liberal democracy, and they are raised by prohibitionists in the United States, including many feminists and racial scholars. Unlike neutralism, my account of value democracy can answer legitimate concerns about defending free and equal citizenship against hateful viewpoints. But unlike prohibitionism, which coercively bans viewpoints, value democracy protects rights and is more compatible with respect for citizens as free and equal. There is thus a key distinction between viewpoint neutrality and neutralism, as I will elaborate in chapter 3. Viewpoint neutrality is the legal doctrine that rights should protect the expression of all opinions. Neutralism is a political theory that the state should not promote or express any particular set of values. Although I apply viewpoint neutrality to rights, I reject neutralism. I ground viewpoint neutrality in an affirmative, non-neutral set of democratic values, namely those of free and equal citizenship.

Before turning to value democracy's account of how we might promote equality at the same time that we defend rights, in the next section I describe in greater depth what is at stake in the theoretical divide between the neutralists who defend robust rights protections and the prohibition-ists who seek to limit rights to protect an ideal of equal citizenship. I then introduce value democracy as an alternative to both of these accounts. Value democracy and democratic persuasion suggest how liberal democ-racies can simultaneously protect rights and promote a democratic ideal of free and equal citizenship.

I. Two Dystopias: The Invasive State and Hateful Society

In formulating a political theory, it is often useful to begin by thinking about the kind of society that one wants to avoid rather than the ideal one wishes to realize. Theorizing in reference to dystopias rather than utopias may, in fact, clarify the kind of values that a legitimate society should as-pire to fulfill. In liberal theory, the dystopia that is most feared could aptly be described as "the Invasive State." In the Invasive State, roving police vehicles constantly monitor citizens. Citizens are prosecuted for having conversations and engaging in practices that are antagonistic to the public values of free and equal citizenship, even when these conversations occur in the private space of the home.

In the liberal imagination, fears about the Invasive State often focus on governments that violate rights in the name of illiberal values. The Inva-sive State is usually characterized as a fascist or authoritarian government that intervenes to promote discrimination or to preserve the power of the rulers. But the liberal worry about the Invasive State might also extend to interventions on behalf of liberal values. While authoritarian interven-tions are problematic because of the reasons for the government's actions, liberal interventions raise a distinct difficulty. In the latter case, liber-als might endorse the substantive values behind the intervention, but not the method of achieving them. For instance, attempts to ban hate speech might reflect a liberal concern to protect equality and condemn racism. In this version of the Invasive State, the government uses coercion to enforce the values of free and equal citizenship. However, liberals would resist heavy-handed means to enforce the defining values of a liberal polity. They would see the Invasive State as dystopian, since it respects no re-straint on the state's coercive interventions to enforce equality. Liberal rights to privacy are intended precisely to guarantee against such a dysto-pian role of the state and to ensure the integrity of private spaces such as the "marital bedroom."[19]

While liberals fear the Invasive State, feminist critics of liberalism, es-pecially those tempted by militant democracy's willingness to use coercive means to challenge anti-egalitarian viewpoints, arguably fear a different dystopia, which I call "the Hateful Society." In this dystopia, the state maintains robust liberal rights protections, such as rights to privacy, free speech, and freedom of conscience, but the culture that is protected by these rights deeply opposes public values, particularly equality. In the Hateful Society, rights to privacy protect families that assign subordinate tasks to women and that teach female members to believe they are worth less their male counterparts. Beyond the family, negative comments about women's roles predominate in the workplace and in civil associations; a pervasive culture of chauvinism reinforces the notion that women are less valuable than men. While the citizens of the Hateful Society enjoy rights to free speech that protect them against state intervention, inegalitarian speech and behavior are routine and unsanctioned within the culture of its civil society. The culture of sexism may be so pervasive that women are "silenced," in that they are marginalized in politics, despite their formal rights to participate.

Along with sexism, racism also predominates in the culture of the Hateful Society. Although the law might afford certain formal protections against racial discrimination by the state, civil society is characterized by a discriminatory culture that treats minorities as inferior to the majority race. This widespread private inequality inevitably results in political inequality.[20] While racial minorities may retain a formal set of rights, extensive racism results in "silencing." Racism silences minorities by discouraging them from believing that they can fully exercise their rights to participate as equals in public life. The rights remain merely formal in that they are proclaimed on paper, but they fail to be protected due to the racist culture of the Hateful Society. Citizens may deny loans to minority applicants, refuse to admit minority students into their schools, and pass over minority workers for promotion. Although laws ban discrimination, citizens in the Hateful Society can ignore those laws, and public officials can fail to enforce them. In the broader culture, rights of free speech allow civil society groups to spread racism by burning crosses, painting swastikas, and preaching a message of racial inferiority to minorities. Even if the state bans violence and direct threats, minority citizens feel that their safety is threatened and that the state's neutrality ignores their fundamental interests. Constrained by a doctrine of neutrality, the state is prohibited in the Hateful Society from criticizing discriminatory viewpoints or stopping their proliferation. In extreme cases, hateful viewpoints can inspire acts of violence. Although the violence can be punished and coercion employed to stop it, rights protect the culture that leads to violent acts against minorities in the first place.

The divide between those who fear the Hateful Society and those who fear the Invasive State seems unbridgeable. Liberals fear coercive intervention into the "private" realms of the family and civil society, regardless of the ways these spheres might reinforce inequality. In the extreme case, this fear of state action might lead liberals to think that political theory can offer no response to inequality in the family and in civil society. While some liberals acknowledge that private life has a variety of "moral rights" that might be violated, as a political matter, they believe that the state should not intervene to counter these violations. These liberals argue that political rights cordon off the "private" realm from public scrutiny. In short, the reaction of liberals to the dangers and excesses of the Invasive State sometimes leads them to endorse a kind of neutralist liberalism, which is incapable of responding to the problems of the dystopian Hateful Society.

Indeed, some critics have maintained that an inability to respond to the Hateful Society is a fundamental problem with liberalism itself. As I have noted, these critics argue that liberal theory faces a paradox of rights in its treatment of hateful viewpoints and hate groups. To recall the paradox, liberal rights recognize the status of citizens as free and as equal, yet the protection of rights to free association, expression, and conscience provides cover for groups and individuals who attack the equality of citizens. The paradox is that, in the name of freedom and equality, liberalism shields groups such as the Ku Klux Klan, the American Nazis, and chauvinists who threaten to undermine the very entitlement of women and minorities to free and equal status.

In the chapters to come, I attempt to bridge the divide between liberal theories that seek to protect rights and feminist theories that seek to promote certain fundamental values, such as equality. On my view, a fully articulated theory of rights will offer a way to address both of these concerns, avoiding the pitfalls of both the Invasive State and the Hateful Society. The resolution of the paradox of rights is found when we expand our focus to examine not only the content of rights, but the reasons for rights. Although rights such as free speech are defined by their neutrality toward the content of the views expressed, the reasons for rights are not value- or viewpoint neutral. When we seek to explain why such legal protections are afforded to citizens in the legitimate state, we should appeal to the non-neutral, affirmative values of freedom and equality that characterize the status of all who are subject to law. Although free speech doctrines regulating coercion are rightly "viewpoint neutral," in that all views are protected by rights, the reasons for rights are not themselves neutral with regard to the content or the viewpoint of ideas.

My account of value democracy highlights the important role of the state in promulgating the reasons for rights. While the idea that the content of rights should be promulgated by the state is a familiar one in law, value democracy adds that the reasons and values that justify rights should also be expressed to and promoted among the citizenry. The values of freedom and equality do not apply only in the so-called public sphere.

Instead, I argue that the state should promote these values even when it requires seeking to persuade individuals to abandon or transform certain beliefs that are at odds with the ideal of free and equal citizenship. Value democracy is thus a transformative theory of rights. This account shows that the concern to promote equality is not only compatible with rights, but it is based on the very reasons and values that justify rights themselves. While the paradox of rights is a real problem, value democracy resolves the paradox by protecting the rights of citizens from coercive intervention, while using democratic persuasion to promote the values of freedom and equality that underlie rights.

The reasons for rights, I argue, should be promoted by an appeal to the "expressive" and "persuasive" capacities of the state, and not by coercion. On my view, the exaggerated divide between those who fear the Hateful Society and those who fear the Invasive State is partly a result of an overemphasis on issues related to the justification of coercion in contemporary political theory. In many of the debates, the exclusive question theorists often ask is: "to coerce or not to coerce?" By contrast, value democracy highlights a role of the state distinct from its role as coercer. I focus on when and why the state should employ its non-coercive, persuasive powers.

Rights such as freedom of expression correctly protect citizens against coercive intervention, but I argue that these rights do not extend to a right not to be persuaded by the state. As John Stuart Mill famously writes, alongside a set of rights protecting freedom of conscience and speech, there should be a wide role for citizens in defending the core liberal democratic values.[21] I extend this argument in highlighting a role for the state—in its non-coercive, persuasive capacities—to defend the reasons for rights, namely, the ideal of free and equal citizenship. Indeed, as John Locke argues in *A Letter Concerning Toleration*, it is legitimate for a rights-respecting state to persuade using reason. Locke notes the distinction between the state's persuasive and coercive power when he writes: "In teaching, instructing, and redressing the erroneous by reason, he [the magistrate] may certainly do what becomes any good man to do. . . . [It] is one thing to persuade, another to command; one thing to press with arguments, another with penalties."[22] Since state persuasion, on my view, is not tantamount to coercion, the legitimate state can articulate the reasons for rights and convince citizens to adopt these reasons as their own.

Value democracy relies on two features in responding to the paradox of rights. On the one hand, it emphasizes the central role of the state's persuasive, as opposed to its coercive, capacities. On the other hand, value democracy also stresses the proper limits on the content of the message that the state promulgates to its citizens. As I argue in later chapters, the state should not promote any account of equality or any set of values, but it should focus on the specific kind of equality that justifies rights. While the reasons for rights are grounded in a non-neutral conception of equal citizenship, they do not include a comprehensive or sectarian account of egalitarianism. Rather, the reasons for rights are focused on expressing a respect for the equal status of citizens, a status that the state must respect for it to be legitimate and for the laws to be justifiable to all. The ideal of free and equal citizenship is therefore a public and not a comprehensive ideal.

The legitimate state should seek to change discriminatory views to the extent that they challenge the democratic value that all persons should be regarded as free and equal. However, to avoid having the state impose a "comprehensive doctrine," I argue that persuasive attempts at transformation should only be aimed at those beliefs that are openly hostile to or implausibly consistent with the ideal of public equality.[23] Comprehensive doctrines are those that seek to go beyond a theory of what is owed to people by virtue of their common status as political beings subject to state power. The doctrines are comprehensive in that they are accounts of how persons should act in all parts of their life, including the conception of the good that they should endorse.[24] By contrast, I hope to sketch an ideal of citizen status that is solely related to their role as political beings in a democracy. I signify my break with comprehensive conceptions of liberalism by referring to individuals as "free and equal citizens." I do not wish to limit my view or to confuse it with legal or de jure citizenship, but rather to invoke the broader tradition of a conception of citizenship within the domain of political morality. Many potentially inegalitarian views, which are nevertheless arguably consistent with an ideal of political equality, are rightly left alone by the state. I signify my more limited concern with political equality, rather than with equality in some more comprehensive sense, by discussing an ideal of free and equal citizenship.

Value democracy is a theory that attempts to incorporate both liberal protections of rights and the promotion of egalitarian values. As such, it has both traditional liberal and democratic elements. Its liberal elements are found in its concern to limit the coercive power of the state. Its democratic elements are found in its concern to ensure that the democratic values of freedom and equality are widely respected by the state and by the broader culture of civil society. Value democracy is thus consistent with democrats' concern—dating back to Tocqueville—to think about democratic culture, not only democratic procedures.[25]

In my previous book, *Democratic Rights: The Substance of Self-Government*, I argued that the respect for equal status is rightly understood as among the values of self-government. These core values justify democracy itself and are more basic to the democratic ideal than procedures alone.[26] But while I was concerned in *Democratic Rights* to examine the implications of these values for certain basic rights, here I examine the implications of democratic values for the beliefs and practices of family members and participants in civil society. Value democracy, in the following chapters, applies democratic values beyond formal procedures and institutions directly to what many liberals have thought of as "private" life. Understood as a synthesis of liberal and democratic commitments, my theory of value democracy is rightly understood as an account of liberal democracy.

Value democracy is thus not limited to formal democratic procedures. A state is not fully democratic if it formally guarantees rights and democratic procedures, while failing to endorse the underlying values of self-government in its broader culture. A culture of racism and sexism in civil society, as illustrated by the Hateful Society, can dis-empower minorities through non-formal means, preventing them from participating in politics and from achieving positions of influence. In this way, the Hateful Society leaves the values of self-government empty and abstract. Value democracy, by contrast, seeks to present an account of liberal democracy that more substantively respects and promotes self-government, avoiding the dystopia of the Hateful Society while also steering clear of the pervasive coercion and rights violations of the Invasive State.

Some might challenge my emphasis on promoting democratic values as being elitist, not democratic. For instance, I do not contend that public officials should merely echo the beliefs that are widely held by people at any given period. Value democracy is not limited to only reflecting public opinion. Rather, my claim is that the reason why we have democratic procedures in the first place is to respect the equality and autonomy of citizens. The values of free and equal citizenship are therefore the values that justify and undergird our entitlements to vote in elections and to have a say in public policy. As I argued in *Democratic Rights*, these values give rise not only to entitlements to participate and rights to the franchise, but also to rights that stem from the values that undergird democratic procedures. In short, on my view, democracy requires not only rights to participate, but also other rights that are based on the very values that justify the freedom to participate. These rights include entitlements to free speech, religion, and association.

Now that I have described my theory of value democracy, I am in a position to articulate more fully its response to the challenge that the paradox of rights poses to liberal democracy. A first challenge noted that liberal democracy's commitment to rights makes it complicit in condoning or being silent toward views that attack the foundations of liberal democracy. But value democracy offers a way to protect rights at the same time that the state makes clear through its expressive capacity that it criticizes hateful or discriminatory viewpoints. A second challenge raised by the paradox of rights concerns the stability of democracy. Militant democrats contend that liberals offer no way to prevent the collapse of liberal democratic regimes. On this view, the rights protections afforded to illiberal groups might result in the spread of hateful viewpoints and the demise of liberal democratic protections, as in the case of Weimar Germany. But it is important to point out here that a clear tradeoff would come from abandoning rights in order to coercively suppress hateful viewpoints. It would result in a loss to a major aspect of democratic legitimacy. I will argue that for government to be fully democratically legitimate, it must respect the free and equal status of citizens. To be treated as free and equal, citizens must have the liberty to express and to hear any political viewpoint. Without this ability, citizens would be denied the capacity to accept or reject laws and public policies.

I think, however, that value democracy offers a third alternative between this hard choice of either sacrificing rights to prevent democratic collapse or protecting robust rights to free speech in regard to all political opinions. In response to the militant democrat, I suggest that there is another way of protecting democracy and its core values aside from coercively limiting rights. Value democracy has the advantage of recognizing the concerns of militant democrats without sacrificing the rights that are fundamental to the liberal polity. In response to liberals, I contend that there is no tradeoff between my view and the concern to protect rights. Value democracy maintains robust rights protections alongside a concern to promote and promulgate the reasons for rights.

Value democracy is not limited to stating in the abstract the democratic values of free and equal citizenship that justify the protection of rights. It also criticizes specific hateful or discriminatory viewpoints, such as racism or segregationism.[27] Value democracy explains why those views are wrong, and seeks to persuade citizens to reject them. One reason for active criticism, and not just stating the reasons for rights, is that without an explanation of why discriminatory viewpoints are wrong, those views might be mistakenly seen as compatible with free and equal citizenship. For instance, the segregationists claimed that their policy of "separate but equal" public schools for different races was compatible with the equal protection of the law for all citizens. The Supreme Court rejected these claims in *Brown v. Board of Education,* and criticized the public policies advocated by the segregationists. In its unanimous decision, the Court explained why segregationist policies were incompatible with equal protection, despite the segregationists' claims to the contrary.[28] To avoid the problem of democratic values being co-opted, or wrongly thought to be compatible with specific discriminatory viewpoints, the state and its citizens should criticize views that conflict with the ideal of free and equal citizenship.

A second and related reason for active criticism is to avoid the potential problem of state complicity. There is a danger that the state may be considered complicit with hateful or discriminatory viewpoints, because it protects their right to be expressed. Citizens may then believe that the state is neutral toward the opponents of free and equal citizenship. The state can avoid complicity by not only promulgating the reasons for rights, but criticizing discriminatory viewpoints. This criticism clarifies that the state's protection of free speech rights for racists and other holders of discriminatory views does not imply complicity with or neutrality toward them.

A third reason why value democracy engages in criticism is to counter the concerns of militant democrats, who worry about the stability of democracy in the face of challenges from hateful or discriminatory viewpoints. Militant democrats will likely argue that a mere abstract statement of democratic values would be unable to dissuade the opponents of liberal democracy or convince undecided citizens. This failure would raise the specter of the Hateful Society, where discriminatory viewpoints spread unchecked. One of the aims of value democracy, like that of militant democrats, is to counter the spread of discriminatory viewpoints and to change the minds of those who hold or hear them. While sharing this aim, value democracy rejects militant democracy's coercive bans on speech and other Invasive State methods. Value democracy instead uses persuasive reasoning and criticism. To defend democracy against its opponents, and to avoid the emergence of the Hateful Society without resorting to the Invasive State, value democracy criticizes their arguments and shows why they should be rejected.

Militant democrats might contend, however, that value democracy is not strong enough in its protection of liberal democratic values, and still risks the weakening of liberal democratic regimes by the illiberal forces protected by rights. I offer two responses to this contention. First, it is not clear that persuasion will fare less well than coercion in promoting and protecting democratic values. Indeed, as many defenders of liberal democratic rights have pointed out, coercive laws banning the expression of hateful viewpoints and the free association of hate groups may not be effective. It might cause citizens who hold these views to go underground and to become even more hostile to liberal democratic regimes, as Nancy Rosenblum argues.[29] Such groups may garner sympathy from third parties by resisting coercive persecution. In contrast, value democracy protects the rights of persons who hold viewpoints hostile to free and equal citizenship, and it exposes those viewpoints to public criticism. At the same time, value democracy offers a method for the state and citizens to seek to change minds. It offers respect for holders of even the most hateful viewpoints by protecting their rights, but it also seeks to transform their views so that they are compatible with the foundations of liberal democracy. Value democracy can publicly engage these viewpoints, challenge their premises, and seek to change the minds of the citizens who hold them. In the eyes of third parties, this approach of persuasion and criticism robs hateful viewpoints of their possible outlaw allure, and instead publicly refutes them. Even if the most radical among these groups do not have their minds changed, in the eyes of the polity, value democracy and democratic persuasion can combat the spread of ideas that are inimical to liberal democracy.

Second, even if coercion proves more effective than democratic persuasion endorsed by value democracy, we should not simply favor the view that most effectively combats hateful viewpoints. Even if value democracy is less effective in transforming these views, it is important to respect the rights of citizens in order to treat them as free and equal. The state's respect for citizens as free and equal is the basis for its democratic legitimacy. Less effectiveness in reducing hateful viewpoints may be justified by the overall gain to democratic legitimacy that comes from a strategy that embraces rights, instead of rejecting them.

I concede, however, that there might be some empirical situations in which my argument might fail. In some historical circumstances, value democracy might lack the tools to stave off threats to democracy. In such circumstances, there might be a need to abandon democracy temporarily in order to reinstitute it. But such emergency situations should be viewed with much skepticism, and value democracy offers a way to avoid reaching such a dire choice. Even if value-neutral conceptions fail to combat a rising tide of anti-democratic viewpoints, value democracy might offer an effective approach to defending democracy without abandoning core democratic rights.

In sum, my ambition in this book is to offer a third alternative both to neutralist liberals and to militant democrats. Value democracy stands in contrast to value-neutralist conceptions of liberalism and democracy, in that it posits a clear set of affirmative values that undergird rights and democratic procedures. Value democracy also offers a constructive role for the state in promoting these values among the citizenry. But it resists the militant democratic strategy of coercively defending these values at the expense of rights. Rather than sacrificing rights in the name of democratic values, I suggest that a legitimate democracy has the duty both to protect rights in the most robust sense and to promulgate the values that justify these rights. This third alternative, presented by value democracy, should be attractive primarily because it addresses the concerns of liberals who fear the intervention of the Invasive State as well as militant democrats who worry about defending democratic values in the face of the threat from the Hateful Society. Value democracy thus answers the concerns about complicity raised by the paradox of rights and the problem of stability stressed by militant democrats.

II. How Value Democracy Is Distinct from Other Views

Value democracy shares much with the traditional feminist belief that the "personal is political." I will argue that democratic persuasion is important in convincing citizens to adopt the values, principles, and reasons that underlie a commitment to rights. It is worth mentioning, however, another distinct project which has also taken the feminist mantra as its starting point. The work of the late political philosopher Gerry Cohen is largely an attempt to explore why the public and private realms could not be sharply divided in a just society. But unlike my account, Cohen is not concerned with defending rights or showing the compatibility of his view with the liberal tradition more generally. Indeed, much of Cohen's effort reflects the belief of Karl Marx that a focus on public rights can undermine private equality. Specifically, for Marx, an emphasis on the public rights of the citizen ignores the way private egoism pervades society.

Cohen's work is specifically concerned with demonstrating why John Rawls fails to recognize the relevance of public, egalitarian values to personal decision-making.[30] Cohen thinks that individuals undermine a society's claim to justice when they are inegalitarian in their personal decision-making, pursuing personal wealth in a way that increases inequality. Cohen and I share the view that equality is relevant not only to laws governing and limiting coercion, but also more broadly to citizens' beliefs and practices. But while a concern for citizens' equality is present in Cohen's view and my account of value democracy, our definitions of equality differ significantly.

For Cohen, equality is a comprehensive value that pervades all aspects of personal choice. In contrast to Cohen, I have adopted a different kind of egalitarianism that concentrates more on protecting the values of free and equal citizenship, and that does not require all substantive decisions to be made in an egalitarian fashion. For instance, Cohen is concerned with both the choices that citizens make in spending their money to pursue their own conception of the good and the impact of personal consumption on the value of equality. By contrast, my ideal of free and equal citizenship does not pervade every aspect of citizens' choices in that way. Cohen also differs in that he is not concerned to elaborate how, if at all, his account of equality is compatible with robust rights to freedom of conscience. He does not distinguish himself from theories of rights that seek to combat inequality through the use of force, accounts which lend themselves to the excesses of the Invasive State. Value democracy, by contrast, has at its core the ambition of reconciling the promotion of public values with the protection of rights.[31]

My view is also distinct from many prominent accounts of how the state should promote the values of free and equal citizenship through education. For instance, Amy Gutmann's *Democratic Education*, Eamonn Callan's *Creating Citizens*, and Stephen Macedo's *Diversity and Distrust* are all concerned with the importance of instilling a set of liberal values in citizens before they are entitled to the full rights of adults.[32] These accounts suggest that, because children have not yet developed their full capacities, they can be coerced into a liberal education in a way that adults cannot. My book also concerns education, but in a broader sense that is not limited to children. For Gutmann, Callan, and Macedo, state education is largely pursued chronologically in youth before rights are granted. In contrast, throughout this book, I discuss the possibility that the state can be concerned to educate the citizenry about the values that underlie rights even after those rights are granted in adulthood. Because I am concerned with the state's broadly expressive and educative functions regarding adults, however, the balance between the concern for rights and the concern for democratic values cannot be resolved chronologically by age. Rather, drawing on the concepts of public relevance and the non-coercive, expressive capacities of the state, I attempt to show how value democracy can simultaneously protect rights and seek to educate the citizenry about the values that are at the core of a legitimate state.

A second difference between my account compared to the approaches of Gutmann, Callan, and Macedo is that these authors argue for the compatibility of rights and a robust approach to promoting liberal values through education. By contrast, my account goes beyond an argument for compatibility to suggest why the commitment to rights themselves entails a commitment to promote public values in private life. In addition, I offer a theory of rights and the reasons of rights, not an account of virtues which would need to be balanced against rights. Because my approach is rights-based, it avoids promoting a particular or sectarian conception of the good. The reasons for rights on my account are based on neither virtue nor conceptions of the good.[33] Instead, the basis for rights is free and equal citizenship.

Finally, my view can be contrasted with liberal perfectionist thinkers such as Joseph Raz and, as has become clear in his latest work, Ronald Dworkin. These thinkers also see values as at the basis of rights, but they articulate comprehensive conceptions of these values and suggest that they should be promoted as conceptions of the good life.[34] For instance, Dworkin ties the value of autonomy to the obligation to lead a reflective life and even to pursue one's life as a "work of art."[35] Such visions are much more comprehensive than mine and would justify an expressive role for the state well beyond articulating the reasons for rights. In contrast, as I suggest in chapter 3, my distinctly political ideal of free and equal citizenship offers a way for the state to counter the Hateful Society, without using the state to bring about a particular vision of the good life.

III. Outline of the Book

The theory of value democracy explains how the state can avoid the two dystopias of the Hateful Society and the Invasive State. Unlike the Hateful Society, value democracy seeks to challenge beliefs in civil society that threaten equal citizenship. But unlike the Invasive State, value democracy protects the freedom and equality of citizens through the state's persuasive capacity, and not through coercion.

In chapter 1, I propose a "principle of public relevance," which claims that when beliefs, expression, and practices conflict with the ideal of free and equal citizenship, they should be changed to make them compatible with that ideal. In this book, I suggest two ways to fulfill the principle of public relevance, consistent with a respect for rights. The first way, "reflective revision," emphasizes the duty of *citizens* to incorporate the ideal of free and equal citizenship into their *own* set of beliefs and practices. The second way to fulfill the principle of public relevance is "democratic persuasion." It gives the *state and citizens* two duties: they should convince other citizens to adopt the ideal of free and equal citizenship, and they should criticize policies and positions that oppose free and equal citizenship. Democratic persuasion suggests how the state can respond to the problem of hate groups and promote the public values of free and equal citizenship in the family and civil society. Together, reflective revision and democratic persuasion specify how the principle of public relevance can be realized. The book will use the concepts of reflective revision and democratic persuasion to explain how democracies can avoid the excesses of both the Invasive State and the Hateful Society.

I continue in chapter 2 with a discussion of the role of the family and civil society within my theory. While the family and civil society should be protected by basic rights, I argue that the extent to which public values apply there is a normative question. I propose a conception of "publicly justifiable privacy" to clarify the implications of the principle of public relevance for thinking about the divide between public and private. My conception of publicly justifiable privacy challenges the traditional liberal approach of separating public values from the internal dynamics of the family and civil society. According to publicly justifiable privacy, family and civil society practices that conflict with free and equal citizenship should be protected by rights, but ideally should be amended to be compatible with public values. Drawing on and critiquing the work of Susan Okin, I argue that even "thin" values of free and equal citizenship have relevance within the family. Ideally, I argue, people should engage in reflective revision to change those personal beliefs and practices within the family and civil society that conflict with the ideal of free and equal citizenship.

The principle of public relevance suggests why some beliefs and practices, though they are protected by rights, ideally should be amended to be compatible with free and equal citizenship. But a question remains about what the state should do to address these protected yet publicly relevant beliefs. In particular, what should the state do if people fail to adopt the ideal of free and equal citizenship? In chapter 3, I outline a theory of freedom of expression that offers an account of how the state should simultaneously seek to transform discriminatory or hateful beliefs while defending them from coercive interference.

On my view, freedom of expression, rightly understood, has two components. First, it protects all viewpoints, short of threats to particular persons and incitements to imminent violence, from coercive intervention. Second, it provides a role for the state—in its capacities as speaker, educator, and spender—in expressing the reasons why these viewpoints are protected. In this persuasive, non-coercive role, the state should actively seek to promote the values of free and equal citizenship. Chapter 3 explains that the reach of this persuasive role is broad in the sense that it aims to affect the beliefs not only of family members, but more generally, of groups in civil society. I refer to this account of the state's role in value democracy as democratic persuasion. Although democratic persuasion stresses the importance of an active role for the legitimate state in promoting democratic values, value democracy does not abandon all accounts of neutrality in thinking about freedom of expression. I argue in chapter 3 that the Supreme Court's doctrine of viewpoint neutrality is appropriate as a standard for limiting state coercion. Viewpoint neutrality means that all viewpoints, regardless of their content, should be protected by freedom of expression, provided they are not direct threats to individuals. However, while viewpoint neutrality is appropriate as a standard for applying the right of free expression to citizens, I argue that it is misplaced as a guide to determining the state's own expression and what it should say. On my view, the state should be non-neutral in its persuasive and expressive roles. It should pursue a robust, non-neutral policy of persuading citizens to change their discriminatory views and to respect the ideal of free and equal citizenship.

Although acts of pure persuasion are central to my theory, they sometimes are not capable of changing minds or of influencing the culture widely. In chapter 4 I defend the notion that, while persuasion should not be backed by coercive force, it should be backed by the state's subsidy power. I define subsidy power as the ability of the state to spend money and, as crucially, to refuse to spend money on certain organizations. The state's subsidy power includes the ability to grant or withdraw tax-exempt, tax-deductible non-profit status. Its use is compatible with the right of free expression. Indeed, I argue that the reasons justifying free expression require the state to withdraw subsidies from groups that oppose the core values of free and equal citizenship.

An important challenge to the principle of public relevance is raised by a concern for freedom of religion. Should the state seek to transform inegalitarian religious beliefs using its persuasive capacity? On some accounts of religious freedom, religious beliefs deserve a presumptive protection from state influence. In chapter 5, I argue against such "static" views of religious freedom, and claim that rights should not entail the absence of public justification. Not only are some religious beliefs publicly relevant, but the state should seek to transform them through its persuasive capacity. In making this argument, I appeal to the ideal of religious freedom itself. Some religious conceptions, I argue, are at odds with the ideal of religious freedom—suggesting that religious freedom itself requires an account of the public relevance of hateful religious beliefs and a role for state transformation in the realm of religion. Whereas I argue in chapters 3 and 4 that freedom of expression requires both legal protections in form of rights and the state's active promotion of public values, so too, I argue in chapter 5, religious freedom requires these two roles for the state. In chapters 3, 4, and 5, I attempt to show that the state should protect rights and promote the public reasons that justify and underlie them.

CHAPTER ONE

· · · · · · · · · · · · ·

The Principle of Public Relevance
and Democratic Persuasion

VALUE DEMOCRACY'S TWO GUIDING IDEAS

I. Introduction

Value democracy seeks to avoid the dystopias of both the Invasive State and the Hateful Society. Unlike the Invasive State, value democracy respects rights, and unlike the Hateful Society, it criticizes inegalitarian viewpoints that oppose the values central to democratic legitimacy. Since value democracy criticizes hateful or discriminatory viewpoints, it can answer the problem of complicity and the concern about regime stability raised by the paradox of rights. Value democracy aims to respond to the paradox of rights by demonstrating that the democratic state can give voice to its own values without abandoning its core commitments to freedom of speech, conscience, and religion for all citizens.

In this chapter, I introduce several concepts that will serve as the building blocks for the theory of value democracy elaborated in the rest of the book. I begin section II of this chapter by introducing a principle of public relevance. According to this principle, beliefs and practices that conflict with the ideal of free and equal citizenship can be of public concern, and should be changed to make them compatible with democratic values. The principle of public relevance applies even when beliefs and practices are protected by rights against state coercion. Under the principle of public relevance, families and civil society organizations are not cordoned off as "private spaces" where discrimination can spread, free from public criticism. I emphasize, however, that the principle of public relevance is limited to beliefs and practices that oppose democratic values; it does not construe all areas of life as political.

I go on in section III to elaborate the meaning of the democratic ideal of free and equal citizenship. I define it in political terms, and distinguish it from more comprehensive notions of equality. In section IV I explain how the individual members of a democratic society can fulfill the principle of public relevance. I present several arguments for why citizens should adopt the values of free and equal citizenship as part of their beliefs. I also introduce the notion of reflective revision as a way of elaborating how citizens might evaluate and change their views.

In section V, I introduce the notion of democratic persuasion to describe how the state can promote democratic values. Value democracy accepts that the state's coercive power might be appropriate for protecting rights in certain cases, such as using the police to stop violence or enforcing the Civil Rights Act to uphold non-discrimination in the workplace. However, an important puzzle arises when citizens use their rights of free expression to advocate discriminatory beliefs. For example, citizens might exercise their freedom of expression to advocate denying equality for women or minorities. When confronted with viewpoints that are inegalitarian but protected by rights, value democracy calls for what I refer to as democratic persuasion. I will suggest that the state rightly engages in democratic persuasion when it exercises its expressive capacity to promote the values of free and equal citizenship. Democratic persuasion helps the state to avoid the charge that its protection of free expression for hateful or discriminatory viewpoints makes it complicit in them. The state avoids complicity by using democratic persuasion to criticize these viewpoints and to clarify that it does not condone them. Democratic persuasion also serves to answer concerns from militant democrats about the stability of liberal democracy. By engaging in democratic persuasion, the state can defend itself against the viewpoints that are inimical to its most basic values.

In sum, this chapter shows that value democracy can address the problems of the Hateful Society without straying into the dystopia of the Invasive State. It does so by recognizing that some beliefs, which are protected by rights, are publicly relevant when they conflict with the values of free and equal citizenship. To counter hateful viewpoints, value democracy offers two non-coercive ways of promoting democratic values. The first is reflective revision by citizens, and the second is democratic persuasion by the state. After introducing the ideas of public relevance, free and equal citizenship, reflective revision, and democratic persuasion in this chapter, subsequent chapters build on the discussion to develop and defend more fully these key ideas, which are central to my account of value democracy.

II. The Principle of Public Relevance: Challenging Beliefs That Are Hostile to Free and Equal Citizenship

The dominant metaphor for understanding the divide between the public and private spheres in liberal theory has been a spatial one. It is common to speak of the family and civil society as "private spaces" protected by liberal rights. The metaphor suggests a private haven, free from the concerns and interventions of political life in the "public square." But even in regard to rights protections, the spatial metaphor is misleading; in many instances, the metaphor fails to capture the right understanding of the public and the private in American law. The metaphor overlooks how privacy rights can potentially be overridden, even within the family and civil society. For instance, a right of sexual privacy may guarantee a certain amount of freedom from state intervention within relationships, but it does not protect against conviction for sexual crimes such as rape. Although this was not always the case, "marital rape" is now rightly classified as a crime.

But even short of extreme instances like marital rape in which rights are violated, the activities protected by privacy rights can still be, in an important sense, relevant to our identities as political actors. Consider a family that resembles the Hateful Society by raising its female children to feel inferior to male children. Provided there is no abuse, this form of childrearing does not necessarily justify the state's coercive intervention, such as removing the children from the home. However, raising young women to feel inferior is still relevant to the public values of free and equal citizenship. It is important, therefore, to distinguish a category of "public relevance" even within spaces protected by privacy rights. What makes certain beliefs and practices publicly relevant is that they conflict with our public status as free and equal citizens. According to the principle of public relevance, these beliefs and practices are of public concern, and ideally should be changed to make them consistent with the ideal of free and equal citizenship. The beliefs and practices can be publicly relevant, even when they are protected by rights against coercion. The public relevance of these discriminatory beliefs and practices suggests that citizens and the state should find a way to respond to them.

Actions that undermine public values can occur not only within the family, but within other "spaces" like the workplace or civil society associations that are often considered to be private. The ideal of free and equal citizenship is not geographically limited. Consider the case of "bad civil society" hate groups that stop short of committing crimes but express an ideology that opposes the idea of equality.[1] Such groups are justly protected by basic rights against coercion. These rights protect groups from being compelled to disclose their membership lists, and they entitle groups to assemble at sites not owned or funded by the state.[2] Although hate groups are protected by basic rights, their views clearly are publicly relevant in that they deeply oppose the values of free and equal citizenship. Indeed, hate groups are defined by their clear and explicit opposition to these values.

Just as rights of privacy and free association protect civil society groups, these rights protect the integrity of the home from arbitrary invasion and prevent the kinds of excesses that characterize the Invasive State.

We should not be compelled to disclose our actions within the marital bedroom, for instance, or within any room so long as no rights are violated.[3] The state should not place surveillance equipment in our living rooms to monitor our speech. In this sense, privacy rights do protect some actual spaces from state-sanctioned invasion. However, in my view, it is wrong to interpret the inviolability of these "spaces" as a metaphor for the irrelevance of public values within the family and civil society. Although the family and civil society should be protected by rights against coercion, their beliefs and practices should be open to criticism if they are hostile to free and equal citizenship.

My rejection of the spatial metaphor is sure to raise the specter of the Invasive State for some liberals, who will no doubt fear that I have abandoned what should be a neutral stance toward private spaces. But, as I will argue in chapter 3, such a concern badly misunderstands neutrality. While liberal rights should be neutral in the sense that they protect all citizens regardless of the viewpoints they hold and express, the public values that underlie those rights cannot be neutral. They must speak to why we should respect rights. Such a normative account cannot itself be value neutral; it must articulate the values that give us a reason to uphold rights of privacy in the first place. But it follows that these values, which are public in the sense that they provide the foundation for political rights, can be opposed by beliefs that are protected by rights. This opposition is publicly relevant, because it challenges the foundations of rights.

On my view, privacy rights are based on respect for all citizens as free and equal. Thus, the democratic state's understanding of privacy must itself be justified, so that privacy is consistent with the underlying value of respect for free and equal citizenship. This democratic value justifies protecting privacy in the first place. Proponents of the spatial metaphor, however, construe privacy as drawing spaces that are immune from justification or criticism, even when illiberal beliefs are spreading in civil society or the family. If we pull apart this conception, we see that the spatial metaphor begins to break down. The very reasons that justify privacy might be challenged and even undermined by illiberal behaviors and beliefs in "private" spaces. At times, these behaviors might violate rights and call for a coercive response. For example, the state would be justified in coercively stopping marital rape. At other times, behaviors might not violate rights, but they may oppose the values of free and equal citizenship, which comprise the reasons for rights. The spatial metaphor is thus flawed in two senses. First, no actual space can be always free of government coercion because rights violations, such as rape, potentially can happen everywhere and should be stopped by state action. Second, even when no right is violated and individuals are protected by rights of free expression and privacy, viewpoints might be expressed that oppose the values of free and equal citizenship. Public values are relevant here in the sense that they are in need of a defense, not a coercive response.

For instance, I will argue that raising children as racists does not justify coercive intervention within the family or the forcible removal of the child from the home, but it is publicly relevant and may call for a persuasive response by fellow citizens and the state. It is central to value democracy that all citizens retain rights against the state spying on our conversations or coercively discovering our beliefs. But at times, these views come to light without unjustifiable coercive interventions. For instance, if a young child came to school dressed in Nazi or Klan attire, this might reveal something about his or her racist upbringing. The parents in these cases have flouted their duty to endorse and support the democratic ideal. Even protected practices and beliefs, if they are discriminatory, should be criticized and, if hateful enough, condemned by the state in its persuasive capacity. Beliefs and actions within the family and civil society can still be publicly relevant and subject to criticism, because they can impact the norms of free and equal citizenship. The spatial metaphor is flawed and should be rejected, since it wrongly regards all of the actions that take place within the realm of the family or other private spheres as immune from public justification and the concerns of equal citizenship. As an alternative, I present a conception of publicly justifiable privacy, which regards practices and beliefs in civil society and the family as publicly relevant when they conflict with the values of free and equal citizenship.

Public relevance and the ideal of publicly justifiable privacy, however, only potentially justify a state response in the form of what I call "democratic persuasion." I will argue that one fundamental implication of these ideals concerns the obligations, not only of the state, but more broadly of citizens. Moreover, democratic persuasion is limited by a robust set of rights to be free from coercive interventions. This freedom includes rights against the state spying or forcibly obtaining information about our lives in the family and civil society.

A publicly justifiable conception of privacy seeks to avoid both the indifference of the Hateful Society and the excessive coercion of the Invasive State in response to hate groups and individuals who oppose an ideal of public equality. Consider a recent case from Canada, which I discuss at length in the next chapter. Canadian authorities removed a child from a home after they discovered that she was being taught racist views by her mother. Although removal in instances of abuse would not violate the family's privacy rights, it would be a mistake to remove a child solely because the parents taught abhorrent beliefs. For instance, removal might threaten the child's long-term well-being. It would also be a coercive sanction that would violate the parent's right to freedom of expression and conscience. If we are free to express our ideas anywhere, arguably we should be free to express them in the home. Coercion would therefore raise the threat of the Invasive State. Yet, while removal of the children would be an excessive response to hateful viewpoints when there is no child abuse, we should not settle for claiming that such beliefs are simply private and therefore must be ignored. They inculcate in the next generation a set of values that violates the very principles of a legitimate society. In particular, hateful viewpoints directly challenge what I have called the core values of democracy, especially the idea that all subject to law should be treated as being entitled to equal status. The spatial metaphor's assumption that the family is a private space cordoned off from public evaluation ignores how, as an institution for education, the family can pass on viewpoints that oppose public values, thus raising the danger of the Hateful Society.

The previous example suggests the limits of the spatial metaphor as a paradigm for thinking about public relevance, and it demonstrates the need for a more nuanced normative approach. To replace the spatial metaphor, I propose a conception of publicly justifiable privacy. Whereas the spatial metaphor cordons off some areas of life, such as the family and civil society, from any kind of public concern or criticism, the notion of publicly justifiable privacy appeals to the principle of public relevance in drawing the distinction between public and private. The principle of public relevance claims that personal beliefs and actions should be in accordance with public values to the extent that private life affects the ability of citizens to function in society and to see others as free and equal citizens. According to this principle, private beliefs, communications, and actions are not immune to public evaluation. Rather, the family and civil society are potentially subject to public evaluation and criticism when they oppose the values of free and equal citizenship in a manner that comes to light publicly without violating the rights of these groups.

Practices within the family or civil society that violate democratic values do not always call for a coercive response. Sometimes publicly relevant practices and beliefs should be protected by rights. In these instances, the principle of public relevance can be fulfilled in two ways. First, citizens ideally would engage in what I call reflective revision. When they engage in reflective revision, citizens internalize the reasons and values that underlie rights, and they transform their beliefs to make them consistent with free and equal citizenship. I describe reflective revision in more detail in section IV of this chapter. But when citizens do not engage in reflective revision on their own, I suggest that the principle of public relevance should be fulfilled in a second way, which I call democratic persuasion. The state uses democratic persuasion when it exercises its expressive capacity to criticize racist and other discriminatory beliefs in the family and civil society. This criticism is intended to protect free and equal citizenship, and to prompt greater reflective revision among citizens. I argue for democratic persuasion at greater length in section V of this chapter.

In sum, by subjecting the family and civil society to normative scrutiny, the principle of public relevance provides a way of recognizing what is problematic about the Hateful Society. Although it might formally respect the rights of equal citizenship in its laws, the Hateful Society permits the unabated spread of racism and discrimination within the "private sphere" of the family and civil society. Discriminatory beliefs directly challenge the ideals that justify rights in the first place. Soon I will describe value democracy's response to beliefs and practices that are protected by rights but that oppose the ideal of free and equal citizenship. Before doing so, it is necessary to clarify the meaning of the ideal of free and equal citizenship.

III. THE MEANING OF FREE AND EQUAL CITIZENSHIP

Defenders of a traditional division between public and private spaces might worry that the principle of public relevance is potentially limitless, opening every aspect of life to public scrutiny. After all, I have suggested that matters of equal citizenship might occur both within the family and within the associations of civil society. I acknowledge that the principle of public relevance is potentially quite broad because it concerns citizens' beliefs and practices across multiple domains, including those tradition- ally thought of as "private." For example, citizens' beliefs about whether other citizens should be treated as equal will influence their thinking and behavior in the domains of civil society, private clubs, and family life. In this sense the principle of public relevance goes beyond the traditional liberal concern to divide public from private life. If a belief is publicly rel- evant, in that it conflicts with free and equal citizenship, it maintains that relevance across different domains. Thus, the principle of public relevance is broadly applicable; even if beliefs are expressed in the most private of domains, they are publicly relevant to the degree that they conflict with the ideal of free and equal citizenship.

Despite the potentially broad application of the ideal of free and equal citizenship across a variety of domains, however, its limits come from the fact that this is a distinctly public kind of value. Specifically, the principle of public relevance is not "deep" in terms of either its justification or the types of beliefs to which it applies. To use a phrase from John Rawls, the principle is "political, not metaphysical."[4] To show why the principle is not deep in justification, we must clarify what kind of equality is entailed by free and equal citizenship. Although the ideal is a normative one that potentially conflicts with a wide variety of beliefs and practices, it does not concern many of the deepest theological or philosophical questions.

Instead, the ideal of free and equal citizenship regards the equal status of persons who are subject to coercive law in a democratic society.

According to value democracy, citizens must be treated as having equal status in that the rights of all citizens must be equally respected. These rights include freedom of expression, association, and religion, as well as rights of political participation and the rule of law. Citizens are to be regarded as "free" in the sense of being able to possess and exercise the rights of citizenship. Beliefs that relegate women, minorities, or other groups to second-class citizenship directly challenge this ideal. Beliefs that call for citizenship to be denied altogether on the basis of race, gender, sexual orientation, or other categories are also publicly relevant. Moreover, free and equal citizenship is incompatible with public discrimination, such as in education and employment. In sum, the ideal of free and equal citizenship in value democracy centers around the political ideal that all citizens have equal status under law. This in turn entails an anti-caste principle: to affirm the ideals of free and equal citizenship, we must reject the idea that some citizens are to be regarded as second class.

Much work in political and legal theory concerns hard cases about whether citizens are treated as second class in certain situations. However, I want to start with a set of relatively easy, concrete cases that involve paradigmatic violations of the ideal of free and equal citizenship. Doing so will give us a fixed point from which to work toward a more nuanced understanding of the ideal of free and equal citizenship. We should not limit ourselves to applying general principles to specific cases in a "top-down" fashion. Rather, we should also work from the "bottom up" by considering core cases of protecting free and equal citizenship. These cases can then shape our understanding of moral principles. Decisions that uphold the equal protection of the law for African Americans, women, or gays, like *Brown v. Board of Education* and *Romer v. Evans*, serve as bedrocks in thinking about the meaning of free and equal citizenship. Core cases of protecting free and equal citizenship function in this way as "considered convictions," which can be extended to more controversial cases and inform our general principles. Our understanding of free and equal citizenship should therefore begin with both general principles and considered convictions about specific cases.[5]

Which laws and practices most obviously violate that ideal? The most obvious violations of the ideal of free and equal citizenship occur when race, ethnicity, or gender are used to make discriminatory legal distinctions between classes of persons. The institution of slavery, present in the United States before the passage of the Thirteenth and Fourteenth Amendments, placed African Americans into bondage and was perhaps the most visible and evident violation of free and equal citizenship. Informal and formal racial segregation in the American South after the Civil

War also served to distinguish between classes of citizens in the United States. The end of Jim Crow laws through *Brown v. Board of Education*, the 1964 Civil Rights Act, and other extensions of the Fourteenth Amendment of the U.S. Constitution have brought the United States closer to the ideal of free and equal citizenship. Some of these measures have sought to end the state's direct role in creating a subordinate class of citizens, such as when the Court ruled that the government must end segregation in public schools. Other measures have banned segregation in public accommodations, including hotels or restaurants, on the grounds that segregation unjustly created a second class of citizenship for African Americans.

In addition to racial subordination, the history of gender discrimination in the United States provides a clear example of the violation of free and equal citizenship. The denial of the vote to women, for instance, enshrined into law differences based on gender and stigmatized women as second-class citizens. The extension of the franchise to women was an important move in the direction of free and equal citizenship.[6]

Although it is a more controversial area, I take the rights of gay citizens also to be fundamental to the ideal of free and equal citizenship. In its *Lawrence v. Texas* and *Romer v. Evans* decisions, the Supreme Court struck down laws that openly stigmatize gay citizens and deny rights on the basis of sexual orientation. These cases, respectively, held that a law banning gay sodomy and another law allowing discrimination against gay citizens were unconstitutional. On my view, the Court decisions in *Lawrence* and *Romer* stand for the principle that laws discriminating against gays are at odds with the ideal of free and equal citizenship.[7]

What both cases have in common is the claim that some laws not only deny gays rights, but are based on an idea of animus, which disregards the fundamental equal status of citizens who are gay. I want to briefly explore the Supreme Court's animus doctrine, because it helps to show why a theory of rights must examine citizens' beliefs and the reasons for legislation. More specifically, the animus doctrine helps us to elucidate which kinds of reasons underlie rights. Just as importantly, the doctrine articulates the kinds of reasons that have no place as a basis for law, and it clarifies how the reasons for rights can conflict with a variety of inegalitarian kinds of reasoning. Indeed, the animus doctrine can explain why the beliefs prevalent in the Hateful Society are illegitimate as the basis for law.

The animus doctrine is central to the Court's gay rights jurisprudence. According to the Court, when a law makes distinctions between people based on categories such as sexual orientation, the state must demonstrate a "rational basis" for the law to avoid violating the Equal Protection Clause of the Fourteenth Amendment. In rational basis review, the burden is that the state must have a rational goal available to it, and the law itself must be a rational way to meet the goal. Even if the goal is not articulated, the Court will often seek to try to reconstruct such a reason for the law. The issue, therefore, is not actual reasons, but possible reasons for a law. The Court ruled in *Romer* that the plebiscite revoking the civil rights protections of gay citizens was so lacking in rational basis that its only motivation could be "animus." No other basis was even available as an explanation of the plebiscite. Although this term literally means "hatred," it is used by the Court to strike down laws that might be based on either religious or secular reasons that fail a basic standard of rationality.

What is significant about the doctrine of animus as a whole is that it suggests that, in order to determine whether a law violates a right, we need to examine the available reasons and motivations for that law. This means that the reasons and beliefs of citizens, and not only their actions, are relevant to the constitutional jurisprudence of rights. In short, to understand which rights citizens are entitled to hold in the first place, we must dig beneath the surface of rights violation claims to examine the reasons for rights.

However, I differ from the Court, in that I do not think a sensible account of the animus doctrine can be based strictly on "rationality" without appealing to affirmative, democratic values. Many hate groups, for instance, are quite rational in the sense that they have clearly articulated goals. Moreover, a law denying civil rights protections to a minority group could have a purpose that is rational in the sense of being "clearly defined." Therefore, the "rationality" standard should be interpreted as meaning that the goal of a law must respect the democratic value of equal status for all citizens. As I reconstruct the animus doctrine at the basis of the *Romer* and *Lawrence* decisions, it should stand for the proposition that laws criminalizing sexual relations and denying civil rights protections fail to respect the entitlements of gay people to be treated as having equal status. Regardless of how popular these laws may have been, they lack a democratic basis because they are hostile to the fundamental democratic value of free and equal citizenship.

Some critics might object to my inclusion of equal status for gay citizens as central to democratic persuasion. While the Supreme Court has relatively recently extended its jurisprudence to protection in this area, gay rights remain contested among the polity. It might be claimed that some people might embrace the ideal of free and equal citizenship, and yet reasonably refuse to apply these values to gay citizens. However, like the Supreme Court in its *Romer v. Evans* decision, I reject this claim.[8] It is inconsistent to say that one endorses the ideal of free and equal citizenship while rejecting gay rights, or for that matter, equal rights for women and African Americans.

Indeed, it would be a mistake for the state to wait for non-discrimination to be widely accepted before promulgating the reasons for rights. Waiting for wide acceptance would have prevented state officials from promoting racial non-discrimination when it was controversial during the 1950s and 1960s. Hence I do not think the idea of "reasonable disagreement" should refer to whether the disagreement is widespread, as an empirical matter. Rather, reasonable disagreement is disagreement with a particular moral basis that is compatible with respect for free and equal citizenship. Opposition to extending free and equal citizenship to gay citizens therefore does not qualify as reasonable disagreement.

The animus doctrine is relevant to rights more generally, beyond the context of gay rights. Even if a wide variety of viewpoints are protected by rights, the animus doctrine implies that viewpoints should be criticized if they oppose the basis for rights and disrespect the fundamental equal status of all citizens. I will argue in depth in chapter 5 that some religious views may display animus and oppose the reasons underlying religious liberty. Although the animus doctrine is formally used in discerning the kinds of discriminatory beliefs that lead to unconstitutional laws, chapter 5 goes beyond the question whether certain laws are unconstitutional, and asks what the state can do to criticize and check the spread of discriminatory beliefs themselves. The animus doctrine helps us to identify the kinds of beliefs that oppose the ideal of free and equal citizenship and that are rightly subject to democratic persuasion, as I argue in greater detail in chapter 3. Indeed, the case of *Romer* suggests why democratic persuasion in defense of free and equal citizenship might need to be aimed at large segments of the population. In that case, a majority of Colorado's citizens passed a plebiscite limiting civil rights for gays that the U.S. Supreme Court struck down as unconstitutional, arguing that it was motivated by animus against gays. Although the expression of animus-based beliefs is protected by the right of free speech, I will argue that the legitimate state will not only disallow laws based on this motivation, it will seek to transform animus-based beliefs in its expressive capacity.[9]

More generally, I contend throughout this book that the idea central to legitimacy—that citizens should all be treated as free and equal—is incompatible with the notion that some should be regarded by the law as second-class citizens. The entitlement to first-class citizenship carries with it a commitment to regard all persons subject to law as having two fundamental political capacities. They are entitled to be recognized as politically autonomous and equal. In a democracy, laws are not merely imposed upon citizens; they are entitled to debate the laws and to vote for their representatives. This requires a respect for what John Rawls calls a "capacity for a sense of justice."[10] If citizens do not have rights of expression and political participation to decide what they think of laws and policies, the state would not respect their capacity to reflect upon and debate the laws and policies of a democratic state. But it is not enough for any one individual or group to enjoy this capacity and to have the freedom to exercise it. The "equal" in free and equal citizenship suggests that a respect for a capacity for the sense of justice must be extended to all citizens in a democracy, because all persons who are subject to coercive laws must have the ability to endorse them.

In addition to an equal capacity for a sense of justice, Rawls proposes that we respect free and equal citizens as having a distinct "capacity for a conception of the good." While the capacity for a sense of justice is used by citizens to exercise political autonomy and to judge the laws and policies of the state, the capacity for a conception of the good is used by citizens to exercise personal autonomy and to pursue their life plans, based on what they value. To be fully exercised, the capacity for a conception of the good requires the rights of free expression, association, and religion. In short, the "freedom" in free and equal citizenship requires respect for both the political and personal autonomy that citizens need to develop opinions about politics and the good life. The "equal" in free and equal citizenship reflects a concern to ensure that these capacities are respected equally regardless of one's race, ethnicity, or gender. An important reason why slavery, segregation, and the limitation of the franchise are violations of the ideal of free and equal citizenship is because they deny the equality of all citizens in possessing the two moral capacities.

I have emphasized the ideal of free and equal citizenship as opposed to values and policies that endorse a subordinate notion of citizenship. I have also appealed to well-established, considered judgments about policies that violate this ideal, with some of these judgments from the domain of civil rights protections and Supreme Court jurisprudence. In chapter 3, I emphasize how the ideal of free and equal citizenship also underlies civil liberties protections more broadly, such as free speech, free association, and religious freedom. In this sense, the ideal underlies the wide array of rights protected in a liberal democracy.

In elaborating the ideal of free and equal citizenship, it is important to contrast it with some notions of equality that go beyond the realm of the political. As I noted, the normative ideal of free and equal citizenship is political, and not a religious or metaphysical conception of equality. By contrast, there are theological conceptions of inequality that do not necessarily bear upon the idea of equal citizenship and that can be bracketed from this principle. For example, in his recent work Robert Putnam asks a sample of Americans whether they believe that there is salvation outside their church.[11] He uses this question as a proxy for whether Americans endorse toleration and equality. But it is possible to profess that there is no salvation outside one's church, while holding beliefs that are consistent with equal citizenship. One might believe that persons are not equals before God, because some will enter the Kingdom of Heaven and others will not. However, someone who endorses this view might still believe that all citizens should be afforded equal rights of citizenship, because of a division between divine and human law. Such a belief would not contradict the principle of equal citizenship, although it would be evidence of a kind of inequality at a deeper theological level. Therefore, on my account, it is not necessary that one hold a theological egalitarianism at the deepest level regarding salvation, or that one hold a metaphysical notion that persons are possessed of equal dignity. The principle of equal citizenship is thinner in that it lies closer to the notion of equal rights and non-discrimination in access to education and opportunities for employment. Although I will develop a notion of equal citizenship that will apply to several domains, it remains shallow in justification, because it is based on a principle that underlies basic constitutional protections instead of underlying deeper matters of religion or metaphysics.

The ideal of free and equal citizenship can also be distinguished from more secular forms of "metaphysical" equality. We need not accept a Kantian ethics that permeates every decision to endorse an idea of equal citizenship. Kant famously argues that treating each person as an equal requires that all actions be guided by the categorical imperative. The potential murderer who appears at our door is entitled to a deep kind of respect that requires that we not lie to him or her, even to save the life of another person.[12] Nothing in the idea of equal citizenship, however, requires a commitment to that kind of equality any more than it requires an idea of equality before God. In short, the ideal of free and equal citizenship is distinct from metaphysical or religious ideas of equality in that it is meant to be a principle that underlies the rights and entitlements of those persons subject to laws in a liberal democracy. This is a principle compatible with a wide range of religious and metaphysical doctrines that might not be fully egalitarian.

A more controversial issue is how far to extend the ideal of free and equal citizenship to the realm of material equality. On my view, I do not think that first-class citizenship or the need to respect citizens' capacities for a sense of justice or a conception of the good requires strict equality of income.[13] I take it that although economists in public universities might be paid more money than political scientists, this does not violate the equal citizenship of political scientists, provided that women and minorities have equal opportunity to enter either profession. Nothing in the pay differential between these two groups, for instance, inhibits the ability of political scientists to speak out about policy in a democracy as equals or relegates them to second-class citizenship. Economists and political scientists, despite their income differential, might retain the same capacity to pursue conceptions of the good and to pursue a robust role in public life.

In contrast, this acceptable differential is different from pay differentials based on race or sex, which are rightly limited by a principle of free and equal citizenship. Although there are difficulties in discerning when discrimination is purposeful, intentional pay differentials based on race or gender, which treat women or African Americans as subordinate to men and whites, are incompatible with equal citizenship, because they are likely to reflect broader conceptions of blacks and women as inferior to whites and men in the general political and social world.

In sum, the ideal of free and equal citizenship is not deep in its justification. Its justification is limited to democratic values, and it applies only to beliefs that affect citizens' public status. Although the rights of free speech, conscience, and religious freedom protect all beliefs against coercion, the principle of public relevance in section II has suggested that these beliefs should be revised when they conflict with free and equal citizenship. In section III, I defined the value of free and equal citizenship, which determines what beliefs are publicly relevant. I am now in a position to begin to sketch the two ways that the principle of public relevance can be fulfilled—through citizens revising their own beliefs, as described in section IV, and through the state responding to hateful or discriminatory views, in section V.

IV. Why Citizens Should Adopt the Values of Free and Equal Citizenship as Their Own

On my view, the right of citizens to free speech protects them from state coercion. This right gives citizens an entitlement to say and believe whatever they wish. As a matter of right, citizens should be free to reject the ideal of free and equal citizenship without coercive interference or punishment from the government. But, as I will argue at length in chapter 2, individuals have an obligation to endorse and internalize a commitment to public values through a process of reflective revision. This way of fulfilling the principle of public relevance obligates citizens to make their beliefs consistent with the ideal of free and equal citizenship. In chapter 3, I argue that citizens are also obliged to promote the ideal of free and equal citizenship through democratic persuasion.

But now, I want to ask the more basic question of why the ideal of free and equal citizenship should be embraced by citizens. It is widely thought that the reasons for laws must be consistent with free and equal citizenship. But a separate issue concerns whether it is important for citizens themselves to adopt democratic values. Some might object that it is not a matter of public concern when citizens' beliefs conflict with the ideal of free and equal citizenship. In the rest of this section, I present arguments against that contention and in defense of the principle of public relevance. The principle of public relevance claims that citizens should adopt the ideal of free and equal citizenship and change their discriminatory beliefs and practices which conflict with democratic values. In defense of the principle of public relevance, I provide several arguments for why citizens themselves should endorse the ideal of free and equal citizenship. These arguments help to further answer the concerns about the stability of democracy raised by the paradox of rights.

The first argument for why it is important for citizens to endorse the democratic values of free and equal citizenship focuses on democratic congruence. This concerns the importance of wide endorsement of the reasons for rights and shows why it is a problem for legitimacy if only elites endorse the reasons for laws and rights. To see why a lack of democratic agreement undermines the legitimacy of the state, it is helpful to think of the example of a society in which all of the laws are legitimate, but 90 percent of citizens do not endorse the principles for these rights and institutions. In such a state, legislatures would enact the right laws, but at the expense of ignoring the beliefs of their constituents. Such a state is legitimate when we consider only its laws and policies, which protect the basic rights of citizens. But the lack of agreement between the egalitarian principles behind the laws and the discriminatory beliefs that citizens actually hold is problematic from a democratic point of view. It is difficult to say that such a state is fully democratic or governed by the citizens in a robust sense when it is ruled by an elite opinion which is not widely shared. Of course, such a society is more legitimate than one upholding laws that conflict with democratic values. But I take it that democratic legitimacy would increase if there were greater agreement between the beliefs of actual citizens and the principles governing their society. Although I will argue that it is a mistake to think that every aspect of democratic citizens' lives should directly mirror their public commitment to equality, I use the phrase democratic congruence to refer to the importance of consistency between democratic public values and personal commitments. Therefore, democratic legitimacy is based not only on whether the state protects democratic rights, but also on democratic endorsement or citizens' agreement with the values that justify rights.

In some ways, democratic congruence might seem contrary to a popular understanding of the relation between policy and popular opinion. On some views of democracy, policy should be restricted to reflecting popular opinion. Democratic congruence on this interpretation would mean changing policy to reflect the opinions of most people. This would imply, in the context of the 1950s or earlier, that public officials could not advocate for more equal treatment for African Americans, because equality was widely opposed by popular opinion. But as I have argued at length in my previous book, *Democratic Rights*, strict deference to popular opinion would mean the enactment of policies that potentially undermine the very values that undergird the right to participate in democracy in the first place. Imagine, for instance, if a substantial majority of the population believed in disenfranchising African Americans from the vote. Because such a policy would reject the very reason why we allow participation, namely out of respect for citizens as equals to participate in their own governance, it would not be a democratic policy. In my view, when public opinion opposes the very values that give rise to the right to participate, such policies are rightly struck down by courts in the name of democracy. The challenge in a democracy, however, is to avoid such conflicts between popular opinion and elite institutions, such as the Supreme Court. It would be better from the perspective of democracy if a majority of people supported rather than opposed democratic policies.[14] In order to obtain a more robust legitimacy, it is important for a polity to consider how it can make public policy consistent with democratic values, while respecting rights. I do not suggest that the government should mold opinion on matters about which there is reasonable disagreement. There are many cases where there is reasonable disagreement about the meaning of democratic values. But in extreme instances, such as the case of majorities opposing equal citizenship for a minority race, democratic legitimacy requires at minimum that there be an attempt to change public opinion.

I have suggested so far that there is a problem from the standpoint of legitimacy if only elites endorse the values of free and equal citizenship, which are central to the ideal of democracy. For a democratic ideal to be fully realized, it is important for those values to be endorsed and embraced by the citizenry, and not only instantiated in public policy. Although I have couched this need in largely moral terms, there is also a concern about the empirical stability of a democracy that only relies on elites to pass laws consistent with these values. Such a democracy might lack empirical stability. If many citizens were to reject a commitment to free and equal citizenship, as in the German, Italian, and Japanese democracies of the interwar years, there is a risk that democracy itself might be undermined in the long term. Indeed, recent examples have shown that even when small but politically active groups dissent from core democratic values, they can undermine democratic stability. For instance, the Dutch politician Geert Wilders started a one-man political party, the PVV, that has expressed hostility toward Muslims and has called for banning the Koran. Despite its extremism, the PVV has grown to become one of the ruling coalition's most influential allies in Parliament.[15] If democratic rights, both procedural and substantive, do not rest on a foundation of widespread endorsement, there is no reason to think that these rights are going to be stable over time. This empirical worry and the broader idea that the values of free and equal citizenship should be widely supported are at the heart of Rawls' concern to ensure that a regime has "stability for the right reasons."[16]

In addition to democratic congruence and stability, another argument for citizens to internalize the ideal of equal citizenship and the reasons for rights is what I call the argument from interconnection. The values of freedom and equality could be undermined by non-governmental institu-tions if most citizens opposed these values and the rights of free and equal citizenship. For example, if families promoted discrimination in educating their children, it would risk undermining the formal respect for equality in the constitution. The same might be said of a company with a workplace environment that is influenced by discriminatory beliefs opposing the basic rights of free and equal citizens. This would potentially undermine the formal, legal guarantees of free and equal citizenship. If we hope to have a democratic society, and not merely a justifiable state, the argument from interconnection suggests that actual citizens should endorse the rea-sons for constitutional rights. This would reduce the problem of practices in the private sphere undermining public values.

There are two important empirical considerations that will affect the power of the argument from interconnection. First, the arguments apply to those groups in civil society that specifically oppose the ideal of free and equal citizenship.[17] For instance, the argument from interconnection would apply to groups that opposed women's suffrage early in the twen-tieth century and that more generally sought to restrict the role of women in the professions and the workplace. More recently, it would apply to groups that seek to deny civil rights to gays, including their qualifications to serve as educators. For example, the Traditional Values Education and Legal Institute has argued that gays should be barred from the classroom, since they allegedly "recruit children into a deviant lifestyle."[18] On my conception, equal opportunity in the workplace and education is a matter of free and equal citizenship, since it concerns the ability of persons to have access to positions of power and influence in the wider social world.

The second important empirical consideration for the argument from interconnection is to show that discriminatory beliefs translate into dis-criminatory actions that can undermine the rights of individuals to par-ticipate as equals in the workplace. In recent work, social psychologists have linked beliefs to the kind of discrimination that actively undermines women's rights. As Margaret Bull Kovera and Eugene Borgida write in the influential *Handbook of Social Psychology*, "Extensive research has established a reliable scientific relationship between gender stereotypes and a range of work-related outcomes."[19] For instance, Alice Eagly and Linda Carli cite President Richard Nixon's dismissal of the role of women as equal citizens to explain why the culture of the workplace in the 1970s did not offer women a chance to compete as equals.[20] Nixon was recorded on White House audiotape as declaring that women had no role in govern-ment: "I don't think a woman should be in any government job whatso-ever mainly because they are erratic. And emotional. Men are erratic and emotional, too, but the point is a woman is more likely to be."[21] Eagly and Carli point out that "in a culture where such opinions were widely held, women had virtually no chance of attaining influential leadership roles."[22] Indeed, Nixon's statement suggests not only a culture of discrimination in his administration, but a wider culture in which women faced significant obstacles in attaining the status of free and equal citizenship. Even if laws were on the books protecting women's rights to equal employment, these sorts of beliefs and attitudes undermined their equal opportunity in the workplace.[23]

In addition to the argument from interconnection, I want to introduce a related argument from public trust. Regardless of what the law formally states, the law is carried out by public officials and bureaucrats who will often be influenced by their own beliefs. These officials could weaken the legal protection of free and equal citizenship if they live and are raised in a society that widely rejects the reasons for rights. Consider, for instance, the failure of some prosecutors to take seriously the crime of domestic violence. The prosecutors are influenced by having grown up in a society that wrongly ignores violence that takes place within the family. The argument from public trust shows that for public officials, including prosecutors, to be trusted to reliably protect free and equal citizenship, the values of freedom and equality need to be widely endorsed by citizens in the broader society, including in the so-called private sphere.

The argument from public trust also suggests that public officials and those occupying governmental roles have a distinct obligation to promulgate the values of free and equal citizenship. Although all citizens should endorse these values and internalize them, it is particularly important for the representatives of the people to articulate democratic values. Consider, for instance, the issue of state apologies for past injustices. Although a citizen can recognize that a racist policy was wrong and condemn it, it is only a representative of the people as a whole that can speak on behalf of the polity in condemning and apologizing for past injustices.

When the president of the United States apologizes for previous acts of discrimination and racism by the nation, there is a different force than when a private citizen apologizes. For example, in the infamous Tuskegee experiments from 1932 to 1972, the U.S. federal government deliberately withheld life-saving medical treatment from hundreds of poor African American men with syphilis, and did not disclose that they were suffering from the disease. The purpose of the study was to observe the course of untreated syphilis in patients until their deaths. The patients were experimented on "without their knowledge and consent."[24] In 1997, President Clinton officially apologized for the Tuskegee experiments. President Clinton engaged in a form of democratic persuasion, in that he not only apologized for the unjust acts of the government, but he explicitly cited the reasons for rights when he declared that the experiment "was an outrage to our commitment to integrity and equality for all our citizens."[25]

His speech also upheld the ideal of free and equal citizenship in condemning the racism behind the study: "To our African American citizens, I am sorry that your federal government orchestrated a study so clearly racist. That can never be allowed to happen again."[26]

It was significant that the apology came from a public official, since it evoked an issue of public trust regarding whether officials would act on their responsibility to protect the equal rights of all citizens. As President Clinton said, "An apology is the first step, and we take it with a commitment to rebuild that broken trust. We can begin by making sure there is never again another episode like this one."[27] It is thus essential in a democracy that the reasons for rights and free and equal citizenship are articulated on behalf of the state as a whole, and not only by private individuals. Only a public official could make an apology on behalf of the American people, as President Clinton did when he said: "The American people are sorry—for the loss, for the years of hurt. You did nothing wrong, but you were grievously wronged. I apologize and I am sorry that this apology has been so long in coming."[28]

Of course, public officials should enjoy the right to hold their own religious beliefs and express their personal opinions. But if judges, police officers, and teachers hold beliefs at odds with the egalitarian values that underlie rights, they might fail in the course of their duties to fully protect those persons they regard as unequal or inferior. The challenge for value democracy is to think about how the argument from public trust can be resolved while simultaneously protecting rights and ensuring that public officials do not hold beliefs at odds with core liberal commitments to free and equal citizenship.

V. Democratic Persuasion: Using the State's Expressive Capacities to Promote Free and Equal Citizenship

So far I have argued that citizens should embrace the value of free and equal citizenship. Ideally, citizens will adopt democratic values and seek to persuade others to do the same. In instances of bigotry, discrimination, and other practices that violate the core values, citizens should criticize discriminatory behavior and seek to transform the beliefs behind it. But while citizens ideally should pursue these activities, there is nothing about rights as such that ensures citizens will transform discriminatory beliefs on their own. In spite of Mill's hope that free speech will result in truth, such a process does not unfold only by protecting rights. On my view, an active citizenry is necessary to promote public values when citizens are granted freedom of expression.[29] But in cases where the citizenry does not succeed in instilling such values, does the state have a role in expressing the value of equal citizenship?

Although Mill does not develop a notion of state persuasion, I suggest throughout the book that the state, as well as citizens, should promote public values. I have already touched on why it is important that public officials embrace the ideal of free and equal citizenship. But in my view, the state also should try to convince citizens to embrace the values of free and equal citizenship through democratic persuasion. Democratic persuasion does not refer to any form of state expression, but rather to the specific obligation of the state (and citizens more generally) to promote the democratic value of free and equal citizenship. I emphasize that the state should respect rights and the free thought of citizens in this process. The idea is to prompt the embrace of the values of free and equal citizenship, as opposed to coercing them. Coercion would violate the rights of citizens and would be incompatible with reflective revision. But reasons, unlike coercion, allow citizens the choice of adopting what is advanced by the state. Citizens can adopt the reason because they see its value, or they can reject it because they either do not see its value or wish to ignore it. In short, a conscious attempt to pursue democratic persuasion should focus on giving reasons as an alternative to state coercion.

It is common in contemporary political theory to think that the status of citizens as free and equal entitles them to a justification for law that respects them as being capable of reasoning.[30] But, as I will argue, this respect too often has stopped short of actually engaging citizens in reasoning or challenging them when they reject the democratic grounds for an entitlement to justification. On my view, citizens deserve not only a potential or a hypothetical justification for law, but they have a fundamental entitlement for the justification to be articulated. Such a defense of democratic values is not only consistent with rights protections, as I will argue in chapter 3; it is required by rights.

There are two main reasons why the state, and not only citizens, should be concerned with promoting public values. The first concerns a possible lack of initiative on the part of citizens to endorse the values of free and equal citizenship. If citizens are protected in their ability to say and believe whatever they wish by a set of liberal rights, there is no guarantee that they will engage in reflective revision, as shown by the spread of hate groups in the United States and Europe. If a failure to engage in endorsement of these values is widespread, the arguments I have given about democratic congruence, stability, interconnection, and public trust become all the more salient. In order to answer these concerns, it is important to ensure that there is an effective way of promoting free and equal citizenship in the absence of citizens' decision to do so.

In addition to concerns about stability and effective promotion of the values of free and equal citizenship, a second reason why the state should promote democratic values concerns its complicity in views that oppose freedom and equality for all citizens. A state that fails to answer these critics would risk being seen as being neutral about its democratic values, or worse, complicit in protecting the views of liberal democracy's own opponents. To articulate how democratic persuasion avoids complicity and to bolster the claim that the state should seek to express the reasons for rights, I turn first to the idea of promulgating law. It is commonly thought that the state has an obligation to ensure the content of law is promulgated or made known to citizens. While citizens are obligated to know the law, it is also the responsibility of the state to provide ways for citizens to receive this information. Similarly, I want to claim that citizens are not only obligated to internalize the reasons for rights, but that the state should promulgate these reasons. It is essential in a legitimate society for the state to express why it is protecting rights and to explain the reasons underlying those rights.

This state role in promulgating the reasons for rights is particularly important with respect to certain negative rights. As I will suggest, rights to free speech should protect even the most heinous political viewpoints, including those promoted by hate groups, such as the Ku Klux Klan. The state's protection of these viewpoints, however, is not equivalent to the state's indifference to them. The state is not neutral toward the values expressed by hate groups. But when the state protects hate groups such as the Klan, the reasons for the protection are inverted with respect to the content of the speech and beliefs that are protected. Negative rights that protect individuals from the state in matters such as free expression and privacy have, as I call it, an inverted character that leads to possible confusions about the state's indifference or even complicity in views that seek the demise of liberal democracy. In the absence of the state clarifying its reasons for rights, it might be commonly mistaken that the state is neutral or indifferent to the content of viewpoints that are protected by rights. It is thus incumbent on the state to promulgate its reasons for rights in order to clarify the confusion that might accompany inverted rights. In extreme instances, the state has an obligation to criticize hateful viewpoints and to persuade citizens that these views are incompatible with the values that underlie the state's legitimacy. In this way, the state can avoid the excesses of the Hateful Society with its indifference toward the basic reasons for equal citizenship. But the state can also avoid the excesses of the Invasive State by employing its persuasive as opposed to its coercive capacities.

The kind of criticism that the state might use will vary depending on the degree that the criticized viewpoint opposes free and equal citizenship. For instance, some groups and persons might hold specific opinions that are at odds with these democratic values, while also holding a vast array of opinions consistent with free and equal citizenship. In such instances, it is the specific discriminatory views that the state should seek to criticize, while avoiding censuring these groups as a whole. Indeed, such specific views might best be criticized not through direct confrontation, but through the general promulgation of the reasons and arguments for rights. But the Ku Klux Klan is a different case, in that the entire reason why this group exists is to oppose the ideal of equal status and equal protection before the law. Such a group arguably should not only be criticized; it should be condemned by the state in its expressive capacity. Of course, such condemnation might not result in a change of viewpoint by members of hate groups. But condemnation clearly answers concerns about the state's complicity in such views. It is also part of an effort to create an ethos in liberal democracy to combat the spread of these ideas among society at large. Condemnation recognizes and responds to the threat of the Hateful Society.

Although hate groups and those that endorse their ideology might be subject to criticism by the state, the audience for democratic persuasion is not limited to only the groups themselves. The audience is also the citizenry as a whole. The people of a liberal democracy have an interest in hearing the central values of democracy articulated and defended. Although I will argue at length that individuals and groups should retain robust rights to free speech, including entitlements to racist viewpoints that reject the ideal of equality before the law, these rights exist alongside the interest of the citizenry in seeing democratic values hold a prominent place in public deliberation and discourse. The right to express racist viewpoints should not be confused with the right to see these viewpoints win a prominent place in democratic society. To the contrary, value democracy suggests why the democratic citizenry has an interest in opposing the spread of these hateful or discriminatory views.

In order to effectively challenge and limit views opposed to the ideal of free and equal citizenship, it is important that the state amplify the reasons for rights. While I draw on the Supreme Court as a prime example of an institution concerned to promote the reasons for rights, its lengthy legal opinions are not widely read. State institutions need to do more to amplify the reasons for rights besides making the court opinions available to the public. I attempt, therefore, to seek more effective ways of persuading citizens through reasoning. But I recognize, too, that reasoning alone might be insufficient to successfully promulgate public values and the reasons for rights.

While state expression takes its most obvious form when public officials speak, there are other ways the state can use its expressive functions to defend the core values. For example, the state can celebrate Martin Luther King Day and build public monuments to honor the civil rights movement. In his speech on the Tuskegee syphilis study, President Clinton spoke not only for himself but on behalf of the state as a whole in an effort to promulgate democratic values and to apologize for times when the country failed to live up to the ideals of free and equal citizenship. Such apologies call not only for the response of a particular person or politician, but for the response of a democracy as a whole to articulate its fundamental values. Such instances of the "state speaking" are fundamental to clarifying what makes a society legitimate in the first place.

But importantly, Clinton's apology was not limited to state speech. He not only apologized for the government experimenting on African American men without their knowledge or consent, but he funded a public memorial for the victims of the study, and provided government funding for a National Center for Bioethics in Research and Health Care at Tuskegee University. These forms of state spending reinforced Clinton's condemnation of racist medical experimentation. The message here and in celebrations of civil rights, such as Martin Luther King Day, not only articulates democratic rights; it also criticizes the practices of racism and segregation in American history. As I suggest in chapter 3, these forms of democratic persuasion are also rightly interpreted to criticize contemporary private organizations that are segregated or discriminatory.

In addition to the state's role as a speaker and spender, it often acts as an educator. In educating students, the curriculum should not be neutral with respect to equal citizenship, but it should promote the public value of equality in the beliefs of future citizens. Thus, the civil rights movement's struggle against segregation is not usually taught in value-neutral terms. The state takes a side when it distinguishes between the actions of Bull Connor and Martin Luther King Jr., and celebrates King's birthday instead of Connor's. In holding a public holiday in honor of King, and in teaching students the lessons of the civil rights movement, the state condemns the viewpoint of racial segregation. Moreover, students not only should be educated about the content of the Constitution, but they should also learn the reasons for the rights it protects.[31] Using the state expression in this way does not violate privacy, even though the teaching might conflict with the beliefs students are being taught by their own parents at the dinner table. Parental control over children's beliefs does not extend to the right to prevent children from hearing views that support equal citizenship or that conflict with parental beliefs.

To develop the notion of the state's expressive capacities and its obligation to pursue democratic persuasion on behalf of the values of free and equal citizenship, I draw in part from First Amendment jurisprudence. As I discuss in chapters 3 and 4, the Supreme Court has held that when the state threatens to punish or otherwise act coercively, it must be viewpoint neutral, but when the state does not act in its coercive capacity, but as a promoter of its own values, it is entitled to a great deal of leeway. According to the Supreme Court's "state as speaker" doctrine, the various organs of government often have an entitlement to promote specific viewpoints and specific messages. These include the kind of symbolic statements and public holidays I have just mentioned. More broadly, the Supreme Court has recognized that the state can promote a particular message when it provides formal education to students. Perhaps most controversially, state spending is sometimes, but not always, treated as a type of expression that can promote a particular viewpoint. However, Supreme Court jurisprudence, as I suggest in chapter 3, is often couched in excessively value-neutral terms. A value-neutral approach would allow the state to promote whatever message it wishes, even if it expresses a message directly opposing the reasons for rights. In contrast to a value-neutral theory of state expression, democratic persuasion is distinctly non-neutral, and calls for the state to express a message that promotes the values of free and equal citizenship. This is an obligation, not distinct from rights, but that comes from the obligation to promote the reasons for rights.

Sometimes two opposing sides will accuse the other of being hostile to democratic values. Should the state take sides in such disputes? I acknowledge there will be hard cases in deciding whether viewpoints conflict or are consistent with public ideals. There will be what theorists refer to as "reasonable disagreement" about the meaning of public values.[32] I propose that the state should criticize beliefs, not in controversial cases of reasonable disagreement, but only when viewpoints clearly conflict with the ideal of free and equal citizenship. Democratic persuasion moves from hard cases at the boundary of reasonable disagreement to focus on beliefs that most fundamentally conflict with the values of freedom and equality. Individuals, as they engage in reflective revision based on their public commitments, may re-examine their private beliefs regarding cases of reasonable disagreement. However, when the state uses its expressive capacities, it should be more reticent and focus instead on cases of clear conflict. The reason for this reticence is that the state is much more powerful than individuals, even when it employs its expressive rather than its coercive capacity. The president of the United States can speak to the country at will in a way that ordinary citizens cannot. When the state makes mistakes in criticizing viewpoints hostile to the values of free and equal citizenship, the potential drawbacks are greater than when individuals make mistakes in their own moral evaluation. Greater reticence should therefore be used in cases of reasonable disagreement.[33]

Viewpoints hostile to the ideal of free and equal citizenship need not be explicit; they can also be thinly veiled. When hate groups "dress up" their beliefs in language that only barely conceals their hostility to the core values, they are nonetheless acting in opposition to those values. For example, hate groups might claim that their opposition to interracial marriage is not based on an idea of racial inferiority, but on the idea that the races should be segregated. Such openly hostile and thinly veiled attacks on the core values are the clearest instances of arguments and beliefs that cannot plausibly be thought to be consistent with the core values of free and equal citizenship. I propose this criterion of "implausibility" as a tool for characterizing some of those beliefs and arguments within non-state areas of life that are publicly relevant.

While hate groups characterize paradigmatically implausible views, other groups may hold equally discriminatory beliefs for reasons that are less obviously ill-intentioned. For instance, some deeply discriminatory religious views, which challenge the equal role of women or of minorities in public life, might genuinely be motivated by a love or desire to save the souls of one's fellow citizens. But regardless of these motivations, these beliefs remain deeply incompatible with core values, and so I suggest that even such religious beliefs should be treated as publicly relevant. I examine the unique case of discriminatory religious beliefs separately in chapter 5.

Nothing in this argument about convincing citizens rests on the notion that any single state agency or public official has a monopoly on the right reasons for law. I take it that just as individuals can be wrong about these reasons, so too can the state officials who attempt to promulgate these reasons. The fact that an agent of the state says something does not automatically make the statement an instance of democratic persuasion. Just as state agents can act wrongly by violating the law or by seeking to enact laws that are flawed, so too state agents can speak wrongly in a way inconsistent with democratic persuasion.

In an important sense, then, the reasons that rightfully justify law are independent of any one state official or agency. The reasons are "institution-independent." I develop this feature of value democracy by drawing on arguments against judicial supremacy, which is the view that the Supreme Court has a monopoly on constitutional interpretation.[34] I argue, by contrast, that no one institution should serve as the exclusive or only voice for the reasons for rights. Although the Court potentially acts as one "exemplar" in defending the reasons for rights, a role in promoting democratic values applies broadly, and is the responsibility of citizens, state officials, and public agencies. Far from being a "statist" conception, then, value democracy appeals to the institution-independent standard of free and equal citizenship as a source to which all can look in evaluating both the actions and the expression of state officials and law. Democratic persuasion is defined by the obligation to express and defend the values and reasons that underlie rights; it is rightly pursued by both state actors and persons in their capacity as citizens.

The idea of institution-independence allows value democracy to serve as a normative standard to examine the legitimacy of a wide range of state actions and expression. It is well established in law and in political theory that a theoretical frame is necessary to evaluate the coercive actions of the state's diverse agents, from elected officials to judges, police officers, and administrators. Traditionally, the fundamental problem of legitimacy has been focused on discussions of when state actions are morally justified. But in addition to acting coercively, the state can also use its non-coercive capacities to defend the core democratic values. These non-coercive capacities include expressing democratic values by both giving reasons and promoting the ideal of free and equal citizenship through state funding. Political theory has been silent for too long about these various forms of non-coercive state expression and funding. I argue that, in the same way that we need a theory to determine when state action is legitimate, we also need a theory to determine when state expression is normatively required and what content it should have.

Before I conclude this section, it is important to acknowledge a difference between some ideas of representation and the notion of value democracy. On some accounts of democracy, the role of public officials—in particular, of elected officials—is merely to reflect the opinion of their constituents. Value democracy modifies this understanding of democracy. On my account, regardless of the empirical beliefs of the persons that occupy any particular democracy, there exists a core set of values fundamental to the democratic ideal itself. To be democratic in the first place, a state must respect the ideal of treating each person who is subject to the law as possessing equal status. The state should also regard persons who are subject to law as free citizens. Citizens should only be coerced when there are justifying reasons that respect each citizen's status as both free and equal. This ideal is central to the legitimacy of the democratic state. Of course, in any society, some public officials and some persons might reject this ideal. I take it, though, that if public officials and citizens are to articulate reasons consistent with the foundational justification of democracy, they should embrace the ideal of equal citizenship. While some citizens and public officials might reject this ideal, when they do, they are speaking against democratic values. While they may be using the state's expressive capacities, they would be failing to engage in democratic persuasion.

VI. Conclusion

In the introduction, we explored the dilemma posed by the paradox of rights. On the one hand, rights are grounded in an affirmative set of values, including a concern to respect equal citizenship. Yet the beliefs, practices, and expression protected by these rights can potentially undermine the ideal of equal citizenship. The Hateful Society served as a paradigm of how rights might give rise to discriminatory beliefs in the general culture.

While the Hateful Society avoids the rights violations that plague the Invasive State, it still allows for a culture of widespread racism, sexism, and other beliefs that oppose the values of equal citizenship underlying rights.

In this chapter, I have sketched two concepts that are meant to avoid the excesses of the Invasive State with its violation of rights, and the Hateful Society with its beliefs that undermine the reasons for rights. First, the principle of public relevance avoids the misconceptions of the spatial metaphor by recognizing that public values can be undermined in a variety of spaces. Public relevance, however, does not eliminate privacy altogether. Publicly relevant values do not run so deep that they address every question in life, including issues of the good life. Rather, public relevance posits a minimal standard of equal citizenship that might apply to a broad array of activities and beliefs without dictating how citizens should think about each issue that arises in their lives. Thus, I do not propose to abolish privacy; my aim instead is to offer a publicly justifiable conception of privacy to replace the misleading idea, often associated with the spatial metaphor, that public values have no place in civil society and the family. Moreover, I provided arguments based on democratic congruence, stability, interconnection, and public trust for why it is important for individual citizens to endorse and incorporate the values of free and equal citizenship into their set of beliefs. In the next chapter I elaborate on citizen endorsement of these values, what I call "reflective revision," and its implication for the public/private distinction.

Although the principle of public relevance proposes that citizens should ideally adopt the values of free and equal citizenship as their own, a question arises concerning the state's role in promoting this principle. How can it promote the ideal of equal citizenship without undermining the rights that are also required by this ideal? I have suggested that the key to resolving this aspect of the paradox of rights is found in the distinction between the state's coercive and expressive capacities. When the state is acting in its coercive capacity, it cannot seek to enforce the principle of public relevance. But when the state is acting in its non-coercive, expressive capacity, it should seek to persuade citizens of the value of equal citizenship. Thus, even when beliefs are protected by rights, the state can seek to transform those beliefs through its expressive capacity. While the state's expressive capacity might be used to promote a variety of messages, I hope in the following pages to expand on a normative theory of what the state should "say" when it "speaks." I argue that the state has an obligation, similar to the one that citizens have, to expressively defend the values of free and equal citizenship. I call this account "democratic persuasion."

CHAPTER TWO

. . . .

Publicly Justifiable Privacy and Reflective Revision by Citizens

I. INTRODUCTION

IN THE PROVINCE OF MANITOBA, the Canadian government's restrictions on hate speech reached into the domain of the family when a girl raised by racist parents was removed from her home. The judge in the case made clear that one of the reasons for the removal was the fact that the girl's parents had decorated their home with Nazi paraphernalia and were teaching their child the most heinous of racist views. For instance, the girl stated in school that black people should "die." An investigation of the family's home also revealed that the house was decorated with swastikas celebrating the genocidal politics of the Nazi regime. Although there were other factors in the decision to remove the child, such as the kind of care the child received, the content of the parents' political views played a major role in the decision to remove her. As the judge in the case stated, "Advocating genocide and the willful promotion of hatred against an identifiable group are crimes in this country. These children have a right to be protected from these things."[1]

Although the actual Manitoba case had complications involving potential abuse, we can imagine a hypothetical example in which the parents are non-abusive, but teach their children racist views. Such a case would raise the question of whether a government could coercively extend its values into family life through the use of child removal. Some versions of the Invasive State, or even of militant democracy, might deem the girl's racist upbringing in this example to be so unacceptable to a democratic society that the child should be forcibly removed from her home. On such a view, the government's reason for removing a child would not require proof of physical or emotional abuse, but only evidence of the child being taught hateful viewpoints. Such an approach would raise the kind of worry that I suggested liberals would have about the Invasive State. The dystopia of the Invasive State uses coercion, such as the threat of taking away one's child, to impose congruence between family and political values. But even if we reject the heavy-handed method of child removal in cases of parents with hateful viewpoints, should teaching children hateful viewpoints be immune from public scrutiny? Are the teachings of the parent in this case irrelevant to public values?

Freedom of conscience, expression, and association should protect all political beliefs—even hateful ones—from being coercively banned or punished.[2] But to say that a family should not be coerced into rejecting hateful viewpoints does not imply that their beliefs are entirely private. I argue in this chapter against a view of privacy that regards hateful and discriminatory beliefs and actions in the family and civil society as being immune from normative evaluation and irrelevant from the perspective of public values. Against this view, I argue that, while illiberal beliefs and practices should be protected from coercive intervention, they are also publicly relevant because they conflict with the ideals of free and equal citizenship.

Fundamental to the idea of value democracy is the notion that, as a matter of normative justification, hateful or discriminatory practices and beliefs are potentially matters of public concern—regardless of what "spaces" they occupy. In contrast to a spatial metaphor of privacy, I defend a notion of publicly justifiable privacy. In judging what beliefs should be subject to public scrutiny, I appeal to the "principle of public relevance." As I suggested in the previous chapter, the principle claims that personal beliefs and actions should be consistent with public values to the extent that private life affects the ability of citizens to see others as free and equal citizens.[3] On my view, the boundaries between public and private should not be determined in a manner that automatically considers all practices and beliefs in the family or civil society to be beyond criticism. Instead, the boundaries should be drawn by reference to what practices and beliefs are relevant to the ideal of free and equal citizenship.

In the next chapter, I explore the role of the state in attempting to fulfill the principle of public relevance. The difficulty there will be to theorize about how the state can both respect rights and challenge publicly relevant beliefs that are at odds with the ideal of free and equal citizenship. However, in this chapter I have a more modest goal. I want to examine the principle of public relevance and its implications for privacy. Specifically, I defend the view that citizens in liberal democracy should engage in "reflective revision." Citizens engage in reflective revision when they endorse the ideal of free and equal citizenship and appeal to it to evaluate more general beliefs. In some instances, if there is conflict between democratic values and a set of beliefs held by citizens, they should find a way to reflectively revise their beliefs in order to incorporate the ideal of free and equal citizenship. To the extent that public values might conflict with the existing worldview held by citizens, a political conception of free and equal citizenship requires reforming and changing existing beliefs.[4]

I begin by examining possible conflicts between the political values of free and equal citizenship and the more general moral and theoretical commitments of individuals, or what many theorists refer to as "comprehensive conceptions."[5] I argue that while a commitment to free and equal citizenship only entails endorsing a "thin" set of values, this endorsement potentially challenges the comprehensive conceptions of citizens and some practices often regarded as private. I go on to explain why the notion of reflective revision requires amending and transforming certain doctrines that are incompatible with the idea of free and equal citizenship. I argue that the relevance of value democracy for beliefs is compatible with the claim that my account of free and equal citizenship relies on a "thin" conception of democratic values. Finally, I consider and respond to some liberal arguments against the notion of publicly justifiable privacy. These arguments suggest why issues of coercive state action or what some call "the basic structure" should be the exclusive subject of political theory.

II. WHEN EQUAL CITIZENSHIP AND COMPREHENSIVE DOCTRINES CLASH

Often the concern to politicize the personal and to argue that equality is relevant within the family is associated with political theories that assume a single vision of the human good, or what it means to live a valuable life. These theories propose specific ways of life as the best kinds that all people ought to lead. In some contemporary political theory, however, there has been a move away from seeing politics as concerned with a vision of the human good. This move has been motivated by the recognition that there are many reasonable ways of life and religions that people may follow. The state should therefore allow people to choose their own conception of the good and not interfere with that choice. For example, Rawls in his theory of "political liberalism" distinguishes comprehensive conceptions, which deal with metaphysics, personal ethics, and conceptions of the good, from "political conceptions of justice," which regard what laws can be coercively enforced by the state.[6] The state is properly concerned, according to Rawls, with "thin" political conceptions of free and equal citizenship, and not with comprehensive conceptions of good.

But what has troubled some feminists about this distinction is that it cordons off private life from concerns about equality. Famously, Susan Okin criticizes Rawls for his divide between public and private conceptions of politics.[7] Equality, she argues, is a value that should be present not just in the public realm, but in the private realm as well. For example, it would do girls little good to have formal rights of equal citizenship if they were raised in homes that did not instill and respect private equality. Drawing on this criticism, feminists might contend that the values of equal citizenship, because they are strictly public, are too thin to apply within the family.

I suggest, however, that the values of equal citizenship and equality under law should commit us to the notion that girls within the family should be treated as equals. It is incumbent on families to teach not only gender equality within the family, but also that all citizens should be treated as equals regardless of race or gender. I will argue that this conclusion about the role of equality within family life derives from a "thin" or non-comprehensive conception of free and equal citizenship. Contrary to Okin, we need not adopt a comprehensive view of the human good as requiring equality to see that our public commitments demand much of us in private life. Instead, we can "work backward" from our public commitments to evaluate the degree of conflict between our personal beliefs and the democratic values that we believe should govern society. I will suggest why a coherent endorsement of democratic values requires that we revise our personal commitments to make them consistent with an ideal of free and equal citizenship. I begin this section by critically examining Okin's and Rawls' views of the family. I then show the implications of the notion of reflective revision for life within the family.

The ideal of equal citizenship is most obviously relevant to how citizens should be treated by the law in the legitimate state. Namely, the principle of equal citizenship suggests that the legitimacy of the state and its actions depends on its recognition that all persons subject to the law have the entitlements to be treated as free and to have their interests considered equally. If distinctions among citizens are to be made, they must be drawn while respecting the value of equal citizenship, and not determined arbitrarily. From the standpoint of law, unchosen characteristics such as sex and race cannot serve as the basis for unequal treatment.[8] This principle is enshrined in the Fourteenth Amendment's guarantee of "equal protection of the laws," and it is also the bedrock principle of justification in liberal political theory. For political liberals, a central idea is that state action must be justified to individuals who are recognized as free and equal citizens. Discerning what counts as a justification to individuals requires bracketing comprehensive views about the good life, and searching for reasons that can be shared among reasonable citizens who respect each other's status as free and equal. When I refer to the reasons that can be shared, I do not mean reasons that are defined empirically as merely being popular. Instead, I refer to reasons that are defined normatively as being grounded in the concern to recognize the common status of all citizens as free and equal persons.

Many have thought that the emphasis on equal citizenship, rather than on equal personhood, entails an overly "thin" conception of equality. Our status as equals in the political realm, in particular, might be regarded as divisible from our status as equals in everyday life. Equal treatment might then be viewed as requiring equal treatment only by the state, and not by our family members, co-workers, or fellow participants in civil society. Critics of such thin accounts have contended we might endorse a principle of equal citizenship and yet hold problematic, inegalitarian beliefs. For instance, some people might regard their fellow citizens as equals in politics, but unequal in the family or associations because of their belief that women are inferior or do not deserve respect.

Such a division between public and private, however, has led critics of political liberalism to worry that a political ideal of equal citizenship is too shallow to secure real equality. These critics point out that real inequality in power often lies within more informal realms than those that can be influenced by the state. For instance, the internal dynamics of the family might have more to do with whether we are raised as equals than the way we are treated by the law. Thus, feminist critics such as Okin argue that parents who raise their female children in inegalitarian ways might undermine the state's formal guarantees of equal citizenship. Okin develops this argument in her criticism of Rawls. She claims that Rawls' emphasis on the public idea of equal citizenship leads him to ignore inequalities in the private realm. According to Okin, Rawls "strongly implies that in the nonpolitical aspects of [citizens'] lives—personal morality or religion for example—they may hold views such as that there is a fixed natural order or a 'hierarchy justified by religious or aristocratic values.'"[9] In other words, Rawls posits a dichotomy between persons as private individuals and citizens as political persons.

This feature of political liberalism, in Okin's view, is "reminiscent of those aspects of liberal theory that Marx criticized for splitting persons into 'abstract citizens' and 'human beings.'"[10] The division between the actual person and the citizen is a problem for Okin because many real inequalities exist in the private realm. Despite formal equality in the public realm, women will not see themselves as equals if they are raised in families that treat them as inferiors. It does women little good to have equal representation as citizens if in their actual life they are the victims of domestic inequality. As Okin argues, by leaving public reason out of family relationships, Rawls renders his own theory powerless to secure real equality.[11]

I want to contend that, despite Okin's criticisms, an ideal of equal citizenship can address power inequality in the family and civil society. Although equal citizenship is a political, as opposed to a comprehensive, value, it reaches broadly into what many liberals have considered to be the private sphere. In my view, the ideal of free and equal citizenship is both limited to a political conception and yet broadly relevant to citizens' beliefs and practices within the family and civil society. In some cases, personal identities and comprehensive beliefs are clearly compatible with the ideal of public citizenship. For instance, figures such as Martin Luther King Jr. famously combined religious, and thus highly personal, arguments with a political vision of equal citizenship. Indeed, as I argue in chapter 5, part of King's genius lay in his ability to articulate a shared, public ideal of equal citizenship using apparently comprehensive, religious language. King's "moral identity," however—by which I mean the ordering of his personal and political views—was defined by his use of religious reasons to reinforce public reasons that appealed to free and equal citizenship.[12]

A more difficult and complex relationship occurs, however, when personal reasons conflict with the shared public ideal of equal citizenship. Some comprehensive views, rather than reinforcing an ideal of public reason, might serve to undermine it. In such instances, comprehensive views will ideally give way to the ideal of free and equal citizenship. In the legitimate state, it is not enough for citizens in public forums to proclaim an allegiance to an ideal of equal citizenship, while in their personal or "private" lives they hold beliefs that are inconsistent with this ideal. But I also want to claim that acknowledging the relevance to all citizens of these personal comprehensive doctrines follows from the solely political ideal of equal citizenship.

For instance, imagine that a male citizen, a member of the town school board, is faced with voting on a measure that would ensure equal funding for girls' and boys' sports programs. Suppose that he votes in favor of equal funding, saying publicly not only that all citizens should be treated equally on the basis of gender, but that equal access to sports is essential to girls' ability to compete, and the ability to compete is essential to future citizenship. But suppose this male citizen forbids his own daughters from participating in sports because of his belief, as a father, that girls should be confined to learning domestic tasks. On my view, this citizen's apparently contradictory behavior seems to indicate that he has not internalized the value of equal citizenship.

I take the father's actions to be problematic from the standpoint of equal citizenship for three reasons, which relate to the arguments from democratic congruence, interconnection, and public trust that I mentioned in chapter 1. First, there is the question of democratic congruence, or whether the father has sincerely endorsed the decision he is willing to make in public. It seems that while he has claimed to endorse a policy based on equal citizenship, he does not truly believe the public values he claims to endorse. At minimum, he has failed to see the implications of his political viewpoint for his decisions within the family, because he denies in his personal decision the same values and arguments that he has endorsed publicly. If these are the right values to guide policy, and if they require equal funding because of the importance of sports to girls' future citizenship, the father should also follow and endorse these principles at home.

The second worry about the father's behavior is that arguably, his supposedly "private" decision has had more of an impact than his public, official one in actually affecting the degree to which his daughters are treated as equal citizens. His refusal to allow his daughters to play sports undermines any public commitment that the state has to their equal citizenship. This second concern derives from what I have called the "argument from interconnection," which suggests that decisions by non-state actors have the potential to undermine their fellow citizens' chances to attain real-life equal citizenship. This argument from interconnection applies to all citizens regardless of whether they occupy a formal office. A private citizen, for instance, would be wrong to vote for a similar ballot initiative guaranteeing equal access to sports on grounds of equal citizenship and then to deny his daughter the right to play out of a belief that she should be confined to domestic tasks.

A third problem with the contradiction between private belief and public commitment derives from the "argument from public trust." This argument suggests the distinct importance of public officials' following through on their public commitments and pronouncements. For example, imagine that, after the school board reaches the decision to equalize funding for girls' sports, members of the group ask the father in question to write a letter to parents explaining the decision and encouraging them to sign their daughters up for new programs. We can imagine that, because of his "private" views about raising children, this father will not be able to write a sincerely persuasive letter as a school board member to the parents. We can also imagine that the policy's effectiveness might be further undermined by other school officials who claim to publicly endorse the policy but who refuse to follow it in their family lives. For example, imagine the father is also the head of the school athletic department, and serves as a source of advice for parents who are choosing athletic activities for their children. Despite his public statements, the head of the athletic department is likely to be less supportive in private regarding parents signing up their daughters to play sports.

Just as the argument from interconnection suggests why citizens occupying informal roles could potentially undermine public values, so the argument from public trust is meant to illustrate why public officials might undermine these values in ways distinct from and more subtle than their roles as lawmakers. We might think more broadly, for instance, about the role that public officials play in mentoring future state officials. The choice of whom to mentor might be affected by the comprehensive beliefs of public officials. Here, a subtle sexism might dissuade women from entering public service or prevent them from advancing, because of the difficulty of finding mentors who can promote their careers and introduce them to important professional networks. It is therefore essential that a transformation of comprehensive beliefs occurs to ensure that these informal interactions are consistent with the ideal of free and equal citizenship.

I take these three arguments from democratic congruence, public trust, and interconnection to show why the political principles of free and equal citizenship ideally should require the transformation of discriminatory or hateful comprehensive doctrines. When comprehensive doctrines are at odds with the values of freedom and equality, citizens should engage in reflective revision, a concept I have previously mentioned but that I now want to discuss in further depth. Reflective revision entails that citizens should "work backwards" from the ideal of equal citizenship, using this political value to reevaluate and transform the discriminatory aspects of their comprehensive doctrines. If free and equal citizenship is an ideal that should be endorsed by all citizens, it follows that it is problematic in a legitimate liberal democracy when beliefs denigrate democratic values. The ideal of free and equal citizenship therefore is not just relevant to justifying coercion; it is relevant to our own moral identities, to the way we order our various public and private commitments. Indeed, because these kinds of commitments may conflict with democratic values, we cannot starkly divide the need to endorse an ideal of free and equal citizenship from the rest of our beliefs.

Before considering the implications of reflective revision, I want to clarify when citizens have the duty to engage in this process. The need for reflective revision is most evident when a comprehensive doctrine rejects the idea of equal citizenship altogether. In the most drastic case, hate groups or religions that endorse apartheid-like political policies should be transformed so as to incorporate the ideal of equal citizenship. Members of these groups may refuse to engage in reflective revision on their own, and I will have much more to say about the appropriate state and citizen responses to this failure in the pages to come. In other instances, such as that of the school board member and father, a comprehensive doctrine will seem to incorporate an ideal of equal citizenship, but ultimately aspects of the doctrine will undermine the ideal. In these cases, the process of reflective revision is less drastic than in instances when the ideal of equal citizenship is rejected altogether. A more subtle form of transformation is necessary to make comprehensive beliefs compatible with equality.

However, I take it that not all beliefs and inequality are inconsistent with the political ideal of equal citizenship. Certainly, some comprehensive forms of inequality might not be publicly relevant, and should not be subject to attempts at transformation. For instance, a belief in heaven and hell is ultimately in some sense inegalitarian, and yet it is not per se a violation of equal citizenship. One can believe in the existence of hell as a theological matter and yet still think those condemned to go there should be treated as equal citizens on earth. Such a person might think that judgments about whether others deserve one afterlife or another are not matters for humans to decide. The challenge in thinking about public relevance and its implications is to discern precisely which kinds of inegalitarian beliefs violate the public ideal of free and equal citizenship.

We can further clarify the meaning of the principle of public relevance by recalling the example of the father who is a school board member. The board member supports equal school funding for boys' and girls' sports, but he does not allow his daughter to participate in athletics. The reason why the school board member's decision within his own family is publicly relevant concerns the role of sports in public culture—namely, participation in sports is an important way that girls learn to compete, and this skill is important to achieving success and equality in adult life. But the example would work very differently in a world where sports lacked any social or political significance. For instance, if the issue was the father's decision whether or not to let his daughters play Tiddlywinks, there would not be as much public relevance at issue. His decision not to allow participation in this game might be arbitrary, but it is not obviously linked to a denial of his daughters' future political equality.

This principle of public relevance implies a new understanding of the way to divide public and private life. To quote one of the more feminist passages from Rawls, "if the so-called private sphere is alleged to be a space exempt from justice, then there is no such thing."[13] I draw from this thought when I argue that the scope of what is private should itself be determined using the principle of public relevance. Thus, I have developed an account of publicly justifiable privacy to show that the very line between the public and private must be drawn by a normative inquiry.[14] Specifically, we determine what is public and what is private by considering whether comprehensive beliefs in the family and civil society might conflict with free and equal citizenship. But, as I argue, the public relevance of a belief or practice does not imply a lack of protection from coercion. Beliefs and practices are still protected by rights of conscience and expression. It is consistent, without violating these rights, to invoke public relevance to discuss the implications for equal citizenship of these practices and beliefs. In particular, I will argue that public scrutiny of the family and civil society using expression is consistent with protections against coercive intervention into these domains.

III. The Varieties of Reflective Revision

So far I have attempted to articulate how beliefs and practices both about and within the family might be publicly relevant. Public values can conflict with so-called private beliefs and commitments, even when individuals do not voice those commitments in public forums. Ideally, citizens will work to recognize these contradictions and resolve them through a process of reflective revision. Citizens engage in reflective revision when they appeal to a public ideal of free and equal citizenship, not only in evaluating coercive law, but also in evaluating their own beliefs and practices. The process of determining through reflective revision how the values of free and equal citizenship fit into one's own set of beliefs is an individualized one. Although the ideal of free and equal citizenship is fixed, the particular path of reflective revision will differ from person to person because comprehensive beliefs will vary widely. Similarly, when citizens employing reflective revision find conflicts between their own beliefs and public values, their responses will vary in how they seek to adjudicate these conflicts and internalize the ideal of free and equal citizenship.

Reflective revision about the fit between one's commitment to the public values of free and equal citizenship and beliefs about and within traditionally private spaces such as the family can happen in two distinct ways, full or partial. First, citizens might employ reflective revision to voluntarily reorder the way their various public and private commitments fit together. In full reflective revision, citizens scrutinize all aspects of their conceptions in the light of public values. Citizens would then connect their private beliefs to a political commitment to the public values of free and equal citizenship. Full reflective revision entails that all beliefs that conflict with democratic values are examined and reconciled through internal reflection and perhaps deliberation with other citizens.

But this kind of full reflective revision is not necessarily required by value democracy. A second, more partial kind of transformation would be limited in response to discriminatory beliefs that have an effect on other citizens. In partial reflective revision, the private beliefs of individuals could remain incompatible with public values, as long as their publicly relevant actions and deliberations are guided by respect for the freedom and equality of all citizens. This would require something like the cognitive dissonance of a scientist who publicly follows the rules of his trade as a matter of professionalism, while privately doubting the validity of the scientific method. But in order to qualify as a case of partial reflective revision, private beliefs that clash with free and equal citizenship should not influence publicly relevant actions, including certain actions within the family and civil society. When these citizens hold publicly unjustifiable beliefs in a way that has no effect on the freedom or equality of others, they should be left free from public scrutiny.

Although it may be a conceptual possibility for a person to live this double life of private person and public citizen, some commentators have argued that this position would be quite difficult to maintain psychologi-

cally. A split existence would deny the individual a coherent moral identity and would require a significant divide between the public beliefs that
guide actions and private beliefs that are inconsistent with those actions.[15]
However, value democracy and its account of reflective revision only seek
to achieve the second or partial kind of transformation, though it might
often result in the first or full kind of transformation.

Why not abandon the limitation of promoting only thin values, and
instead endorse a full-fledged conception of equality in all aspects of life?
The answer to this question rightly stresses the importance of reflection.
For citizens to think freely about whether they endorse the ideal of equal
citizenship, it is important that they be able to reflect about what they
take to be a good life. Part of equal respect entails a respect for citizens
to reflect on matters of the good and to make up their own minds freely
about which particular conception of the good they choose to endorse. The
value of equal respect is central to the idea that we should limit ourselves
to a conception of equal citizenship in thinking about the kind of equality
that is relevant within the family.

The transformation of some beliefs in the family and civil society
might be thought to impose a culture of comprehensive liberalism, rather
than merely one of free and equal citizenship. Does my notion of public
relevance risk transforming not only beliefs, but cultures themselves? Will
persons who engage in reflective revision risk having to give up a fundamental part of their cultural identity? I grant that it is true that, as is
the case of full transformation, it is conceptually possible that the values
of free and equal citizenship will displace cultures that were previously
incompatible with these values. However, such a process is unlikely. As
with partial transformation, comprehensive conceptions and cultures will
likely be changed but not displaced if they seek compatibility with the
ideal of free and equal citizenship. The fact that a conception has been
transformed does not indicate that one's identity has been destroyed. As
H.L.A. Hart points out in his famous reply to Lord Devlin, it is wrong to
think that "any deviation from a society's shared morality threatens its
existence."[16] Similarly, the transformation of individual identity is not
equivalent to its destruction. While comprehensive conceptions need to be
consistent with public reason—and may even need to be transformed to
become consistent—individuals can still have "private" reasons for their
substantive political beliefs. Individuals can therefore understand their
political views in a variety of ways. The point is only that these private
beliefs should not undermine the treatment of all citizens as free and
equal.

Although concepts prominent in contemporary political theory such
as "public reason" and "public justification" seem to suggest an inherent divide between public and private life, there is no such clear or prior

divide. Rather, the boundaries of privacy must be determined by and normatively defended through public justification. This has a major implication for traditional understandings of privacy: democratic values apply to the family and civil society. This means that even if an individual is able to maintain a double life, the "public" commitment to shared values and public reason potentially applies to his or her interactions with the family, because the freedom and equality of other family members may be at stake. The double life might allow citizens to retain private beliefs at odds with public reason, given freedom of speech and conscience. However, public justification requires that citizens in a democratic state should be committed to transforming these beliefs through reflective revision to make them consistent with public reason's demand for equality. Although freedom of conscience is essential to value democracy, it should not cordon off the family as a protected "private" space exempt from the requirements of public reason. Beliefs and actions in the family can be publicly relevant, given that they can disempower women and girls to an extent that is inconsistent with the ideal of equal citizenship.

The principle of public relevance shares many feminists' concerns about life in the family. However, it leaves many significant life decisions untouched. It requires some congruence between public beliefs and commitments within families and civil society. But it does not require that all aspects of one's belief system are dictated by democratic values. Following Nancy Rosenblum, we might say that, although the values of free and equal citizenship apply broadly to politics, civil society, and the family, they do not go "all the way down" into every single issue of personal choice.[17] Rather, these values create a minimum standard of justice for evaluating familial decisions without dictating answers to every issue within the family. Thus, my account of the role public values should play in private life can be distinguished from the more radical feminism of thinkers such as Carole Pateman[18] and Catharine MacKinnon.[19] For these thinkers, many of whom suggest that the public/private distinction is untenable, feminism is a comprehensive conception of complete human emancipation.[20]

One difference between value democracy's emphasis on equal citizenship and the theories of feminists who emphasize comprehensive conceptions of equality is found in debates about marriage. Value democracy rejects the idea that marriage is inherently problematic on egalitarian grounds, because it is not clear why all forms of marriage would be incompatible with a concern for equal citizenship. This distinction between comprehensive feminist theories and my own ideal of free and equal citizenship also has implications for education. An education based on a comprehensive account of women's equality might prescribe any and all matters of the good life. For instance, it might stress the importance of avoiding marriage on the grounds that it is inconsistent with the full emancipation of women. By contrast, my own theory would encourage educators to stress how some institutional arrangements and some decisions within the family threaten women's equal citizenship, but it would avoid taking positions on issues of the good life that are not matters of fundamental justice. For instance, it would avoid taking a position on whether women should marry, so long as the conditions in the family are consistent with the values of free and equal citizenship.

Since the values of free and equal citizenship do not "go all the way down," they leave open a place for non-public values, such as love and other emotions, in the family. The internal regulation of a family need not be governed solely by public values; these principles are not sufficient to account for many of the subtleties of family life. Concerns about equality, for instance, should not drive every interaction among family members. Expressions of affection or humor, although integral to the family dynamic, are not reducible to questions of equal citizenship, nor are they necessarily inconsistent with this ideal. In short, a distinction can remain between the styles of governance in the family and the public realm, but this need not mean that all aspects of the family are immune from public scrutiny. Of course, the boundary between questions of equal citizenship and a more comprehensive ideal of equality within the family is sometimes blurry, and some hard cases will emerge. I therefore suggest in the next section that when it comes to a state role in promoting democratic values, the state should limit itself to pursuing clear cases in which citizens have failed to incorporate an ideal of equal citizenship.

But why should the process of reflective revision be voluntary? Why not punish citizens who refuse to engage in it? Although value democracy suggests why citizens should engage in the personal moral transformation that is morally required by the ideal of free and equal citizenship, it does not give the state license to directly coerce citizens into a process of reflective revision. Indeed, coercion would deny the kind of autonomy required for reflective revision. Attempting to coerce citizens into reflective revision would fail to respect them as free and equal, and it would violate the freedom of conscience that I defend at length in the next chapter as central to value democracy. I therefore emphasize in the next two chapters the importance of a right to "opt out" of attempts at transformation. This does not mean that democratic persuasion in defense of the ideal of free and equal citizenship cannot seek to be effective in prompting reflective revision or more generally in creating a social ethos where democratic ideals are endorsed. It means that democratic persuasion will be limited to non-coercive means that respect rights of freedom of speech and conscience. These rights include the freedom to reject reflective revision and to openly oppose the ideals of free and equal citizenship. Unlike militant democrats, I do not support coercive restrictions on hate speech, provided there is no direct threat or danger of imminent harm. But I do suggest that hateful or discriminatory views violate the democratic ideal and should be publicly criticized.

IV. The Implications of Public Relevance for Citizens and Policy

The notion of a publicly justifiable privacy differs significantly from another way of distinguishing the public from the private. Alternatively, the public/private distinction might be drawn by looking at matters of state coercion rather than principles of political morality. The question of what is private might be conceived along the lines of the spaces protected by a right to privacy. But such a distinction would focus excessively on the role of state coercion into political theory. The resulting theory would respond to the danger of the Invasive State, but it would ignore entirely the dangers, described by feminists, of the Hateful Society. If we ask only about a one-dimensional use of state force in formulating the distinction between public and private, we are left with a truncated choice between two undesirable alternatives: the coercive policies of the Invasive State or the indifference to the ways public values are undermined in the Hateful Society.

But if we open up the question of what is public to the domain of political morality, we can begin to see why, although coercive state action might be limited toward the family, as a normative matter, many beliefs and practices that might be protected against the use of force can still be publicly relevant. In contrast to a focus solely on the use of force, an examination of public relevance sheds light on how public values apply to areas that have been regarded as part of private life. But since I discuss the values of freedom and equality as matters of public citizenship, the principle of public relevance is one of political morality, despite its applicability to private life.

By expanding public values beyond questions of coercion, I do not mean to imply that coercive laws are irrelevant to the family. As many feminist theorists have rightly suggested, and as current law reflects, some citizen behavior that takes place within the family and civil society should be banned by coercive law. For instance, it was a grave error that domestic abuse and marital rape were historically not considered crimes. One of the most important contributions of feminist politics and theory is the recognition that such assaults should be punished by criminal law regardless of whether they occur within or outside of the family. Feminist theorists have also rightly argued that hostile work environments and sexual harassment should not be protected from coercive sanction. Without question, these categories of threats and harassment are not only publicly relevant, but rightly met with coercive action.

Though some publicly relevant behavior that takes place in the domain of family or workplace—domains previously thought to be "private"—should be met with coercive sanction, I want to focus in the rest of this book on a distinct category of publicly relevant behavior and beliefs that are not rightly met with coercive sanction, but that still have implications for public policy. These publicly relevant actions and beliefs should be subject to attempts at transformation by the state acting in its persuasive capacity. But they should also be protected by rights from coercive sanction. Controversially, I will emphasize that not only actions can be publicly relevant, but also some beliefs when they are hateful or discriminatory. These publicly relevant beliefs are defined by being opposed to or implausibly consistent with a commitment to free and equal citizenship. Since hateful or discriminatory viewpoints are publicly relevant, they are rightly subject to the process of reflective revision.

In the next chapter I examine how the state can work to fulfill the principle of public relevance. But it is important to consider also its informal implications. Consider again the question of mentorship, which is linked to what I have called the argument from interconnection. This argument claims that some non-governmental relationships risk undermining public values in the manner of what some describe as "institutional racism." For example, there is a vast amount of discretion in the decision of whom to mentor—say, in a university setting—which goes beyond the clearly delineated duties of professors. Yet given the importance of mentorship to students' future success, it is clearly a matter of public significance. The question of mentorship is thus of profound importance as citizens seek to incorporate public reasons within their moral identity. The same issue, of course, can be phrased as one of trust rather than of interconnection if the actors are public as opposed to private. It is important that public officials embrace public values so that citizens can trust them to implement policies that fully respect free and equal citizenship. For example, if public officials do not embrace public values, they might fail to build professional relations with women or with members of different races. This would result in hiring and promotion policies that do not effectively include a diverse population within the government.

But are there any ways to realize the principle of public relevance beyond a duty of individuals to reflectively revise their beliefs? Some liberals will contend that the state should never intervene on behalf of the principle of public relevance, so as to avoid the excesses of the Invasive State. But I will argue that while some forceful interventions into private life are incompatible with the ideal of reflective revision, not all interventions are coercive. For example, it is not coercive but expressive for the state to seek to persuade citizens to adopt ideals of equality. When it engages in democratic persuasion rather than coercion, it advances the principle of public relevance using reason and not force. I will argue that the state can give reasons in support of free and equal citizenship by using its expressive capacities to educate and speak to citizens. In exercising these capacities, the state seeks to persuade citizens to freely adopt public values.

In contrast to coercion, reasoning with individuals differs because it respects their capacity as free and equal citizens to decide upon their own conception of the good and their conception of justice. Unlike force, reasoning attempts to change minds through the active participation and free thought of the citizens whom one is seeking to persuade. This recognition that reasoning respects the freedom of citizens in a way coercion does not is central to much liberal democratic thinking. For John Stuart Mill, citizens should actively seek to persuade one another of the truth, and this kind of persuasion is not only compatible with free speech, but central to it.[21] For Jürgen Habermas, reasoning differs from force in that reason-giving respects the discursive capacity of citizens.[22]

But can reflective revision be prompted by the state and not just by citizens? Ideally, reflective revision might be prompted by the persuasion and reasoning of one's fellow citizens in civil society. In the absence of such persuasion, there is also a role for the state to persuade in its expressive capacity. If reasoning is itself a mode of respecting citizens' capacity in democratic discussion and deliberation, it follows that the state too can use reason to change minds while respecting freedom and equality. I will argue in the next chapter that the state has a role in articulating the reasons and values that are central to its own legitimacy—namely, the values of free and equal citizenship. It is through democratic persuasion that value democracy can address the inequalities ignored in the Hateful Society while avoiding the unjustifiable coercion of the Invasive State.

The move from this chapter's discussion of reflective revision to the account of democratic persuasion in the next chapter also marks a transition from ideal to non-ideal theory. Reflective revision is a process that citizens will ideally engage in. But it is sensible to assume that, on their own, many citizens may not think about the role of public values in their own systems of belief. The move from reflective revision to democratic persuasion is based on the realistic assumption that not all citizens will endorse the ideals of free and equal citizenship, and that some will openly disparage it. In addition, democratic persuasion might be important even for citizens who follow democratic values in public, since it can prompt further reflective revision and make citizens aware of conflicts between personal and public belief where they were not previously recognized.

V. Beyond the Basic Structure

I have argued so far that the idea of public reasoning among free and equal citizens should serve not only as a way of theorizing rights against coercion, but also as a way of scrutinizing beliefs in the family and civil society. I have also begun to describe how the state should have an active role in encouraging citizens to engage in reflective revision. The public reason of citizens, I have argued, serves as a way of scrutinizing beliefs in what has often been regarded as the "private" sphere. Some will reply that I have divorced democratic values from what should be their subject, Rawls' "basic structure," or the formal sphere of coercive state action. By contrast, I have argued that the principle of public relevance applies beyond the basic structure to beliefs themselves—including beliefs in civil society and the family.[23] In this section, I consider arguments for applying democratic values exclusively to the basic structure itself, and not to the family or civil society. The first two of these arguments contend that the basic structure is sufficient to combat beliefs at odds with free and equal citizenship, while the third asserts that the notion of the basic structure is so expansive that there is no need to go beyond it. I reply to these three arguments in this section, and show that value democracy applies beyond the basic structure.

One argument for making the basic structure the exclusive subject of democratic values is that, over time, the creation of just institutions will shape personal beliefs to make them consistent with the requirements of free and equal citizenship. In this spirit, Rawls expresses a "hope" that comprehensive beliefs will evolve to become more reasonable.[24] This approach, however, overlooks why the basic structure's emphasis on rights in many ways prevents equality from spreading to the family, civil society, and other aspects of the so-called private sphere. People can and often do exercise their rights to oppose the values of free and equal citizenship. For example, hate groups use the right of free speech to promote racism. The difficulty, I argue, is that rights are "inverted" in that they permit the expression of views that contradict the reasons for the right itself.

Another argument for regarding the basic structure as the exclusive subject of democratic values might appeal to the role of private emotions and affections within the family. These emotions might have the effect of tracking justice. They might offer at least a "muted" conception of justice within the family.[25] This view, however, does not account for how the emotions within the family—including that of love—might stray far from egalitarian concerns. Certainly, there was love within families before the feminist movement began to show how family dynamics could undermine the public ideals of equal citizenship. But this does not mean that there

was less love in such families. I do not think love itself requires an aware-
ness of the specific principle of equal citizenship. Rather than rely on any
familial affections to realize the ideal of equal citizenship within the family, it is necessary that the culture encourage citizens to engage in the process of reflective revision. Citizens should attempt to become aware of the
contradiction between their private beliefs and their public actions, and
they should work to transform their beliefs, making them consistent with
the public ideal of equal citizenship. In the next chapter, I will argue that
we should not only rely on individuals to reflectively revise their beliefs on
their own, but the state has an obligation to create the kind of culture that
encourages reflective revision.

Another strategy to limit the ideal of equal citizenship to the basic
structure would be to expand the basic structure to include institutions
such as the family. Indeed, Rawls himself seems to vacillate between seeing the basic structure as limited to the coercive apparatus of the state and
viewing it as a broader conception that includes all major social institutions.[26] According to Susan Okin, we should think of the basic structure in
the broader sense, and thus include the family within it.

I think, however, that it would be a mistake to rely on this strategy of
broadening the notion of the basic structure. The way public reason applies to coercive state institutions and the way it applies to more informal
institutions such as the family and civil society are distinct and not paral-
lel. I therefore differ from Okin's suggestion that we should think of the
family in its entirety as part of the basic structure and directly subject to
the same principles of justice that govern coercive institutions. Such an
application would raise a slew of complications. For instance, the commitment to freedom of speech would certainly complicate childrearing.
The value of free speech might trump the value of mutual respect among
adults debating politics, but in family settings where children are still
learning the basics of social interaction the inverse is arguably true. It is
also hard to understand conceptually how a principle regulating the just
distribution of wealth in society might be applied within the family, for
instance, among children. The principles and rights of the basic structure
are crafted to govern state institutions; thus they should not be directly
applied to the family, a non-state institution.

However, even if we disagree with Okin's idea that the family in its
entirety should be viewed as part of the basic structure, the values of free
and equal citizenship can still be used to evaluate certain intra-family
dynamics, even when they are not implicated by the basic structure. As I
have argued in this chapter, the values of free and equal citizenship should
guide reflective revision. For instance, the principles of value democracy
are relevant to personal decisions within the family in matters such as
whether to teach female children that they are equal or inferior to males.

Personal decisions like these are not part of the basic structure, but they are publicly relevant, since they affect free and equal citizenship. Value democracy can thus insist on the political relevance of injustices within the family without regarding the family as part of the coercively defined basic structure.[27]

In this section, I have argued that the basic structure should not be regarded as the exclusive subject of public reason. Contrary to Rawls and Cohen, neither the basic structure nor the emotions within the family are sufficient to ensure that family practices and beliefs will meet the standard of equal citizenship. In order to respect the values of free and equal citizenship within the family, we must engage in reflective revision to ensure that our comprehensive doctrines are not opposed to the ideals of equal citizenship. The principle of public relevance goes beyond the basic structure to apply an ideal of equal citizenship directly to the beliefs of citizens as they occupy roles in the informal domains of civil society and the family.

Finally, some might cite Mill's epistemic argument about free speech to suggest that we need only secure free speech rights to ensure that the values of free and equal citizenship will prevail. Mill argued that truth would be the result of vigorous debate and conversation. But Mill's argument rests on a culture in which democratic values inform how such citizens use their free speech rights. In my view, a democratic culture must have widespread endorsement of the values of free and equal citizenship. To that end, I have suggested how reflective revision is rightly part of such a democratic culture. In the next chapter, I will go on to suggest how the state can also prompt such an ethos.

VI. Conclusion

In this chapter, I have challenged the common but mistaken "spatial metaphor" notion of privacy, whereby the family and civil society are spaces immune from the normative evaluation of public values and justification. I have suggested that the line between the public and the private should itself be held to the standards of free and equal citizenship. Because the ideal of equal citizenship may be undermined by actions, practices, and beliefs in any realm of society, I have suggested that a thin conception of public values potentially reaches domains often regarded as private. The principle of public relevance, therefore, offers a way of conceiving of privacy that is publicly justifiable. My theory of publicly justifiable privacy suggests that we should not cordon off any spaces as immune from public justification.

The first implication of the principle of public relevance and its place within the so-called private sphere is that citizens have an obligation to integrate public values within their own belief systems. I introduced and defended a notion of reflective revision whereby citizens come to recognize the conflicts between certain aspects of their private beliefs and the public commitment to free and equal citizenship. Because it is important to pursue reflective revision in a manner that is freely chosen, the effect on comprehensive doctrines will vary from person to person. Although the democratic values are shared among the citizenry, the way citizens will integrate those values into their beliefs will vary according to their comprehensive conceptions. Some might choose to endorse democratic values from the standpoint of their religion, while others will endorse free and equal citizenship from within a secular conception or freestanding doctrine. All of these changes, however, leave aspects of personal identity and belief open to individual interpretation.

So far I have articulated the principle of public relevance and reflective revision, but I have not yet fully examined their implications for state action. In the next chapter, I explore this central issue. I argue that while rights protect individuals from any state coercive enforcement of the principle of public relevance or reflective revision, there should be an active role for the state in pursuing democratic persuasion on behalf of the values of free and equal citizenship. I emphasize that it is essential for democratic persuasion to avoid coercion. It should respect the rights of citizens and their entitlement to be treated as capable of reasoning on their own. Democratic persuasion should also avoid manipulation that circumvents citizen's ability to reason. Fundamentally, it must reflect respect for citizens' status as free and equal at the same time that it attempts to convince them to adopt democratic values as their own.

CHAPTER THREE

• • • • • • • • • • • • • • • •

When the State Speaks, What Should It Say?

DEMOCRATIC PERSUASION AND THE FREEDOM OF EXPRESSION

I. Introduction

The principle of public relevance elaborated in the last chapter offers a way of avoiding the excesses of the Hateful Society. Life within the family and civil society should not automatically be regarded as immune from considerations of free and equal citizenship. To the contrary, the ideal of public citizenship applies to the beliefs of family members and participants in civil society, according to my publicly relevant conception of privacy. But one might worry that in emphasizing this answer to the Hateful Society, I now risk veering toward the dangers of the Invasive State. How does value democracy protect rights of freedom of speech and conscience?

In this chapter, I articulate why the principle of public relevance is compatible with robust rights of free expression, even for groups that directly oppose the democratic values of free and equal citizenship. Value democracy defends free speech protections for hate groups and other advocates of discriminatory viewpoints. But I argue that while the state should protect the rights of these groups, it also has the duty to make clear that it is not complicit in their opposition to the ideal of free and equal citizenship. The state should criticize discriminatory groups, and in the case of the most extreme hate groups, condemn them. By focusing on the simultaneous role of the state in protecting rights and criticizing discriminatory messages, I hope to clarify how we might avoid the excesses of both the Hateful Society and the Invasive State.

Value democracy offers an alternative to both the prevailing neutralist and prohibitionist approaches to hate speech. Neutralists defend the U.S. Supreme Court's current free speech jurisprudence, which protects hateful political viewpoints from coercive sanction but fails to criticize their discriminatory message. By contrast, prohibitionists have argued that free speech rights should not extend to viewpoints that are at odds with the foundational values of a liberal society. For example, Jeremy Waldron claims that rights protection should not extend to hate speech, because it is a form of group libel. The prohibitionist approach broadly endorses the kind of legal limits on free speech found in countries such as the Netherlands.[1]

Although these two positions have defined the debate over state responses to hate speech, I find both approaches to be problematic because they echo the flaws of the Hateful Society and the Invasive State. Neutralists fail to answer the challenge that hateful viewpoints pose to the core democratic values of freedom and equality. Groups that constitute "bad civil society," such as the Ku Klux Klan and American Nazi Party, challenge the values fundamental to liberal democratic society. Allowing hateful viewpoints to spread unchecked would raise the danger of the Hateful Society. The alternative approach of the prohibitionists, however, runs into the problem of the dystopia of the Invasive State. Theorists who propose to ban hate speech overlook how the core democratic values of freedom and equality require that the state allow citizens to develop and affirm their own political views.

My theory of value democracy proposes a third position that resolves the problems of the two sides. I suggest that we envision the state not only as a coercive power, but also as an expressive power, able to impact beliefs and behavior by "speaking" to hate groups and the larger society. On my view, the state should simultaneously protect the rights of hateful viewpoints in its coercive capacity and use what I refer to as democratic persuasion to criticize their discriminatory message. Democratic persuasion is meant to convey the active and expressive role of the state in seeking to convince citizens to adopt the values of equal citizenship. By presenting this third approach to the dilemma of hate speech, democratic persuasion suggests how we might protect the right to express hateful viewpoints and, at the same time, defend the values of freedom and equality against discriminatory and racist challenges.

In this chapter I extend the notion of promulgating law to develop an account of democratic persuasion. The ideal of the rule of law suggests that the content of legitimate law must be widely publicized. I argue, however, that a proper theory of the freedom of expression also contains an essential role for the democratic state to publicize the reasons that underlie rights and legitimate law. These reasons appeal to the entitlement of each citizen, who is subject to coercion, to be treated as free and equal.[2] Democratic persuasion should not be thought of as in tension or as an idea balanced against the protection of rights, since it makes transparent the meaning and justification of rights to the citizenry at large. Through democratic persuasion, liberty and equality can be reconciled; they need not be on what Catharine MacKinnon has called "a collision course."[3]

My theory is thus expressive in two senses: it protects the entitlement of citizens to express any political viewpoint, and it emphasizes a role for the state in explaining why these free speech protections have been granted.

In this second role, the state appropriately uses its persuasive powers to encourage citizens to engage in reflective revision, thereby adopting the democratic values that underlie legitimate law.[4] I begin the next section by exploring the structure of free speech protections. I draw on the work of Dworkin, Rawls, and Meiklejohn to suggest why the ideal of free and equal citizenship supports the First Amendment doctrine of viewpoint neutrality regarding rights of free expression. The state should be viewpoint neutral in protecting the right to express all opinions, regardless of their content, provided they are not direct threats. I thus endorse aspects of the Supreme Court's legal doctrine of viewpoint neutrality when I argue that viewpoint neutrality should apply to free speech rights against coercion. But I go on to suggest that the state should be non-neutral on the different issue of what beliefs to express itself. I argue that the state should non-neutrally express and promote the values of free and equal citizenship. These values form what I call the "reasons for rights." They explain why we should protect rights in the first place. I thus differ from both the prohibitionists and the neutralists discussed in the book's introduction. Whereas prohibitionists would use coercion to promote democratic values, I suggest that using coercion would violate rights of free expression. But whereas neutralists offer no response to hateful viewpoints and other beliefs that challenge free and equal citizenship, I provide a non-coercive way, through democratic persuasion, for the state to defend freedom and equality for all citizens. It is important, then, to distinguish between viewpoint neutrality and neutralism. Viewpoint neutrality is the legal doctrine that rights should protect the expression of all opinions. Neutralism is a political theory that the state should not promote or express any particular set of values. Although I agree with aspects of viewpoint neutrality, I reject neutralism. In section III, I explain that rights of free expression have an "inverted" structure. They are inverted, because the reasons for rights are often at odds with illiberal views that are protected by the state. The state's protection of hateful or discriminatory views risks sending the message that it is neutral toward or complicit with those views. I suggest in this chapter that democratic persuasion can help the state to avoid the problem of complicity. In sections IV and V, I go on to develop the idea of democratic persuasion by describing the different forms that it can take in promoting the values of free and equal citizenship.

II. Neutrality and Coercion

Value democracy's theory of free expression should incorporate an account of what the state would rightly "say" in its expressive capacity. On my account, democratic persuasion should be primarily concerned to articulate and defend the reasons and values that underlie basic liberal rights. The worry might be raised, however, that the state would violate neutrality if it exercised its expressive capacity on behalf of public values. I answer this worry in the following section by arguing that viewpoint neutrality itself is theoretically grounded in the non-neutral democratic values of free and equal citizenship. Viewpoint neutrality prohibits bans on the expression of viewpoints based on their substantive message. For instance, while the doctrine of viewpoint neutrality would not protect the kind of atrocities committed by the Nazis, it would protect the right to express Nazi ideology.

It is worth clarifying precisely which kind of "hate speech" is protected under the doctrine of viewpoint neutrality. Often, hate speech is used to refer to a variety of speech that can range from threats to the expression of viewpoints. Although viewpoint neutrality requires protecting the right to express certain hateful viewpoints, it does not require the protection of true threats. The Supreme Court recently helped to clarify this distinction between protected expression and prohibited threats in *Virginia v. Black* (2003) by distinguishing two kinds of cross-burning.[5] The Court ruled that an act of cross-burning could be prohibited if it threatened particular individuals and constituted an "intent to intimidate." Justice O'Connor suggested in her plurality opinion for *Virginia v. Black* that it was consistent with the First Amendment to outlaw threats, even if they were based on a specific viewpoint. For example, in one of the cases considered in *Virginia v. Black*, a cross was burned in a family's yard. O'Connor's opinion suggested why this type of cross-burning could qualify as a threat. If it was a threat, it could be legitimately outlawed, consistent with the protection of free speech. Her opinion sought to distinguish this type of cross-burning from cross-burnings that were not threats and were thus protected by the First Amendment.[6] O'Connor's opinion could be interpreted as carving out an exception to the doctrine of viewpoint neutrality when she recognized that threats could be prohibited, even if they were also expressive.[7]

While Justice O'Connor allowed the state to prohibit cross-burning that occurs in a person's yard with an intent to intimidate, her decision clarified that other kinds of cross-burning were protected by the right of free speech. For example, the Court protected a cross-burning that took place on a field during a rally in which no individuals were singled out as targets of the hateful expression. In this case, the Court ruled that the act was not a direct threat but expressed a political viewpoint with no intent to intimidate, albeit a viewpoint with a deeply inegalitarian message. O'Connor argued that banning this kind of cross-burning would unconstitutionally depart from viewpoint neutrality.[8] I call the kind of speech that is not a threat, but that expresses a message inimical to the values of free and equal citizenship, a "hateful viewpoint." Speech that does constitute a threat, however, falls in a separate category than hateful viewpoints. Consistent with the Court's rulings, on my view while hateful viewpoints should be protected from coercive bans, threats can be prohibited. As I suggested in the book's introduction, it is important to emphasize that there is a distinction between the emotion of hate and the content of hateful viewpoints. Hateful viewpoints are defined not necessarily by their emotion, but by their expressing an idea or ideology that opposes free and equal citizenship without constituting a direct threat to particular individuals.

The Court's distinction between threats and viewpoints in *Virginia v. Black* echoed its similar decision in *Brandenburg v. Ohio*, which upheld the right of the Ku Klux Klan to express its hateful viewpoint.[9] *Brandenburg* overruled the Court's previous "clear and present danger" standard that had given the state greater power to ban viewpoints. Under the clear and present danger standard, the Court interpreted the First Amendment as allowing viewpoints to be banned if they were considered subversive and likely to be effective in causing long-term destruction to the security of the United States.[10] The *Brandenburg* decision replaced the clear and present danger standard with a stricter viewpoint-neutral standard that allows limits on speech only in cases of "imminent harm," such as speech that might immediately incite a riot. *Virginia v. Black* reinforced *Brandenburg*'s viewpoint-neutral standard by again protecting the Klan's hateful expression on the grounds that the First Amendment applies to all viewpoints, provided they are not threats or incitements to imminent harm.

Should value democracy endorse the protection of all viewpoints equally by the right of free expression, given its premise that all citizens should be regarded as free and equal? Viewpoint neutrality protects the right to express hateful doctrines, even though they directly challenge value democracy's commitment to freedom and equality. If these hateful doctrines were left to prevail, they could subvert the basic principles of a legitimate democratic state. It might seem then that the appropriate response would be to protect free and equal citizenship by abandoning the Court's doctrine of viewpoint neutrality. I suggest, however, that viewpoint neutrality as a doctrine of free speech can be complemented by the state's use of democratic persuasion in defense of free and equal citizenship. While value democracy's account of free expression strictly protects free speech for all viewpoints, it provides for a robust state role in promoting democratic values and criticizing hateful or discriminatory viewpoints.

Value democracy reinterprets viewpoint neutrality by grounding it in a commitment to treat persons as free and equal. This reinterpretation, drawing on the thought of John Rawls, Ronald Dworkin, and Alexander

Meiklejohn, connects viewpoint neutrality with a wider set of values that are required for political legitimacy. I will offer a value-based argument for adopting the doctrine of viewpoint neutrality.

It is helpful to begin with the value-based defenses of viewpoint neutrality developed by John Rawls, Alexander Meiklejohn, and Ronald Dworkin. According to Rawls, political equality requires a respect for the "two moral powers" of all citizens to develop and exercise what he calls a "capacity for a sense of justice" and a "capacity for a conception of the good."[11] Citizens must be free from coercive threat as they develop their own notion of justice and the good. Otherwise, they would not be able to affirm and choose their own ideas about the most fundamental matters of politics (the just) and what constitutes, in their view, a valuable life (the good). Rawls' argument could be interpreted to support viewpoint neutrality, because the value of equality would be violated if some citizens but not others were free to develop their moral powers. Government discrimination or non-neutrality among viewpoints would make respect for the exercise of the moral powers unequal, and it would deny political freedom to the coerced citizens. Non-neutrality would undermine the equal treatment, not only of the citizens whose viewpoints were banned, but also of the citizens who could potentially listen to and argue with those viewpoints. The state would undermine equal treatment by failing to respect the capacity of citizens to make the free decision to accept or reject any viewpoint. Viewpoint neutrality is therefore necessary for the full and equal exercise of the two moral powers of citizens.[12]

A similar line of egalitarian justification for this doctrine can be found in the work of Meiklejohn and Dworkin. These thinkers may be interpreted as defending viewpoint neutrality in the right of free expression, even for the hateful viewpoints held by the Nazis and the Klan, because neutrality is required to respect the democratic autonomy of citizens to develop their own political opinions.[13] Meiklejohn famously employs the metaphor of a town meeting to argue that all viewpoints must be protected in a democracy. On his view, while the moderator of a town meeting could limit speakers for reasons of time and to ensure that they stay on point, censoring speakers based on the substance of their comments would limit the meeting's democratic aims. Such censorship would prevent fellow meeting participants from hearing a variety of arguments for or against the measure they were considering, and it would constrain their ability to express their own views. This kind of censorship would impede the ability of citizens to be the source of their own democratic decisions, and so would undermine the democratic ideal.

As with Rawls, Meiklejohn argues that any attempt to discriminate based on the content of a particular viewpoint would threaten a regime's democratic credentials, even if those viewpoints were themselves deeply inegalitarian. Coercively limiting or banning an illiberal viewpoint would prevent citizens from actively affirming the core values of democracy. According to this argument, we must have the option to consider and reject egalitarian values if we are to be truly free to affirm them. As Dworkin puts it, "a majority decision is not fair unless everyone has had a fair opportunity to express his or her attitudes or opinions or fears or tastes or presuppositions or prejudices or ideals, not just in the hope of influencing others, though that hope is crucially important, but also just to confirm his or her standing as a responsible agent in, rather than a passive victim of, collective action."[14] In short, citizens are entitled to hear and to make all political arguments, because their status as equal citizens requires it. Neutrality should therefore not be confused with a justification for free speech; it is rather a doctrine that informs us about when it is appropriate to limit coercion.

One might ask, however, whether it is empirically necessary for citizens to have the option to choose inegalitarian principles in order to develop the two moral powers or to deliberate about policy. Perhaps individuals living under censorship would select the same policy views and conceptions of justice and the good that they would choose living under freedom. However, I do not read the defenders of viewpoint neutrality as making an empirical argument, but as presenting a claim about what it means to respect citizens as free and equal. It is not that the protection of all viewpoints is empirically necessary to develop the two moral powers or the capacities for democratic citizenship. Rather, it would disrespect the independent judgment of free and equal citizens, who are regarded as having the two moral powers, if the state were to restrict their options. Even if they ought not to choose views at odds with an ideal of equal citizenship, it is essential to the legitimacy of value democracy that they could choose to embrace inegalitarian principles and policies.[15] As I suggested in the previous chapter, value democracy is not indifferent to whether citizens do choose values of free and equal citizenship. It argues that they should not only choose democratic values, but they should engage in a process of reflective revision to scrutinize their beliefs, including their so-called private beliefs, in the light of democratic values. But it is essential to this process that citizens are free to choose to endorse the values of free and equal citizenship and to pursue reflective revision, rather than being coercively forced to do so.

Much of my emphasis, and that of the familiar free speech tradition following John Stuart Mill, is on the problems posed by coercive or criminal bans on speech. Such bans are blunt instruments with harmful effects. As Mill reminds us, coercive bans risk the loss of partial truths that might, as part of public discourse, serve to enlighten, despite being coached in arguments that are generally wrong.[16] Coercive sanction merely tries to bury opinion and therefore misses the grievances that might be held legitimately even by those with deeply racist views.[17] Mill reminds us too that coercive sanction denies citizens the opportunity to clarify what is wrong with hateful views.[18] As Nancy Rosenblum argues, it also potentially forces these views underground.[19] It would be better for hateful viewpoints to be publicly seen, tracked, and refuted.

I have sought to emphasize why value democracy's defense of viewpoint neutrality should be couched in a wider non–value neutral concern to protect the core values of freedom and equality, which a legitimate society must respect. It follows from the grounding of viewpoint neutrality in a wider non-neutral theory that the legitimate state can and should protect some views that are at odds with its own core values. A ban on certain viewpoints would disrespect the moral powers of free and equal citizens because it would, under threat of punishment, force them to come to particular conclusions about politics.

However, there is a tension between hateful viewpoints and the democratic values that require protecting those viewpoints. For instance, the Klan has been devoted since the time of its founding to eliminating equality from political society. Indeed, its founding ambition in the nineteenth century was to oppose the Equal Protection Clause of the Fourteenth Amendment. The Equal Protection Clause is the clearest constitutional guarantee of the ideal of equal status, and that ideal is the basis of the commitment to freedom of speech.[20]

The question of whether to protect the Klan's right to articulate its viewpoint, as opposed to its acts of violence, therefore offers a clear illustration of a possible tension between the doctrine of viewpoint neutrality as a means of limiting state coercion and the values and reasons underlying that doctrine. There is a clear conflict between the viewpoint of the Ku Klux Klan, which is protected by a right to free speech, and the reasons to protect that viewpoint in the first place. In short, the Klan opposes the values of political equality and autonomy for all persons subject to law, and these values are the very basis for protecting its rights in the first place.

On my view, it is important to retain a doctrine of viewpoint neutrality, but also to give expression to the reasons that underlie that protection. The state should protect the rights of hate groups, while also criticizing their discriminatory views. To see why there is an interest in both protecting and criticizing the Klan's viewpoint, it is important to consider three perspectives that reflect the different interests related to free speech: those of the speaker, the listener, and the democratic polity as a whole.

Ronald Dworkin describes the interest of citizens as speakers in being able to say whatever they wish. If citizens want to articulate a view that is at odds with the basis for the state's legitimacy, coercively preventing them from doing so would directly limit their autonomy. Denying speakers the ability to say what they want thus restricts one of the most basic capacities of citizens to decide and express their own political positions. Dworkin therefore emphasizes the importance of the citizen qua speaker in his defense of viewpoint neutrality. Dworkin's view clearly articulates why the affirmative value of autonomy requires respect and protection of all viewpoints expressed by speakers.

Another interest at stake in free speech rights is that of listeners, as Alexander Meiklejohn points out in his account of viewpoint neutrality. If citizens wish to hear a viewpoint, they should be free to consider it without government intrusion. Indeed, this interest of the listener might be held by citizens who are critical of hateful viewpoints. For instance, if I want to argue against a hateful viewpoint, I should be free to seek it out, understand it, and then criticize it.

A third perspective in discussions of free speech, according to Charles Beitz and T. M. Scanlon, is that of the citizenry as an audience in a democratic polity.[21] The interest of citizens as an audience is distinct from their interest as listeners. The perspective of citizens as listeners is an individual one, whereas the perspective of citizens as an audience concerns them collectively, and emphasizes the importance of the polity as a whole being democratic. Citizens as a democratic audience have interests at stake in deciding what beliefs should prevail in their democracy. In particular, they have an interest in seeing that democratic values thrive in the polity as a whole, so that the right to vote and other procedural and substantive democratic rights are preserved for all citizens.

However, if these institutions are to be preserved, the democratic values that support them must also be defended. Some viewpoints, such as the Klan's, which oppose the values of free and equal citizenship, are hostile to the values that underlie democratic institutions. On my view, the appropriate response by the state to this conflict is to protect the free speech rights of citizens to make all arguments as speakers and to hear all arguments as listeners. At the same time, the state should criticize antidemocratic and discriminatory viewpoints in order to uphold the interests of citizens as an audience in preserving democracy.

It might be objected that my view is not fair to discriminatory viewpoints, because it does not allow them the equal chance to spread. However, this objection rests on a mistaken conception of fairness. Respect is owned not to specific viewpoints per se, but to individual citizens. Viewpoint neutrality requires that the state not coercively limit the free speech rights of citizens, but it does not give the state the obligation to be neutral when it comes to the expression and defense of the values central to its own legitimacy. Viewpoint neutrality does not mean value neutrality. On my account, the state should protect the right of free speech to express all viewpoints, but it should not be neutral in its own expression or endorsement of values. The state and its citizens should promote the democratic values of free and equal citizenship, while criticizing hateful or discriminatory values.

It would be implausible to interpret neutrality as instead guaranteeing equal success for all viewpoints. This misguided interpretation of neutrality would commit the state to bolstering viewpoints that seek to deny the rights of some citizens. Consider, for instance, whether the state should seek to revive Nazi ideology, in the event that it falls to an all-time low in popularity. If neutrality were interpreted as a state obligation to guarantee the equal success of all viewpoints, it would require the state to affirmatively promote Nazi ideology and other racist beliefs that are contrary to its most basic democratic values. The state's promotion of racism would contradict citizens' interest as an audience in preserving the institutions and entitlements of democracy, and in ensuring that the democratic values of freedom and equality are widely shared and endorsed. Thus, the proper interpretation of viewpoint neutrality and of the state's obligation to protect the right of free expression does not imply that everyone has an entitlement for the state to ensure that their own views prevail. On the contrary, the state has no obligation to ensure the equal success of hateful viewpoints. Indeed, the state has an interest on behalf of the democratic citizenry as an audience in seeing that the viewpoints consistent with the values of free and equal citizenship succeed while those inimical to these values fail.

I have outlined the tension between two sets of interests: the first is the interest of speakers and listeners in viewpoint-neutral protections, and the second is the interest of the citizenry as a whole in ensuring that democratic values have a prominent place in public discourse and that hateful viewpoints are combated. One way to resolve this tension is to simply go the way of militant democrats and to ban the speech. Indeed, in a recent series of articles, Jeremy Waldron has denied that there is any tension at all between the right to free speech and the state's commitment to equality, because he believes that there is simply no loss to legitimacy that would come from banning the Klan's speech.[22] He asks whether societies that do ban the expression of hateful viewpoints have less legitimate law, and he argues that they do not. For instance, in countries where hateful viewpoints are banned, Waldron's position would suggest that there is no less legitimacy to the power to tax or to enforce the law.

I agree with Waldron that some viewpoints risk undermining and challenging the equal status of all citizens. As I have emphasized, there is no entitlement of a viewpoint to succeed. I also agree with Waldron that it would go too far to claim that a society which fails to have a doctrine of viewpoint neutrality would lack legitimacy in all of its laws. But on my view, there would be an increase in the degree of democratic legitimacy in a society if it could counter hateful viewpoints while still maintaining viewpoint neutrality when it comes to protecting speakers from being punished for their views.

In order to determine whether it would enhance legitimacy to protect free speech for even hateful viewpoints, we would do well to consider whether there is a difference between a society that has free speech and few hateful viewpoints, and a society that limits free speech but has an equal number of hateful viewpoints. If it is possible to counter hateful viewpoints while still protecting free speech, there would be an overall gain in the degree of democratic legitimacy. Specifically, the gain would come from preserving the entitlement of individuals to make any argument and to hear any argument that they wish. Such guarantees would enhance legitimacy by respecting the autonomy of citizens as speakers and listeners. It would also avoid the limits on autonomy that would come from coercively punishing some speakers. A society that offers this kind of viewpoint-neutral protection of free speech would also more fully realize political equality, because it would extend free speech protections to all citizens. The task, then, is to devise a way for society to protect the entitlements of citizens as speakers and listeners to say and listen to whatever they wish, at the same time that it combats hateful viewpoints that seek to undermine the values of free and equal citizenship. The aim is to ensure that the interests of speakers, listeners, and the "audience" of the democratic citizenry as a whole are all respected and realized.

Value democracy can both protect the rights of autonomous citizens and counter the discriminatory message of hate groups. Value democracy can accomplish this by distinguishing between the state's expressive and coercive capacities. In its coercive capacities, the state has an obligation to respect viewpoint neutrality by not coercing any speakers or listeners on the basis of their viewpoint. But when it acts in its expressive capacities, the legitimate state has an obligation to clarify why some protected viewpoints are at odds with the reasons for free expression in the first place. In this role, the state should both protect and criticize deeply inegalitarian viewpoints. This state duty follows from the recognition that it is important, not only for legitimate law to be justified, but also for the reasons behind the law to be promulgated.

It is often thought that the state should promulgate or make well-known the content of the law. Laws that are passed in secret and never publicized are rightly thought to be a paradigm of illegitimacy.[23] The content of laws must be publicized so that citizens can predict when their actions might be sanctioned. But I would add that citizens should know not only their rights and the rules that are set out by law; they should also know what the reasons are for these rights and legal rules. The key issue is how the state might find a way to express the reasons underlying rights, given that the state must also protect citizens' expression of hateful viewpoints that oppose these reasons. One place to look for expression of the reasons for rights is within the decisions of the Supreme Court. The Court is ideally an "exemplar" of public reason in the sense that it protects democratic values by striking down unconstitutional laws, such as those that constrain the practice of free expression. On my view, however, the Court also acts as an exemplar of public reason in a second sense by promulgating the reasons for rights. Namely, it acts as a model for the wider citizenry, including public officials who deliberate about and make the law, when it explains why certain laws are legitimate or illegitimate and when it speaks in defense of the values of free and equal citizenship.[24] The Court's audience extends to all citizens who are concerned to think and to deliberate publicly about lawmaking. This second notion of the Supreme Court as an exemplar of public reason is an instance of the state relying on its expressive capacity to promulgate the reasons for rights. Ideally, the Court should clarify to the citizenry that the state's protection of hateful viewpoints does not imply its approval of these viewpoints. In other words, the Court should affirm the importance of rights such as free speech, while giving reasons to criticize discriminatory views.

I take the idea of promulgating the reasons for rights to be the first step in what I call "democratic persuasion," which is a central feature of value democracy. Although the state should act in a viewpoint-neutral way when exercising its coercive capacity, it has an obligation to explain why it respects viewpoint neutrality in the first place. The state should use democratic persuasion, promulgating or publicly offering the reasons for rights, in an attempt to convince citizens that its reasons are good ones. Democratic persuasion encourages citizens to engage in reflective revision, with the aim of respecting and incorporating the public values of equal citizenship in their own lives, families, and civic associations. But the state must be careful to make reasoning central and to avoid force when pursuing democratic persuasion.

III. Free Speech as an Inverted Right

In the pages to follow, I will elaborate on how, according to value democracy, other branches of the government can follow the Supreme Court's example in promulgating the reasons for rights. In this section, however, I want to further clarify value democracy's theory of freedom of expression by contrasting it with a noted "expressivist" notion of law. The expressivist view was developed in the areas of Establishment and Equal Protection jurisprudence.[25] According to Elizabeth Anderson and Richard Pildes, rights should be understood, not as based on the interests of the individual, but rather as delineated by the expressive capacities of the state.

Establishment Clause jurisprudence, for example, can be best understood in terms of what the state should or should not express. On this account, a cross in a public school classroom is problematic because it suggests that the state is endorsing Christianity. According to the expressivist view, it is a mistake to think that we should understand why the cross would be problematic by looking to the interests of the students. None of these students is coerced directly; nor are their interests obviously affected. They might, for instance, simply ignore the cross. Instead, displaying the cross in a public school classroom is problematic for the expressivists because it violates what Anderson and Pildes regard as the state's fundamental identity: it implies that the state is Christian. Anderson and Pildes helpfully demonstrate that issues concerning religious establishment are linked to what the state should or should not say when it "speaks." Inevitably, the state will express a message in many circumstances. It is unlikely, for example, that classrooms could entirely avoid conveying any state message. The issue, as they demonstrate, is what the state should say, given that it will inevitably express itself.

I do not wish here to dispute Anderson and Pildes' influential and important account of the Establishment Clause. Instead, I want to discuss a kind of problem that can arise in the tension between state expression and the protection of negative rights against coercive intervention. This problem is distinct from their focus on direct state expression relevant to the Establishment Clause, so it is not surprising that their theory does not address it.[26] The right to be free from state coercion in matters of individual expression requires a distinct kind of expressivist theory, because the way the state conveys its message in protecting free speech is inevitably more ambiguous than in the Establishment context. What is distinctive about the jurisprudence of the rights related to the Establishment Clause is that it concerns direct limits on what the state can say. To the extent that citizens have a right against the establishment of religion, they possess a right against the state endorsing a particular religion. In the Establishment context, the relationship between state expression and rights is perfectly congruent: the citizen's right against establishment of religion correlates with the state's duty not to establish a religion.

Rights of freedom of expression, however, are importantly different. In the free speech context, I argue, state expression can at times seem to be "inverted" when rights are used to protect speech that opposes the reasons for the right of free expression itself. For example, the state's protection of free speech rights for hate groups might appear to suggest that there should be no judgment about the racist content of the protected expression. In this sense, there is a possible tension between the implicit message of speech protections and the reasons that are rightly understood to underlie rights. Given the possible confusion that inverted rights present for the successful promulgation of the reasons for rights, any workable theory of free expression should explain how the state might overcome this challenge.

Value democracy offers an original answer to the challenge of inverted rights. It argues that the state should protect rights in a neutral way, but that it should not be neutral regarding the values expressed by hateful viewpoints. The state needs to clarify its democratic values because there is a risk that its protection of hateful viewpoints might be seen as approving or condoning them. Value democracy's solution to this problem of inverted rights is for the state to protect the right of free speech, while criticizing hateful or discriminatory viewpoints. The state should engage in democratic persuasion, criticizing hate speech and promulgating the reasons for rights. Democratic persuasion therefore solves the problem of inverted rights by clarifying the state's criticism of protected but hateful viewpoints. In this way, democratic persuasion serves as a necessary complement to the rights protected under a doctrine of viewpoint neutrality.

Democratic persuasion is distinctive in that it uses the state's expressive capacities to promote the ideal of free and equal citizenship to the audience of citizens, while limiting coercion by protecting rights to free expression through the doctrine of viewpoint neutrality. Although it criticizes the viewpoints of discriminatory individuals and groups, it always respects their rights of free expression.

To elaborate on the distinction between the state's coercive capacity and its rights-respecting, expressive capacity in promulgating the reasons for rights, it is helpful to contrast my own view with that of the critical race theorist Charles Lawrence, who in turn draws on the work of Richard Delgado. Lawrence believes that the state is always acting in its expressive capacities, because all state action, including coercive action, is backed by reasons and value judgments. For instance, Lawrence views the decisions to desegregate lunch counters and to prohibit signs that barred entry to African Americans as themselves expressions of the state's support for the values of equal citizenship.[27] Lawrence takes this approach to argue that the state should use criminal law to limit hate speech and prosecute hate groups. He points out, as I have, that hate groups directly threaten the basic values of a free society, and that the state therefore must clearly condemn these groups. Lawrence, however, differs from my approach in suggesting that the state should express its condemnation of hate groups through criminal law. Lawrence, like Catharine MacKinnon, rejects the doctrine of viewpoint neutrality in favor of balancing the approach to issues of equal protection and civil rights.[28]

The problem with Lawrence's account is similar to that of Pildes and Anderson: it does not recognize the distinction between the type of values being expressed when the state acts in its expressive capacities and the type of values being expressed when it protects the speech of citizens and groups within society. When the state bans murder in criminal law, it is clearly expressing the idea that murder violates the rules of a legitimate society. Anti-discrimination law functions similarly; it expresses disapproval of the inegalitarian treatment of citizens. But not all decisions about coercion are similar. If the state protects a Klansman's right not to be murdered, it does not express support for the Klan's values; nor is it neutral about these ideas. It is rather acknowledging that citizens are entitled to rights, even when their viewpoints are deeply illiberal. Likewise, protecting the right of free speech for Klan members acknowledges their entitlement to be treated as free and equal citizens in spite of their beliefs. The state does not endorse the viewpoint of these speakers. Rather, it protects the Klan members' rights to expression for reasons related to respect for liberal principles of freedom, although these values are rejected in the content of the Klan members' speech.

Lawrence's critique, however, is helpful in forcing liberal theory to clarify its reasons for refusing to regulate illiberal expression. When the state refrains from regulating illiberal viewpoints, it is essential that it also use its expressive capacities to clarify that it is not expressing support for the viewpoints themselves. The state instead is guaranteeing an entitlement that stems from the need to respect all citizens as free and equal. On my account, the state can clarify the relationship between rights and the reasons for rights by clearly condemning hateful political viewpoints while protecting them from coercive law. Without this clarification, there is a significant risk that the real meaning of the protection of free expression will be inverted.

I interpret the ideal of equality as being present in both the First Amendment and the Fourteenth Amendment's Equal Protection Clause. The guarantee of "the equal protection of the laws" in the first section of the Fourteenth Amendment, and the enforcement powers granted to Congress in the fifth section, explicitly and directly express the democratic values that are central to my view. It is through the Equal Protection Clause that the Supreme Court has secured free and equal citizenship, such as by attempting to end segregation in public schools and by banning laws that discriminate overtly against women.[29]

The basis for the Equal Protection Clause is the value of equality, and the substance of what it protects is non-discrimination. The Equal Protection Clause thus directly expresses equality, in that the Clause's basis and its substantive protections are clearly consistent. But in the case of the First Amendment, there may be a tension between the justification of the right and the substantive content that the right protects. The right is justified by the value of equality. However, the substantive content that is protected by the right of free speech may include racist or discriminatory expression. The value of equality is therefore not directly expressed, but is inverted or hidden in these First Amendment cases, because rights of free speech and religion protect the liberty of citizens who oppose equality. However, this should not obscure the fact that equality is the foundation for both the First and Fourteenth Amendments. In particular, it is important that we not be misled by the doctrine of viewpoint neutrality into ignoring the central place of the substantive value of free and equal citizenship in the First Amendment. Although the ideal of equality is most explicit and direct in the Equal Protection Clause and anti-discrimination law, it also is the basis for the First Amendment.

Consider in greater depth the Supreme Court opinion in *Virginia v. Black*. There, the Court held that a cross-burning was protected during a rally in which no member of the targeted class was singled out. The Court invoked its doctrine of content neutrality, which includes but is broader than the doctrine of viewpoint neutrality. The important point for our purposes is that the protected "speech" in this case—the burning of the cross—clearly opposes the normative reasons that underlie its legality in the first place. Liberal theories justify the right of free expression based on free and equal citizenship. Yet they also should emphasize why the act of cross-burning is an affront to this ideal because the reasons for the right, which the state has the obligation to express, are at odds with the content of the speech protected by the right. *Virginia v. Black* thus presents a potential paradigm of how and why the meaning of rights to freedom of expression should be clarified to citizens. Without this clarification, there is a significant risk that the real meaning of the protection of free expression and the commonly understood meaning will be inverted.

Part of the Supreme Court's audience in the Black case is legislatures considering passing coercive laws that would ban hateful viewpoints short of direct threats. These state actors should be reminded why such laws violate the ideal of free and equal citizenship. But another audience for Supreme Court opinions is the Klan itself and other hate groups in the marketplace of ideas. The Court is saying to these citizens that, while their rights of free expression are protected, the content of their hateful views conflicts with the reasons for those rights protections. In addressing these citizens, the Court acts as an exemplar of public reason in the first and second senses described previously—it is both protecting a right and promulgating the reasons for the right.

Value democracy argues that the reasons for rights are not meant simply to be expressed publicly; they are also meant to be persuasive. The arguments offered as part of democratic persuasion are intended to challenge and change the minds of those who do not appreciate the importance of free and equal citizenship in a legitimate society. Of course, hate groups including the Ku Klux Klan might not listen to reason or be persuaded, but in those cases, it is important to convince third parties and the population at large of the values of free and equal citizenship. Part of the task here is clarifying that the state is not neutral in regard to groups like the Klan, and that the state instead affirms the freedom and equality of all citizens. In short, the legitimate state should employ democratic persuasion to convince the citizenry as a whole that its reasons for protecting the rights of all citizens are good reasons.

As I have suggested, one example of democratic persuasion is Supreme Court opinions. Admittedly, these Court opinions on their own may not be effective in changing the minds of hate groups that oppose the ideal of equal citizenship. The early Klan membership of Justice Hugo Black aside, I assume that most members of hate groups are not thinking analytically about the nuances of First Amendment doctrine. Although they still have an important expressive purpose, we must acknowledge that Court opinions alone will not effectively persuade the citizenry at large of the reasons for rights. As I mentioned in my discussion of value democracy's institutional independence in chapter 1, no single institution of government has an exclusive monopoly on the reasons that underlie rights. Other state actors in addition to the Court should also appeal to these reasons. In the rest of this chapter, I make the case for a wide expressive role for the state. Indeed, I contend that political theory should be concerned not only with the question of rightful limits on coercion, but also with the question of how to express the reasons for coercion and its limits.

When the state attempts to promulgate the reasons for rights without violating freedom of expression, it is essential that it observe two limits. The first, means-based limit of democratic persuasion requires that the state not pursue the transformation of citizens' views through any method that violates fundamental rights, such as freedom of expression, conscience, and association. For example, the state cannot use criminal sanctions to prohibit meetings of the Klan on the grounds that its members reject the reasons for freedom of expression. However, it would be appropriate for the state and its public officials to articulate why the Klan's views are inconsistent with the reasons for freedom of expression. On my view, the state can avoid crossing the means-based limit by confining its method of communicating its message to its expressive rather than its coercive capacity. For example, public officials and citizens engaged in public discussion may make arguments that seek to transform hateful viewpoints. In addition, I will suggest in the next section that there is a wide role for educators and the state more broadly to teach the importance of the ideal of equal citizenship. The challenge for value democracy, however, lies in simultaneously protecting rights of expression against coercive interference, while criticizing inegalitarian beliefs protected by these rights.

As I suggested earlier, the criticism involved depends on the degree to which the beliefs oppose free and equal citizenship. Hate groups like the Ku Klux Klan should be condemned by the state, as the very mission of the Klan is to undermine democratic values, such as equal protection of all citizens under the law. However, in many instances, it is the specific discriminatory beliefs of citizens that the state should criticize, and the state should make it clear that it is not condemning their entire set of beliefs. In the next chapter, I claim that even though some religious groups might hold discriminatory beliefs that should be challenged, this does not imply the wholesale abandonment of their religion.

Since the notion of coercion is central to the means-based limit, it is worth elaborating on how I will use this term. Drawing on Robert Nozick's work on this subject, I define coercion as the state threatening to impose a sanction or punishment on an individual or group of individuals with the aim of prohibiting a particular action, expression, or holding of a belief.[30] Coercion in this view need not be successful; some people might resist the state's threats. But the mere fact that a state action is coercive does not imply, as some have inferred, that the action is unjustifiable.[31] There are clearly justifiable cases of state coercion. For example, it is justifiable for the state to employ coercive criminal law in an attempt to stop citizens from committing acts of violence, like murder, rape, and assault. The means-based limit, however, suggests that the state should not use coercion to prohibit expression. Coercive threats would deny the ability of persons to decide for themselves what kinds of policy beliefs to express. This denial would fail to respect the entitlement of citizens to develop and exercise their moral powers. In particular, coercively banning viewpoints would impair the ability of citizens to determine autonomously which beliefs they wish to hold and defend.

It should be emphasized, however, that a state's attempt to change people's minds by expressing certain beliefs does not constitute coercion, since the state does not seek to prohibit citizens from holding conflicting beliefs. To the contrary, it is central to the idea of expression and more specifically to the expression and defense of the core values of freedom and equality that citizens are free to reject it. Although I argue that the state should seek to persuade citizens to endorse democratic values, it is essential to values of freedom and equality that the state not attempt to force acceptance. Citizens should be free to reject the state's defenses of the core values of free and equal citizenship. For similar reasons, the state should avoid manipulating citizens into accepting the values of free and equal citizenship through misleading citizens or by subliminally trying to change their minds. To respect autonomy, the means-based limit suggests that democratic persuasion must be transparent. But the requirement that democratic persuasion include explicit reasons does not mean that it must avoid emotion or rhetorical persuasiveness. Indeed, as Sharon Krause has pointed out, there is nothing about the appeal to emotion that need be inconsistent with reasoning.[32]

It is also essential to the means-based limit that even when the state is using democratic persuasion to criticize hateful viewpoints, it does not undermine the status of citizens who hold these viewpoints as free and equal bearers of rights. The means-based limit therefore emphasizes using reasons to attack hateful beliefs, arguments, or positions, but it should avoid demonizing individuals or exiling them from society. The means-based limit bars the kind of propaganda that avoids reasons and relies on character assassination, mockery, or the denial of an individual's humanity. This kind of propaganda is prohibited by the substance-based limit, because it degrades the status of those who hold hateful viewpoints as equal citizens. The challenge posed by the means-based limit is to find ways to criticize hateful viewpoints and to persuade the citizenry to reject them, while still respecting the status of all as free and equal. Persuasive rhetoric is important for this purpose, but it should not be divorced from reason, or resort to subconscious or subliminal methods that shun reason altogether.

Besides being subject to a means-based limit, democratic persuasion is also subject to a second, substance-based limit. The substance-based limit restricts the kind of beliefs the state is rightly concerned to transform through its expressive capacity, and the circumstances under which the state is justified in exercising that capacity. It is necessary for the state to use its expressive capacity to challenge only those beliefs that violate the ideal of free and equal citizenship. In particular, the state should not seek to transform all inegalitarian beliefs, but only those that challenge the ideal of free and equal citizenship.

As I argued in chapter 2, when we think about the reach of free and equal citizenship, we cannot a priori cordon off a private realm as being permanently beyond criticism. Intra-family decisions, for instance, might directly affect female children's chances for future equal citizenship if they were forbidden by their parents from receiving any education or learning to read. I therefore agree with Susan Okin and other theorists of liberal feminism that while the family and groups in civil society might be protected by rights of privacy and association, they still might make decisions that undermine equal citizenship.[33] It is essential to clarify here, as I did in chapter 1, that equal citizenship constitutes a political ideal; it is not the equivalent to equality in every sense. For instance, if I always neglect to pay the check at dinner with my friend, I might violate the ideal of an equal friendship, but not the ideal of equal citizenship. In sum, the substance-based limit of democratic persuasion requires the state to criticize only views that are incompatible with an ideal of free and equal citizenship, and not views that are incompatible with morality per se.

Of course, there will be easy and hard cases—it is not always obvious whether a belief is incompatible with the ideal of equal citizenship and therefore subject to criticism by the state. It is only those views which are openly hostile to the ideal of equal citizenship, or implausibly compatible with it, that the state has an obligation to criticize, according to the substance-based limit. For example, the views of hate groups are paradigmatic of views that are openly hostile to democratic values or implausibly disguised in a language of equality.[34] However, groups or citizens who hold opinions that might be plausible interpretations of equal citizenship— although there might be controversy about them—should not be subject to disapproval by the state in its expressive capacities. For instance, while some might think an ideal of equality requires affirmative action, other citizens who disapprove of this policy are not expressing opinions that are necessarily hostile to or implausibly connected to the ideal of equal citizenship. They might oppose affirmative action on grounds that may be plausibly interpreted as consistent with equal citizenship, such as an ideal of colorblindness in hiring and college admissions. The disagreement would be reasonable in that case, and not subject to democratic persuasion. The substance-based limit therefore makes the state use of democratic persuasion more limited than the principle of public relevance. The principle of public relevance identifies conflicts generally between free and equal citizenship and individual beliefs, and suggests the importance of making these beliefs consistent with democratic values. The substance-based limit, on the other hand, further narrows the instances when the state should engage in democratic persuasion. According to the substance-based limit, the state should use democratic persuasion only when individuals hold or advance ideas that clearly conflict or are implausibly claimed to be consistent with the ideal of free and equal citizenship.

The substance-based limit of democratic persuasion concerns what the state is obligated to say on behalf of its own values. At times, the state articulates these values and their justifying reasons through state actors, and the substance-based limit should then be followed. But this certainly does not mean that state actors cannot articulate opinions on controversial matters when speaking in their own capacities. Particular citizens, politicians, or state actors might have their own opinions on questions about which there is reasonable disagreement, including questions about conflicting interpretations of equal citizenship. Moreover, although my focus is on instances in which the state is obligated to promote an ideal of free and equal citizenship and to criticize viewpoints at odds with it, I hold open the possibility that other kinds of state speech might be neither obligatory nor prohibited. Pronouncements in favor of public health, such as warnings about smoking or trans fats, do not violate an ideal of equal citizenship, but neither are they required to clarify the meaning of equal citizenship. Such pronouncements might be permissible on grounds that are distinct from the ones I explore.

In sum, democratic persuasion is an attempt by the legitimate state to express the reasons and values that underlie rights. In some instances, democratic persuasion requires challenging viewpoints that are protected by rights, especially when the viewpoints are hateful. But the point of democratic persuasion is not merely to express the values of equal citizenship as a philosophical exercise. It is ideally an attempt to change the minds both of the members of hate groups and citizens more generally. Given the choice between expressing the values of freedom and equality in a non-persuasive or persuasive manner, all else being equal, the state should opt for forms of persuasion that are more convincing. If the reasons and values that underlie rights are central to the legitimacy of the state, it follows that the state has a role in defending them, especially when they are under attack. Part of defending democratic values is making persuasive arguments on their behalf.[35]

IV. The Scope of Democratic Persuasion

I have argued so far that an account of free expression should both defend the free speech rights of individuals against state coercion, and allow the state to promote the values that underlie these rights. I have also maintained that the state must respect both the substance-based and means-based limits of democratic persuasion when it promotes the ideal of free and equal citizenship through its expressive capacity. In this section, I begin to explore how the state might fulfill these duties by briefly returning to the question, which we explored in depth in chapter 2, of how value democracy applies to citizens in civil society. I hope to use this account of expression by citizens to begin thinking about how the state might change the minds of those who reject the values of free and equal citizenship and the reasons that underlie rights.

The idea of a role for public values within civil society might seem an odd starting point for a theory of free expression, given the usual understanding of the public/private distinction. In contemporary constitutional law, there is a distinction between "public accommodations" and private clubs. Public accommodations such as hotels and lunch counters are regulated by civil rights law, while private clubs are protected by rights ancillary to freedom of speech, namely rights of free association. One source of debate in contemporary public policy and constitutional law concerns what rightly counts as a public accommodation. I agree that the restaurants and hotels regulated by the 1964 Civil Rights Act are rightly regarded as being so essential to access to public life that they should be regulated as public accommodations. Allowing segregation in these public accommodations would perpetuate a system of subordinate citizenship that has its roots in slavery. It would serve as a "badge" and an "incident" of slavery, given the direct legacy from that heinous institution to segregation. In *Katzenbach v. McClung*, the Supreme Court upheld the 1964 Civil Rights Act ban on segregation in restaurants and hotels on the grounds that these were public accommodations that could be regulated under the Commerce Clause.[36] Value democracy treats this holding as settled law and upholds the entitlement of the state to ban segregation in public accommodations, such as restaurants and hotels.

A harder question from the standpoint of value democracy concerns whether private clubs, including those that lack regular meeting spaces, should be regulated as public accommodations or protected by the First Amendment right to free association. The Court has placed some limits on the ability of the government to define these private associations as public accommodations, which would be subject to the same regulations as hotels and restaurants. In a case regarding sex discrimination by the Jaycees, the Court argued that government regulation was appropriate, because the group qualified as a public accommodation: the Jaycees met consistently under one roof, it sold memberships to the general public, and it affected access to employment opportunities.[37] However, in *Boy Scouts v. Dale*, the Supreme Court struck down an attempt by New Jersey to apply the state's anti-discrimination law to the Boy Scouts.[38] The Court ruled that since the club was not a public accommodation, it was protected by the First Amendment rights of free speech and association. The Court held that the Boy Scouts' policy of discriminating in its membership against gays was central to its mission, and was therefore protected by freedom of speech and association.

I consider *Dale* in greater depth in the next chapter, but I begin my analysis here by suggesting that when the state protects free-association rights and limits coercive law from interfering with discriminatory private clubs, we should acknowledge that these clubs are not immune from public scrutiny and criticism. Although the state should protect the rights of free speech and association for clubs, it should also use democratic persuasion to criticize them for espousing values that are contrary to the ideal of free and equal citizenship. Members of these organizations are also citizens, and in this role, they are obligated as a matter of political morality to embrace the ideal of equal citizenship.[39] For example, because racial discrimination perpetuates the historical exclusion of minorities from equal citizenship, citizens should recognize, through reflective revision, that they should refuse to join or remain members when discriminatory actions come to light.[40] Thus, their right to join can coexist with their duty to reject such memberships or to resign from them.

According to value democracy, individual rights against intervention exist alongside the robust duty of citizens to speak out against hate groups, racists, and others who challenge free and equal citizenship. Drawing on Mill, value democracy suggests that the defenders of inequality should be protected from coercion, but "remonstrating," "reasoning," or "persuading" them is required of citizens.[41] Mill did not, however, develop an account of why the state, and not just citizens, might have a duty to reason and persuade citizens on behalf of the values that underlie rights. Indeed, a sharp distinction between our duty to advocate as citizens and our general moral duties may be difficult to draw in everyday discussion, because our moral and political duties are often intertwined. But when the state speaks, it is essential that it speak for all citizens and thus abide by the substance-based limit I elaborated in the last section.

In demonstrating the proper focus of democratic persuasion, it is helpful to examine the controversy that surrounded Supreme Court Justice Samuel Alito's confirmation hearing, concerning his membership in a private club. During the hearing, reasoning by both the citizenry and state officials sought to transform beliefs and behavior clearly protected by rights. Alito was publicly criticized for his membership in a Princeton University alumni group that allegedly not only excluded African Americans and women, but also publicly opposed the university's policy of recruiting and admitting African Americans and women to Princeton, an institution with a history of excluding both groups.[42] In the Alito case, senators acted in their official capacity to scrutinize the nominee's club membership. The members of the Senate Judiciary Committee asked Alito about his membership and his reasons for membership. The hearings served not only to bring to light the discriminatory views of the club, but also to persuade citizens listening to the hearings that the club's views are incompatible with public values.[43]

This case suggests how and why the duty to defend the values and reasons that underlie rights—in particular a concern for equal citizenship—should be pursued not only by citizens, but also by the state in its expressive capacity. In the Alito case, the Senate was exercising its public power to decide whether to confirm a Supreme Court justice. Given the discretion of judges in deciding cases, it is important that they not oppose the basic values and reasons that justify rights.[44] The confirmation hearing, therefore, should scrutinize whether a potential justice opposes the values of freedom and equality or has acted in a manner that raises questions about his or her commitment to those values. Alito's membership in the Princeton club was rightly subject to scrutiny because it opposed the ideal of equal citizenship. No one in this debate disputed Alito's right to join such a group as a matter of law; rather, the issue was whether his decision to join violated the basic public duties of non-discrimination—particularly when organizations like Alito's are linked to future job opportunities as well as to political power. The threat of being voted down for the job of Supreme Court justice by the Senate is not coercive in my definition, because the vote does not deny him the right to belong to the club.[45]

Exercising the state's expressive capacity to defend the reasons for rights is a duty of state officials more generally. State officials, like the Supreme Court, serve as an exemplar of public reason in the second sense that I described, promulgating the reasons that underlie rights and seeking to change the minds of those who reject the ideal of freedom and equality for all citizens. In these circumstances, state officials are not expressing general moral views, much less a comprehensive good or religion. Rather, they are invoking core democratic values related to equal citizenship. The state officials respect the substance-based limit of democratic persuasion, in that they speak on behalf of the core values of value democracy, and not on behalf of their own comprehensive conceptions.

Other kinds of private behavior, however, should not be subject to democratic persuasion. For instance, I do not believe that questions of sexual morality are obviously connected to public values of equal citizenship. An inquiry centered on whether a nominee to the Court had multiple consenting sexual partners, for example, would violate the substance-based limit on democratic persuasion. By contrast, it was clearly a matter of public relevance when Justice Clarence Thomas was asked about sexual harassment during his confirmation hearing. Sexual harassment was an issue linked to his regard for women as equal citizens, and was therefore publicly relevant in a way that consensual sexual practices are not.

Some might object that there is a difference between citizens having an expressive duty to articulate the values of free and equal citizenship and the state having a similar duty. The difference, according to the objection, is that state action—even when limited to expression—falls into the category of coercion per se. However, I would reply that the state, in some of its roles, is clearly reasoning and persuading—not coercing. For instance, in the Alito hearing, the committee members did not force Alito to reject the values of the Princeton club. Instead, they were using public dialogue and public scrutiny to demonstrate that the club's discriminatory policies violated the wider public value of equality. State expression in this form respected both of the key limits that I have proposed on democratic persuasion. The senators respected the rights of citizens and the means-based limit, in that they never threatened to coercively prohibit the beliefs they criticized. The senators also respected the substance-based limit by focusing only on the publicly relevant matter of whether Alito held beliefs that opposed the ideal of equal citizenship. Insofar as the members of the Senate Judiciary Committee referred to the ideal of equal citizenship, they were speaking on behalf of the democratic values that are fundamental to the state's legitimacy.

The contemporary state can "speak" in favor of its own values—and against those who deny the freedom and equality of citizens—in a variety of ways, ranging from the direct statements of politicians to the establishment of monuments and public holidays. Martin Luther King Day and Black History Month, as I mentioned in chapter 1, are examples of official endorsement of the civil rights movement's struggle for equality. Public officials do not shy away from political viewpoints when they celebrate and commemorate these official holidays. Rather, they articulate the ideal of equal status and celebrate those citizens who have promoted it. Far from being viewpoint-neutral about Southern segregation or groups like the Klan, the state promotes a particular viewpoint in defense of equal protection. Of course, citizens have the right to dissent from such expression. But here the state and its citizens should stand together to express disapproval of those who defend segregation in our society or who, more subtly, lament the end of "states' rights" that would protect segregation.

Another way to frame state expression in defense of these values is through the state's action as educator. When state standards require that the history of civil rights and the struggle against groups like the Klan be taught in schools, for instance, these matters are not taught in a viewpoint-neutral way. The movement and its victories are rightly taught as part of the American effort to live up to our proclaimed values of equality. The hope of public educators in teaching the lessons of Martin Luther King Day and Black History Month is that, regardless of what they are taught at home, students will learn the value of equal status for all citizens.

It is important for democratic persuasion not only to honor the exemplars of free and equal citizenship, but also to criticize the segregationists and the other opponents of civil rights. Students are often taught implicitly to be critical of racial segregation, such as when they learn about the hostile crowds that attempted to block the integration of public schools. On my view, the state should be explicit in teaching why Jim Crow laws violated the democratic value of free and equal citizenship. The state should engage in democratic persuasion, and teach civil rights history in a non-neutral way. It should highlight the defenders of democratic values like King and the first African American students in Little Rock, and give reasons to reject the discriminatory beliefs of the segregationists.

Besides learning about the civil rights movement, students should learn about the defenders of free and equal citizenship from the women's movement and the more recent gay rights movement. For instance, the nineteenth-century feminist Elizabeth Cady Stanton pioneered women's equality and the right to vote. She was the principal author of the landmark Declaration of Sentiments. As Sharon Krause points out in her book *Liberalism with Honor*, the Declaration of Sentiments "explicitly recalled Americans to the nation's founding principles of liberty and equality while reinterpreting the principles so as to include women within their scope."[46]

Just as the history of the civil rights movement is taught in a non–viewpoint neutral way, the history of the women's movement should also be taught in a way that recognizes the defenders of free and equal citizenship. The state rightly honors, through public education and monuments, the contributions of the women's movement to the right to vote and equal opportunity. In my view, the state should also recognize the leaders of the gay rights movement, who followed in the tradition of King and Stanton to secure freedom and equality for all persons. For instance, more schools should teach and honor the contribution of Harvey Milk to equal rights for gays. His example, as an advocate for gay rights and as the first openly gay public official in California, showed that sexual orientation should not be a bar to running for and holding elected office. He defended the right of gays to a full role in public life. But teaching his example requires not only recognizing his defense of free and equal citizenship, but also describing and criticizing the bigotry that he faced, which tragically led to his assassination.

These examples of King, Stanton, and Milk all serve to highlight two lessons. First, they suggest why citizens who stand up to injustice should be publicly recognized for exemplifying democratic persuasion. Second, the public teaching and honoring of their commitment to equality is a familiar means of promoting democratic values. I begin with these paradigms as clear examples of the state engaging in democratic persuasion and rightly taking a side in regard to conflicting viewpoints. We will now go on to extend this position to more complex and controversial areas.

V. Democratic Persuasion and the State as Educator

By using the state's persuasive and not its coercive capacities, democratic persuasion can promote democratic values and respect rights. But some might object that the state's role as educator is not merely persuasive, since it acts coercively in forcing children to attend school. While I admit that the state does act coercively in this instance, compulsory education is compatible with a respect for the rights of children. Although it would violate the rights of freedom of expression and privacy to force adult citizens to attend school, it does not violate children's rights to do so. The liberal tradition has long recognized that while adults rightly enjoy robust rights to freedom of conscience, expression, and autonomy to decide how to spend their time, there is an obligation to ensure that children are educated and understand democratic values. Children, who are not yet full-fledged citizens, do not have the same rights as adults.[47] Instead, children are future citizens. Indeed, John Stuart Mill begins his essay *On Liberty* by noting the distinction between adults and children. Mill argues that, because children are not yet in possession of their full capacities, we cannot treat them as enjoying the complete set of rights enjoyed by citizens.

The real controversy over children's education concerns the rights, not of children, but of parents. It is one thing to claim that children are not entitled to full rights of free expression and can be coerced in a way that adults cannot be, but it is a more controversial claim to suggest that parents should be forced to allow their children to be subject to a civic education. If the state can use its expressive capacity to force children to attend school, does it coerce the parents of children when it pursues democratic persuasion?

Although I have claimed that democratic persuasion requires the protection of rights and non-coercive attempts to change minds, it might be objected that when it comes to parents, they can be coerced if they resist permitting their children to be exposed to an education that seeks to inculcate democratic values. I concede the point and recognize that steps, such as compulsory education laws, will inevitably be a part of promoting democratic values to the extent that it is necessary to coerce parents into allowing their children to be both educated and exposed to the democratic value of equal respect for all citizens. But it is important here to recognize that the parents are not coerced in order to inculcate them; they are coerced to the extent that it is necessary to ensure that children are taught the kind of civic education appropriate for minors in a democracy. This concession, however, suggests that parental rights do not include the ability to raise children free from exposure to the ideas fundamental to liberal democracy.

The coercion of children, in the form of compulsory education laws, does forcibly limit some parental rights, but when we examine what is gained for the future autonomy of children, this will be a balance worth striking. Specifically, the parents retain their free speech rights, but they do not have the right to indoctrinate their children isolated from any countervailing opinion. Democratic persuasion allows parents to express their views freely to their children, even when those views are opposed to the core values of free and equal citizenship. For instance, a parent who endorses the Nazi Party or who denies the Holocaust continues to have the right to express these views at home or in person with their children. But value democracy does not include the right to prevent children from hearing that the Holocaust actually happened or that the Nazis wrongly opposed the basic principles of liberal democracy. What is lost for the parent is complete control over the information that flows to their children, but there are two crucial gains. One is the ability of future citizens to understand the reasons for the rights that they possess and may exercise. This understanding ultimately will allow them to make a decision about whether or not to endorse their parents' views, which would be more difficult if information were entirely controlled by their parents. The second gain is the concern that the future rights of all citizens be equally respected, and not undermined by the unchecked spread of hateful viewpoints in civil society and the family.

As we look through the existing case law on the subject of parental control over children's education, I believe it is plausible to interpret this right as not including the ability to exert total control over the information that children learn or hear. In the twentieth century, the Supreme Court seemed to suggest that there is a fundamental right of parents to control what their children learn, and this might seem to oppose the idea I have just defended that parents may be forced to send their children to school. In one case, *Meyer v. Nebraska*, the court struck down a law that prohibited the teaching of foreign languages, and it ruled that parents possessed a right to ensure their children could learn languages other than English.[48] In another case, *Pierce v. Society of Sisters*, the Court struck down a law that required children to attend public schools.[49] But neither of these cases shows that parents have a right to keep their children free from exposure to democratic persuasion. Indeed, the right of parents to expose children to foreign languages or to choose their children's school is consistent with not allowing parents to withdraw their children from exposure to democratic persuasion altogether. Even if they choose private schools over public schools, the state can legitimately require those schools to teach children a civics curriculum that explains the reasons why all citizens should enjoy equal rights. Both of these cases allow the state to enforce compulsory education or exposure to a civics curriculum.

Of course, some parents with viewpoints opposed to the core values and the reasons for rights might object to this requirement. For instance, in *Mozert v. Hawkins*, Vicki Frost brought suit against the state, claiming that she had a right to remove her child from a class that taught abstract reasoning and informed children about other cultures.[50] A federal appellate court disagreed, ruling that the right of parents to choose their children's school does not extend to a right to exclude children from a basic curriculum advancing democratic values. I agree with the holding in *Mozert*, and suggest that the rights of parents do not include the right to isolate their children from democratic persuasion. A core part of teaching respect for other citizens as free and equal is informing children about diverse cultures at home and abroad.

For similar reasons, I disagree with the conclusion of the Supreme Court in the *Wisconsin v. Yoder* case.[51] In *Yoder*, an Amish group in Wisconsin objected to a state requirement that their children learn a curriculum emphasizing reasoning skills beyond the eighth grade. In the view of the Amish, exposure to this form of reasoning would undermine their teaching of the literal word of the Bible. Drawing on this case, I want to explain why the right of parents to control their children's education does not extend to the right to decide whether they should be exposed to democratic persuasion. Despite the outcome of *Yoder*, the Court did not claim that parents are entitled to teach their children anything they wish. Instead, the Court relied on a specifically religious claim that a failure to be able to teach their children as they wished would infringe on the parents' religious freedom. I believe the Court's decision in *Yoder* confuses the notion that democratic persuasion might ultimately change beliefs with the idea that there is a violation of religious freedom. Indeed, I will argue in chapter 5 that democratic persuasion should intentionally seek to transform some religious beliefs that are at odds with the underlying values of democracy.

In short, the right of parents to control their children's education is far from absolute. It does not include the right to keep them from being exposed to democratic persuasion. The parents' claim is not that the children should be free to decide the course of their own education, but rather that the right of parental control should give them the power to exclude their children from democratic persuasion in schools. By contrast, in my view, there is no parental right to exclude children from democratic persuasion, and parents can be coerced to the extent necessary to ensure that their children receive schooling and are exposed to democratic persuasion.

Another objection, however, to democratic persuasion relies not on parental rights or the rights of children, but on the rights of adults to be free from exposure to democratic persuasion. Although democratic persuasion should not be forced on adults, it might be argued that parents might be exposed to democratic persuasion when their children come home and repeat the lessons that they learned in school. Consider, for instance, the case of a Holocaust-denying parent. The parent might protest that she would be exposed to democratic persuasion regarding the reality and evil of the Holocaust through her child. Teaching children democratic values might result in the parents hearing about those values as well. But there are two reasons why I think this inevitable but indirect exposure of the parents to democratic persuasion can be justified.

First, school curricula can be devised in a way that respects the right of parents to opt out of democratic persuasion by ensuring that the school is not attempting to persuade them when it attempts to persuade their children. For instance, children should not be asked directly about their parents' views or encouraged to go home and persuade the parents to adopt the viewpoints advanced in the classroom. Democratic persuasion aims to convince children that all citizens should be treated as free and equal, but it does not require them to act as the state's teachers. The focus should be on the children's education. Indeed, it is essential that children not be used as a means for pushing parents to endorse the viewpoints advanced in the curriculum. The parents should not be singled out and criticized directly in class for disagreeing with the state's viewpoint. Such an approach would risk using coercion as a means of transforming parental beliefs. Of course, it is likely that parents inevitably will be exposed to the views that their children are learning in school. But I take this to be quite different from what could be coercive and abusive means of employing children in democratic persuasion, such as directly forcing the parents to attend school themselves, or forcing the children to inform on their parents. Respect for the rights of freedom of expression and conscience rules out using children as tools in compelling parents to change their minds. For instance, when children are not abused but are taught racist beliefs by their parents, schools should aim to dissuade their pupils from endorsing racism. But children should not be taken from their home solely on the basis of their parents' beliefs. Nor should schools attempt to force parents to change their beliefs through the use of sanctions.

While parents may be indirectly exposed to democratic persuasion through their children, this is acceptable given that indirect exposure to democratic persuasion is simply inevitable in contemporary society. For example, if a Holocaust memorial is built in the center of town where many shops are located, Holocaust deniers walking in that area may be indirectly exposed to democratic persuasion regarding the reality and evil of the Holocaust. I take this simply to be a fact of life in the contemporary world where views are not isolated in separate spaces. Similarly, the exposure of parents to the civics curriculum of their children might simply be the inevitable result of living in a world where it is very difficult to cordon off exposure to beliefs. It is no objection against legitimate democratic persuasion that it might find its way into the ears of those who disagree with its message.

A second reply to the critics of democratic persuasion is that, given the power imbalance between parents and children, parental exposure to democratic persuasion through their children is non-coercive. Considering the much greater power of the parent, there is nothing in a child holding an opposing viewpoint that forces the parent to adopt it. Such differences between parents and children might strain relationships, but it is not tantamount to coercion.

I have argued that exposure to democratic persuasion as part of a school curriculum is appropriate in the case of children. This might result in the parents' indirect exposure to democratic persuasion. But it is important to recognize that this does not mean that the parents' indirect exposure is coercive, or that they are forced to accept the democratic values promoted by the state.

Although children, unlike adults, should be compelled to attend school, where they can be exposed to democratic persuasion, there are still important limits on how this should be pursued. Namely, I have proposed a means-based limit and substance-based limit to democratic persuasion, which civic education should respect. The way that a civics curriculum is taught must not undermine the democratic value of free and equal citizenship. Teachers, for instance, should be careful not simply to silence dissenting students, even when dealing with inegalitarian views. Teaching should advance the state's expressions as speaker by instilling respect for basic liberal values through reasoning rather than through coercion. Teachers should not force a belief by punishing children, just as the state should not force a belief on its citizens. Indeed, requirements for students merely to pledge or recite fail to capture the value of respect for each individual as free and equal. A more appropriate curriculum would encourage students to reflect on these matters and to debate hard cases. Such encouragement, however, is not value neutral. The teaching methods should follow the means-based limit by reasoning with students, rather than coercively punishing them. Similarly, to follow the substance-based limit, teachers should frame issues for their students to recognize that the state has a duty to respect, not just any values, but those of free and equal citizenship.

I have argued so far that value democracy has an interest in promoting equality through the education of children, which is one of the state's expressive capacities. One potential problem with this account is a potential conflict between state expression and the free speech rights of government employees. Imagine a case in which a public school teacher was fired for promoting hateful views in the classroom—say, those of the Ku Klux Klan. Such a case would pit the free speech interests of the teacher against the school's and the state's interest in promoting the value of equal citizenship.[52] A Klan member who serves as a public school teacher would threaten to undermine the value of equal citizenship that is rightly viewed as at the heart of a civil rights curriculum. In order to promote the fundamental values that underlie rights, the school would be justified in firing the teacher. Protecting the free speech rights of the teacher would be a misplaced invocation of the kind of "inverted" free speech right that was rightly protected in *Virginia v. Black*. Unlike in *Virginia*, the Klan member in the school teacher example is a government employee who serves a public trust in teaching children equal citizenship. Certainly, the teacher could not serve this public trust and express the reasons for rights if he or she advanced the Klan's agenda in class and in school.

More controversially, I suggest that this kind of hateful expression by the teacher could be grounds for dismissal even if done outside the school—say, in a newspaper editorial or in a public speech. This racist expression would likely undermine the teacher's ability to convey the democratic state's message of equal citizenship in the classroom. In short, while "inverted" rights of free speech appropriately protect hateful viewpoints such as the Klan's, they do not entitle racists or members of hate groups to work officially for the state. Although firing might seem coercive and in this case it is carried out by the state, it is not an instance of state coercion that violates rights. The state is not attempting to deprive all individuals of the choice of whether to adopt a hateful viewpoint. The state thus respects viewpoint neutrality more generally. But when it comes to the specific question of whether it will fund views at odds with its core values, it refuses to provide positive support for hateful viewpoints by hiring members of the Klan or American Nazi Party. There is no general right to be employed by a public school any more than there is a right to be a Supreme Court justice. One of the requirements for both official positions is not to undermine the state's duty to promulgate the reasons and values that underlie rights.

Importantly, however, a case in which a teacher was fired for preaching hateful views should be distinguished from an instance in which a teacher was punished for resisting a school policy that has no bearing on questions of free and equal citizenship. For instance, if a teacher were protesting the school administration's budget priorities, this kind of speech ought to be protected, because firing the teacher would violate the substance-based limit on democratic persuasion.[53] Only if the teacher's view were explicitly opposed to the value of equal citizenship, or if it were implausibly connected to that value, could he or she justifiably be fired on the grounds of state promotion of the core values central to legitimacy.

Value democracy's treatment of the teacher firing case differs from the militant democrat approach taken in Canada. In a famous decision, *R. v. Keegstra*, the Canadian Supreme Court examined whether the country's free speech codes allowed a teacher to be punished for teaching anti-semitic views.[54] The teacher had expressed disdain for the Jewish people as part of his classroom lessons. Consistent with the Canadian ban on virulent anti-semitic viewpoints, the teacher was not only fired, but punished. In contrast to this approach, value democracy would advance the interest of the democratic state and its citizens in condemning hateful viewpoints, while defending free speech rights. Value democracy would prohibit hateful viewpoints from entering into the classroom, and in some cases, it would justify firing teachers who spread such views. But when the state goes beyond firing these teachers or refusing to hire them, and proceeds to punish them, it crosses the line into the kind of militant democracy that I have sought to avoid. In *Keegstra*, an individual was punished not as a teacher, but as a citizen. This kind of punishment for an individual as a citizen is unacceptable in a democratic society that should treat all its members as entitled to make and hear all arguments. My position thus contrasts with both a pure neutrality approach, which would allow the teacher to continue spreading his hateful views in the classroom, and militant democracy, which would go beyond firing the teacher to punish him under criminal law.

On my account of freedom of expression, the case of the teacher should be distinguished from that of a student sanctioned for expression of an inegalitarian viewpoint.[55] The question of students' rights in public schools was recently raised in a 2004 incident at a Poway, California high school. Following school-sponsored participation in a national "day of silence" to recognize the plight of homosexual individuals who suffer from widespread anti-gay sentiment, one student wore a t-shirt to school that condemned homosexuality and the school's sponsorship of the day of silence. The t-shirt contained the text, "Homosexuality is shameful. —Romans 1:27. Be ashamed . . . Our school embraced what God has condemned."[56] Asked to remove the t-shirt or cover the words on it, the student refused. The school consequently forced the student to remain in a school office for the remainder of the day. Saying his free speech rights were violated, he sued in federal court.[57]

Value democracy treats the school's sponsorship of the day of silence as a justified form of democratic persuasion. In particular, it importantly served to recognize the way in which the harassment of gay students and potential violence against them are pervasive parts of American culture. It is clearly a publicly relevant concern to call public attention to this matter. If the t-shirt had been worn by a teacher, it would justify sanctions against him or her on the grounds that such a message, expressed by a state employee, would undermine the state's goal of defending the ideal of equal citizenship. But while students are rightly thought to be the audience of the state's message of equality, they are not themselves charged with expressing the state's view. They are the recipients of such legitimate state expression, not the voice through which the state speaks.

At the same time, it is crucial that, in seeking to persuade students to accept this message of equal citizenship, the state does not threaten them into doing so. A coercive threat would be inconsistent with the means-based limit on democratic persuasion. The notion that hateful viewpoints should be opposed through the state's expressive and not coercive capacity requires that students should have the right to retain a viewpoint that is at odds with the ideal of free and equal citizenship, so long as they do not adopt threatening or violent behavior. Unlike teachers, who have a responsibility as public workers to respect free and equal citizenship, stu-

dents should have the entitlement to hold beliefs at odds with equality.[58]
If the state seeks to coerce rather than persuade, it abandons its educative
function and falls into the excesses of the Invasive State.

VI. The Effectiveness of Democratic Persuasion

My view as stated so far may trigger a challenge from militant democrats and others who might worry that democratic persuasion is not active
enough in its opposition to hate groups and other opponents of the values
of free and equal citizenship. Militant democrats will ask what makes
democratic persuasion effective in the face of hateful beliefs. They might
argue that democratic persuasion as stated so far only guarantees that the
values of free and equal citizenship will be expressed, but not actively defended. According to militant democrats, democratic persuasion without
effectiveness cannot answer sufficiently the challenges from democratic
congruence, stability, interconnection, and public trust, which I raised in
the previous chapters. According to the view of militant democrats, the
state should abandon the means-based limit and employ coercion as a
method of promoting the values of free and equal citizenship.

I concede to the militant democrat that democratic persuasion should
not be content to merely express the values of free and equal citizenship.
Expression of the values is essential in responding to worries about complicity that stem from the inverted character of rights to free expression.
But democratic persuasion should also strive to avoid the Hateful Society
and promote a culture in which the values of free and equal citizenship are
embraced. To make democratic persuasion more effective without straying into the realm of coercion, I suggest that the liberal state should fund
democratic persuasion and refuse to subsidize viewpoints that directly
challenge free and equal citizenship. Although it is essential that hateful
or discriminatory views be protected from coercion in order to respect
rights, having a right to express hateful viewpoints does not mean a right
to have those viewpoints funded by the state.

But even if democratic persuasion, which includes giving or withholding state subsidy, is effective in curbing hateful viewpoints, militant democrats will object that coercion would be even more effective. I want to
offer two responses to this contention. First, it is not clear a priori whether
militant democracy will be more effective than democratic persuasion
in challenging beliefs that are at odds with the values of free and equal
citizenship. Coercive interventions may fail to change minds or simply
backfire. As Locke argues in *A Letter Concerning Toleration*, "such is the
nature of the Understanding, that it cannot be compell'd to the belief of
any thing by outward force."[59] I propose democratic persuasion as a non-

coercive alternative that can present convincing reasons, appeal to the understanding, and change belief.

Second, as I stressed in raising the paradox of rights, the question of whether to adopt democratic persuasion or militant democracy does not turn simply on a matter of effectiveness. I take it that even if militant democracy is more effective than democratic persuasion in limiting hate groups, there is an advantage from the standpoint of democratic legitimacy to a conception that can both protect rights and persuade citizens to adopt basic democratic values. The interest of citizens in preserving their autonomy as speakers and listeners suggests they should be free in a democracy to hear and argue all viewpoints, even those that are contrary to the reasons for rights. If citizens are to be treated as autonomous, they must have the right to make arguments, even when they are wrong. My claim is not that a society lacks any legitimacy if it does not protect all viewpoints. But I do want to suggest that protection of this right of free expression can enhance overall democratic legitimacy if it is combined with an approach that answers the problems of complicity and the militant democrats' worries about stability. While coercion would fail to show respect for citizens as autonomous speakers and listeners, giving them reasons to change their mind respects their autonomy. Nothing in the protection of rights to free expression gives individuals the right to hold their viewpoints unchallenged. Indeed, I have suggested why the citizenry as an audience has an interest in seeing the ideal of free and equal citizenship defended and promoted. If value democracy can effectively defend its own values, even if it is empirically less successful in limiting hate groups than militant democracy, it offers overall a better approach from the standpoint of democratic legitimacy.

Another objection to democratic persuasion might suggest that persuasion is most effective when it can draw on citizens' comprehensive doctrines. Democratic persuasion could be more effective if it made use of citizens' own deep ways of understanding the world, including their most deeply held moral views. But again I want to stress that democratic persuasion cannot promote the values of free and equal citizenship with regard only to effectiveness. For the state to respect citizens' freedom of conscience, it must not endorse a particular comprehensive doctrine. Instead, it should seek to find a set of reasons that respect the status of all citizens as free and equal. The substance-based limit thus avoids promoting values on the basis of a particular comprehensive conception of the good, which not all reasonable citizens can share.[60] Such a concern is perhaps best captured by the ban on the establishment or endorsement of one particular religious view as the state's view. The state's promotion of a particular religious viewpoint would undermine the state's role as a speaker on behalf of all citizens.

But this substance-based limit on the state's endorsement of a particular religion or comprehensive conception is compatible with the state encouraging a dialogue among citizens about how to endorse democratic values. The substance-based limit prevents the state from establishing any single comprehensive conception, like Catholicism or Buddhism, as an official doctrine to justify free and equal citizenship. But the state can allow citizens to endorse democratic values from the standpoint of their own deep religious and secular beliefs. As I suggest in chapter 5, this acknowledgment partly takes the form of protecting the free exercise of religion, ensuring a right to reflect on how one's religion might lead the endorsement of free and equal citizenship. It also implies that the state can acknowledge the role of deep religious commitments in the civil rights movement, the antislavery movement, and other efforts to secure freedom and equality for all citizens. Moreover, there is also no substance-based prohibition on the state acknowledging the existence of a wide variety of religious and comprehensive ways of endorsing the values of free and equal citizenship. Indeed, in some public celebrations such acknowledgment is essential. For instance, if the state is to create monuments and memorials to affirm the viewpoints of the civil rights movement, it is essential to acknowledge the fundamental role of the church in that movement. Martin Luther King Day cannot be celebrated without an acknowledgment of King's deep religious commitments. But such acknowledgment does not mean an endorsement of a single religion or other comprehensive doctrine as the sole, official foundation of the values of free and equal citizenship.

Acknowledging the role of a plurality of religious and secular views in endorsing the values of free and equal citizenship serves to prompt, not preempt, reflective revision, which will involve a multitude of ways of endorsing the values of free and equal citizenship from within citizens' various religious and secular comprehensive doctrines. But the state must be careful to prompt reflective revision without undermining it. Telling citizens exactly how they should form deep justifications for the values of free and equal citizenship would undermine reflective revision by needlessly cutting off the various pathways of forging a consensus on these values.

In the next chapter, I focus on state spending as a means of combating ideologies that are hostile to liberal democracy. But before doing so, I want to mention recent research suggesting that certain institutions can strengthen a liberal democratic regime and protect it against the kind of collapse that militant democrats fear. For instance, Samuel Issacharoff's work on institutional design describes how some schemes of democracy may be more stable than others.[61] Issacharoff believes that there are certain features of American democracy that might compare favorably to parliamentary systems. These American institutions might be adopted by a regime that is trying to protect itself against the opponents of liberal democracy.

As important as institutional stability is, I want to emphasize the steps that a liberal democratic regime can take to actively persuade citizens to reject illiberal ideologies. Value democracy suggests two reasons why the promotion of democratic values should supplement institutional mechanisms for promoting stability. First, democratic persuasion can articulate the values that make a democratic society fully legitimate in the first place. While stability is an important value, it is not the only value. If we focus solely on stability and ignore the crucial value of legitimacy, we would have no way of distinguishing between a stable Hobbesian leviathan and a stable rights-protecting liberal society.

Second, if it is possible to combat illiberal ideologies while respecting rights, value democracy can promote stability without making the tradeoffs inherent in militant democracy. Militant democrats present us with a stark choice between the stability of a regime and the protection of rights. Often the choice comes when collapse is imminent. My view offers a way of staving off this difficult choice. We can protect the stability of a liberal society by actively promoting democratic values and by persuading citizens to endorse freedom and equality for all. Value democracy does so without sacrificing rights out of a concern for stability. Even in a society where democracy is not directly threatened, value democracy can reinforce the commitment of citizens to freedom and equality by actively promoting democratic values.

VII. Conclusion

In the previous chapter, I made the case for a principle of public relevance, which suggested the normative import of the public values of free and equal citizenship within domains often regarded as private. But the question remained of how the state can best promote this principle. Value democracy embraces a conception of rights that protects citizens against coercive intervention. So it was a particular challenge to explain how democratic values might be promoted by the state without violating rights such as free expression. In this chapter, I sought to answer this challenge by grounding a conception of free expression within the broader theory of value democracy. Value democracy argues that while it is important to respect the right of citizens to develop their own political views, the same values that ground this right also create a duty for the state to clarify why it is protecting free expression in the first place. Value democracy therefore suggests that while the state in its coercive capacity must not seek to impose democracy's core values, in its persuasive, non-coercive capacity as speaker, it should seek to persuade citizens to respect the values of equal citizenship that ground the freedom of expression. Democratic persuasion, I argued, is compatible not only with the right of free expression, but with the robust protection of that right found in the Supreme Court's doctrine of viewpoint neutrality.

Theorists such as Rawls and Meiklejohn may be interpreted to support a viewpoint-neutral conception of freedom of expression. This viewpoint-neutral conception has been influential in the Supreme Court. I have argued, however, that viewpoint neutrality is actually undergirded by a non-neutral ideal of free and equal citizenship. In addition, I have proposed that the state has a responsibility to promulgate, not only the content of rights, but also the reasons for those rights through its expressive capacity. The state should be viewpoint neutral in protecting rights of free expression, but it should not be value neutral in using democratic persuasion to criticize hateful viewpoints and to promote the ideal of free and equal citizenship.

The challenge presented by freedom of expression is that the viewpoint-neutral right of free speech—unlike rights against the establishment of religion or to equal protection of the laws—is "inverted" with regard to the reasons for that right. Specifically, rights are inverted because they may be seen as condoning or being indifferent toward the content of the views they protect, even when those views attack the reasons for rights. I have therefore argued that protection of free speech should be accompanied by a robust direct expression of the reasons for rights through the state's expressive role as speaker and educator. In these roles, the state should seek actively to criticize the beliefs of groups, such as the Ku Klux Klan and the American Nazi Party, that are opposed to the values and reasons justifying freedom of speech. While viewpoint neutrality has a place within value democracy, it should be complemented by democratic persuasion. The state engages in democratic persuasion when it expresses the reasons and values that justify rights, and criticizes views that deny the freedom and equality of all citizens.

Now that I have elaborated on why the state should pursue democratic persuasion in its capacities as speaker and educator, I turn to a more controversial area. In the next chapter I propose that the state should promote the values of free and equal citizenship in its capacity as spender and subsidizer. This capacity will allow for more effectiveness in pursuing democratic persuasion, while still respecting a robust notion of the rights of free speech, association, and conscience.

CHAPTER FOUR

Democratic Persuasion and State Subsidy

VALUE DEMOCRACY AIMS TO PROTECT RIGHTS and to persuade the opponents of free and equal citizenship to change their views. In the previous chapter, I argued that the state should actively pursue democratic persuasion, given the problem of complicity that can accompany neutralist protections of free speech. The problem of complicity arises because the state's protection of free speech rights might be confused with its condoning the hateful messages that are expressed using those rights. I pointed out that the state can avoid complicity with hateful expression if it engages in democratic persuasion. By criticizing hate groups and promoting the ideal of free and equal citizenship, the state can clarify that its protection of groups from coercive intervention is not tantamount to approval of their message. While it is essential to protect the right to express all viewpoints, it is equally important that this protection be accompanied by the state's defense of the reasons for rights.

I now deal in greater depth with the concern of militant democrats, who question whether democratic persuasion has enough power to change minds and to counter the culture of the Hateful Society. Can more be done, in addition to expressing the reasons for rights, to ensure that democratic persuasion will be effective? In response to militant democrats, I argue in this chapter that the state should pursue democratic persuasion, not only through expression, but also in its capacity as spender or subsidizer. Here, the state's power in contemporary society is significant. If we combine what the state spends directly on various programs with the grants that it provides to private organizations, government expenditure is a large portion of the gross domestic product.[1]

I acknowledge that the pressure brought to bear by financial interests goes beyond pure expression, and it might seem like an inducement that is distinct from mere reasoning. But though democratic persuasion should always include reasoning, it is not limited to pure expression. As I have stressed, democratic persuasion is a term of art meant to describe the various capacities of the state and citizens that can be employed to transform hateful viewpoints while respecting the means and substance-based limits. I emphasize that democratic persuasion should not involve the coercive banning of any viewpoint, but democratic persuasion rightly includes the state's use of financial means to promote the values of free and equal citizenship.

Value democracy's use of state subsidy answers the worry of militant democrats that state expression alone might not be active enough in criticizing hate groups. I reply that state subsidies, combined with expression, can effectively counter the spread of hateful viewpoints while being non-coercive and compatible with the right of free speech. It therefore avoids the problem that militant democracy shares with the Invasive State. Namely, militant democracy does not adequately protect the right of free speech, because it goes beyond state subsidy and expression and relies instead on state coercion.

I begin this chapter by arguing that although the use of the state's funds for democratic persuasion is not viewpoint neutral, it is compatible with the right to free speech. In the next section I analyze the Supreme Court's jurisprudence about the potential conflict between free speech and viewpoint-based state spending. Here I draw on some of the Court's doctrine, while criticizing its at times misplaced focus on neutralism.[2] In the final section, I consider the related issue of whether non-profit status should be denied as a way of expressing disapproval of hate groups and other organizations that directly challenge the ideals of free and equal citizenship. I suggest that the granting of non-profit status, like the granting of funds, should be conditioned on whether groups respect the ideal of freedom and equality for all citizens.

II. State Funding and Freedom of Expression

I argued that the right of free speech should be protected for all citizens, no matter what viewpoint they express. This viewpoint-neutral right of free speech is grounded in respect for citizens as speakers and listeners to hear and make all arguments. The right of free speech prevents the state from coercively banning any argument or viewpoint, provided that there are no direct threats or incitements to immediate violence. However, value democracy rejects the idea that all viewpoints, no matter how hateful, have the entitlement to be immune from criticism and to have equal success in spreading among the citizenry. In many instances, the state should not be neutral when it comes to its own expression and funding. Rather, it should use democratic persuasion to criticize hateful viewpoints and check their advance. Democratic persuasion promotes the crucial interest of citizens as an "audience" that democratic values thrive and that discriminatory viewpoints do not become the governing policy or principles of a polity.

Promoting these values, even with the most purely expressive functions of the state, requires resources. If the state is to promulgate the reasons for rights, it must pay for the use of media to do so. A microphone or camera costs money. Monuments require significant resources to build, and curricula to advance the value of free and equal citizenship depend on significant resources to develop and teach. Public schools that are charged with promoting respect for democratic values in children are expensive to run. In all these cases, the use of state funds is necessary for the most basic state speech.

One form of state funding is direct expenditure. This includes the funding of public education, civics curricula, and monuments. At other times, the state spends money more indirectly by granting money to private organizations for the purpose of subsidizing activities with a public benefit. Value democracy embraces non-neutral criteria in deciding which groups to fund. It claims that groups should be funded only if they respect free and equal citizenship. Discriminatory groups, like the Klan or an alumni organization that seeks to prevent minorities from attending a university, should not receive government grants or funding.

The concern might be raised, however, that when the state gives grants on the basis of non-neutral criteria, it takes a side in affirming some viewpoints. The state then not only speaks for itself, but it affirms the viewpoints of some members of the polity as allies of its own message. I argue, however, that it is often compatible with rights of free speech for the state to refuse to subsidize viewpoints that are hateful or discriminatory. Though it is wrong for the state to coercively ban those viewpoints, under some conditions the state can refuse to fund organizations or individuals that advance these viewpoints. The state rightly uses grants to advance a message of respect for democratic values and to further the interest of the citizenry as an audience in securing freedom and equality for all members of the polity.

Besides direct state expenditure and grants, a third category of state spending is the granting of special tax privileges for certain non-profits. These privileges include tax deductibility for contributions to a group and tax exemption for its property and earnings. While non-profits are wide-ranging in their makeup and goals, almost all of them are required by American law to show that they promote some kind of public benefit in order to receive tax privileges.[3] This requirement is appropriate because non-profit status with tax exemption and tax deductibility is a kind of state subsidy. I argue in section III that the "public benefit" condition for non-profit status should be interpreted as requiring, at minimum, that the group not seek to undermine the values of free and equal citizenship. If a group is opposed to democratic values, the state has an obligation not to grant it non-profit status with tax privileges. The use of non-profit status is thus a valid means of democratic persuasion, like state expression, expenditure, and grants.

Does the use of state expenditure to promote the values of free and equal citizenship constitute coercion by the state? I argue here that there is an important contrast between financial inducements and state coercion. State coercion is employed in an attempt to deny the ability to make a choice. By contrast, financial inducements, like pure persuasion, clearly attempt to convince citizens to make a particular choice, but they do not deny the citizen the right to reject it. Parking fines that are imposed as a penalty for parking in a red zone, for instance, are not meant to give citizens a choice about whether they wish to pay to park in a red zone. Unlike a fine, potential state funding serves as an incentive that citizens might legitimately choose to forgo.

It is central to my analysis in the next two chapters that while democratic persuasion might employ methods of financial inducement and incentive, groups must retain the right to opt out of such persuasion. I acknowledge that such a right cannot merely be a formal entitlement. Individuals need some financial resources to give worth to the ability to use their rights. This minimal requirement of access to resources is necessary for individuals to be able to exercise their right of free speech. The ability to exercise the right of free speech should not be denied to anyone on the basis of their viewpoint. But while I acknowledge that minimal resources are necessary for citizens to exercise their right to express their views in public, this does not mean that they are entitled to see that their views are ultimately successful in spreading among the citizenry. Here it is important to distinguish between the funds that are necessary to exercise a right of free speech, and the claim that there is an entitlement for a particular viewpoint to be successful. Although I defend the use of resources to ensure that rights can be exercised, I also argue that state expenditure is rightfully used to promote viewpoints consistent with the value of free and equal citizenship, and to see that hateful and discriminatory views are defeated. In sum, I distinguish between the use of state expenditure to fund the protection of rights, an ideal I affirm, and the claim that viewpoints have an entitlement to be funded, a belief I reject.

It will be helpful to note ways in which state funds are necessary to secure the entitlement of individuals to exercise the right of free speech before going on to outline how the state should use funds to promote the ideals of free and equal citizenship. On the one hand, I do want to acknowledge some instances when state funds should not be denied to individuals or groups, because denial of funds would be equivalent to restricting their exercise of free speech. Such instances would be coercive or have the equivalent effect of coercion in sanctioning individuals because of their viewpoints. For instance, if the only media outlets were owned by the state, and the state failed to provide access to these outlets for those with hateful or discriminatory viewpoints, then arguably, the right of free speech would be diminished, and perhaps even violated. Or imagine that a state library had access to a set of rare books that were treated as foundational texts by hate groups. Denying access to these books, even if they were used to further a discriminatory ideology, would be equivalent to cutting off a free speech right through coercion, because the state library in this instance would be the only means for citizens to gather the information that they seek. Similarly, the state would cut off a substantial means of communicating one's ideas and would mistakenly impede the right to free speech if the Postal Service refused to deliver letters containing discriminatory messages.

Following Rawls, we might distinguish between a right to freedom of expression and the "worth" of that particular liberty.[4] Without the actual means, including minimal financial resources, to exercise a free speech right, that right might arguably have no real value. This concern about the worth of liberty suggests the general importance of a just distribution of wealth. This distribution would give citizens the ability to exercise their right of free speech, even when their expression resists the state's message or its financial incentives.

In addition to providing the minimum means for citizens to be able to resist democratic persuasion, the state should clarify that its use of subsidy power does not preclude a right to resist its message. Even if some methods of democratic persuasion might not violate the means or substance based limit in the strictest sense, they might be ruled out on the grounds that they could reasonably be confused with punishment or coercion. Later on in this chapter, for instance, I will use this principle to argue against the use of discriminatory taxes on individuals with hateful viewpoints.

It is therefore important that the state, at times, use its financial resources to ensure the right to dissent from the core values of the state. When a group that advances a discriminatory viewpoint wants to exercise its right of free speech and hold a rally, this might require some state expenditure. For instance, the state may have to spend resources in providing police protection to ensure that citizens can exercise their right of free speech. The state, in providing police protection for the demonstrators, helps to make it clear that there is a right to dissent from democratic values.

Funding police protection is a way of guaranteeing the right of free speech. But the state must also make clear that this protection does not imply that it endorses the message of the hate group or its rally. The state is funding the right to march, but it is not funding the message of the marchers. The state might clarify that it is not funding the message of the marchers by also funding police protection for the civil rights protestors who are demonstrating against the hate group's rally. There is thus a crucial distinction between the state funding the protection of a right and the state subsidizing a viewpoint. For example, the discriminatory group is entitled to state funded police protection when it exercises its right of free speech and holds a protest. However, I believe the group is not entitled to the state subsidizing its viewpoint. For instance, the group is not entitled to state funding for audiovisual equipment for its protest, or government money to buy larger and more expensive banners or placards.

Although I recognize the right to resist democratic persuasion as part of the right of free speech, and I acknowledge the entitlement to have these rights guaranteed in more than merely formal ways, this entitlement is not the same as the right to be subsidized by the state in pursuing a mission or promoting a message that is hateful or otherwise opposed to democratic values. There is an important distinction between the need to fund the protection of the right to free expression, and the separate question of whether we should fund a particular viewpoint. While funding a right concerns the use of resources so that all can say what they wish, the question of subsidizing a viewpoint concerns the issue of further funding to make the viewpoint more successful or effective in spreading among the citizenry.

I will argue that hateful or discriminatory organizations have no right to be subsidized by the state. In fact, in some instances, the legitimate state has an obligation not to subsidize these groups. This obligation is based on the duty of the state to avoid potential complicity in the message of hate groups and the duty to ensure that democratic values thrive. Those who advance hateful viewpoints should not succeed in making public policy. The use of state funds to fulfill these duties contributes to promulgating and defending the values of free and equal citizenship and making clear the reasons for rights. As Robert Post puts it, "[B]ecause we do not believe in an equality of status among ideas, we permit the government to advance and accentuate discrete and specific ideas when it itself speaks."[5] State subsidy helps to express these ideas, specifically those of free and equal citizenship, and it is an essential part of democratic persuasion.

Some might criticize the use of state spending for democratic persuasion on the basis of a different objection. They claim that, because state spending relies on taxes, and taxes are coercive, this implies that state spending is coercive. But this is a flawed train of logic. It is true that, under my conception, taxation is coercive since there is no choice about whether or not to pay taxes. The government aims to collect the tax, whether citizens wish to contribute or not. But the fact that the method of obtaining funds is coercive does not mean that the use of funds is necessarily coercive. Certainly, taxes can be used for coercive purposes, such as hiring police officers to stop crime. But they can be used for non-coercive purposes as well. For instance, funding a scholarship program is not itself coercive, though it makes use of funds that were obtained through taxation. In short, the coercive nature of taxes does not tell us whether any particular state use of funds is itself coercive.

Another mistaken reason for thinking that incentives are coercive is their effectiveness. Studies of power often emphasize the role of incentives because they get results. But the question of whether a technique is powerful or effective is clearly distinct from the question of whether it is coercive. Pure reasoning, for instance, might convince other citizens to change their minds. But this does not imply that pure reasoning is coercive.[6] To the contrary, democratic persuasion regards both reasoning and subsidy as effective yet non-coercive means to promote the values of free and equal citizenship.

II. State Speech and the Limited Public Forum: The Supreme Court's Flawed Neutralism

I now want to turn to instances in which the state might or might not use its spending power to promote the value of equal citizenship. In a line of cases that explores whether the government can condition its spending power on certain expressive goals, the Supreme Court has vacillated between two categories. In the first category of cases, it has found that when the state creates or "designates" a "limited public forum" for "private speech," it cannot choose to give or withhold subsidies to groups based on the content of their viewpoints. In this category, the Court has ruled that viewpoint neutrality in the limited public forum is required in order to avoid unconstitutionally limiting free speech. In a second category of cases, the Court has said that when the state speaks it can express or fund any government-sponsored message it wants. On my view, both categories have a distinct but equally flawed conception of neutrality at their core in that they seek to avoid any reference to substantive democratic values. The first wrongly assumes that there should be a viewpoint-neutral test for state subsidies of "private speech." The second of the Court's categories wrongly assumes an open and neutral test for what the state itself can rightly express.

The Court applied the "limited public forum" doctrine in the case of *Rosenberger v. University of Virginia*, concerning whether a public university could decide to withdraw subsidies from a student group that produced a religious publication.[7] The Court decided this case on First Amendment grounds regarding freedom of speech, invoking a standard of viewpoint neutrality. It ruled that when a public university creates a public forum to allow a variety of ideas to be heard, access to that forum, including funding, cannot be based on a group's viewpoint. In the Court's terms, the university established a limited public forum, which in turn triggered a requirement of viewpoint neutrality in access to the forum.

The idea of a "limited public forum" is meant to evoke an analogy with the kind of broad free speech protections that individuals enjoy in a "traditional" public forum such as a park. In these spaces, the government cannot limit what is said based on the viewpoint of a person or group. The traditional public forum is a zone of free speech. Similarly, the Court has suggested that when the government creates a "limited public forum," all views are entitled to free speech. However, a limited public forum differs from a traditional one in that the limited public forum involves funding viewpoints. While I agree with the Court that all views are entitled to free speech, I argue that it is a mistake to hold that all views are equally entitled to state funding or grants.

I do not wish to dispute the specific outcome of the *Rosenberger* case on the grounds I have defended in this book. The group's respect for free and equal citizenship was not at issue in this case. But I do believe it a mistake to suggest that any time a student group receives a subsidy from a state university, freedom of expression requires viewpoint neutrality in funding. This approach would mean that a public subsidy could be demanded by student groups, even if they espouse values that fundamentally seek to undermine the ideals of equal citizenship.[8] Consider the question of whether a state university would have to fund an organization, like Justice Alito's group at Princeton, that opposed the admission of women and racial minorities to the school. I have argued that members of this group might have a right to speak on campus, publish in the student newspaper, or espouse their views in the classroom, but this does not imply a right to be subsidized by the school. Public universities and private universities that seek to advance public purposes have an interest in seeing that some democratic views succeed and others do not. To act on that legitimate interest, universities must be free to condition their subsidies on respect for free and equal citizenship. Universities should not be forced to give funds in a viewpoint-neutral way to all groups, including those that are hateful or discriminatory.

Imagine a case in which discriminatory viewpoints were spreading on a university campus. The university would have an important obligation to challenge these views, and it could use its spending power to do so. The university should use its subsidy power, funding student groups that respect democratic values and withdrawing state support from groups that advance discriminatory views. Nothing in this funding policy would limit the free speech rights of students to associate or organize. Rather, the public university would be acting on its duties to criticize racist or discriminatory views, and to promote the ideal of free and equal citizenship. Groups that do not receive financial support from the university could still exercise the right of free speech and association, since they could continue to organize and raise private funds.

The Supreme Court, in its recent decision *Christian Legal Society v. Martinez*, reached the right conclusion when it ruled that a state university did not violate the right of free speech when it refused to subsidize a discriminatory student group.[9] But the Court's reasoning in the case was flawed, because it focused on which side respected the viewpoint neutrality requirement in funding. After describing the case, I will argue that the state need not be viewpoint neutral in funding student groups because it can and should refuse to fund hateful or discriminatory viewpoints.

In the case, a student group called the Christian Legal Society (CLS) sued the University of California, Hastings College of the Law. The CLS claimed that its First Amendment rights of free speech, free association, and free exercise were violated when Hastings refused to recognize the group as an official student organization. According to Hastings' policy, official student organizations were entitled to receive school funding. The CLS argued that the school's policy of recognizing and funding only non-discriminatory student groups violated the First Amendment guarantee of viewpoint neutrality as applied to the Christian Legal Society. The CLS claimed that the school's policy violated viewpoint neutrality by discriminating against the group's viewpoint that homosexuality is immoral. The group claimed that the First Amendment right of free expression protected its refusal to admit gays as members. In the CLS's view, its discrimination against gays expressed the group's fundamental belief that homosexuality was immoral and contrary to Christian teaching.

The group not only practiced discrimination against gays, it saw that discrimination as fundamental to its expressive purpose. The Hastings branch of the Christian Legal Society specifically claimed that all members had to sign on to the national organization's bylaws. These bylaws say that the group's goal is to "clarify and promote the concept of the Christian lawyer."[10] The Hastings branch of the CLS claimed that lawyers who were engaged in homosexual acts failed to live up to the national bylaws. Hastings Law School replied that the university's commitment to non-discrimination required all student organizations, as a condition of receiving funding, to abide by an "all-comers" membership policy that did not exclude anyone based on sexual orientation, race, or gender. The Law School defended its "all-comers" policy on the grounds that it was a viewpoint-neutral condition on funding. When the Christian Legal Society refused to abide by this policy, its student group subsidy was discontinued. However, it retained the right to meet and speak on campus.

While I agree with the Court's result, which sided with Hastings Law School, its reasoning for that decision wrongly placed viewpoint neutrality at the center of state subsidy cases. Specifically, I think the Court erred in believing that the denial of funds to the Christian Legal Society was consistent with the requirement of viewpoint neutrality in the limited public forum doctrine. On my view, Hastings' all-comers policy was not viewpoint neutral. However, I disagree with the Christian Legal Society's claim that, because the policy was not viewpoint neutral, it was invalid. I argue instead that a non–viewpoint neutral standard of respect for free and equal citizenship is the proper condition for granting state funds.

To see why non-discrimination policies are not viewpoint-neutral, it is helpful to consider the Court's decisions regarding "compelled association." The Court has recognized that, in certain circumstances, the state would violate the right of free expression and association if it "compelled association," or required a group to admit all applicants for membership. For example, discrimination is central to the Ku Klux Klan's expressed purpose for existing. Forcing it to admit black and Jewish members would undermine its ability to express its hateful viewpoint about minorities. For instance, if the Klan were required to allow blacks and Jews to join their marches, it would force upon the Klan a message of inclusion, when their preferred message is one of exclusion. Compelled association in that case would not be viewpoint neutral, because it would interfere with the Klan's expression of its discriminatory viewpoint. Similarly, the Supreme Court upheld the right of an Irish group to exclude gays from a march, on the grounds that exclusion was central to the group's expressed disapproval of homosexuality.[11] In sum, free expression and association rights require the protection of a group's right to discriminate when that discrimination is tied to the expressive purpose of that group. Requiring inclusion is therefore not a viewpoint-neutral policy.

Compelling association in such cases would arguably infringe on these groups' interest in free expression. There are differences between the *Christian Legal Society* case and the jurisprudence on compelled association. Most saliently, cases of compelled association concern whether groups can be coerced into accepting members, whereas the Hastings case is about whether a public university can non-coercively grant or discontinue state subsidies to groups. But while the difference between coercion and state subsidy is an important one, it should not be confused with the question of whether an all-comers policy is viewpoint neutral. An all-comers policy would not be viewpoint neutral as applied to the Klan or Christian Legal Society, because it would be critical of those groups' discriminatory viewpoints as expressed by their membership policies.

The fact that Hastings Law School's non-discrimination policy is not viewpoint-neutral, however, does not imply that it violates freedom of expression. Whether it is consistent with the right of free expression depends on the method that is used to promote non-discrimination. It would violate the right of free expression and association to force the Christian

Legal Society, or the Klan and the Irish parade, to change their membership policies. That would be a coercive case of compelled association. But according to value democracy, it would be compatible with the right of free expression and association if a public university non-coercively discontinued its subsidy to the CLS. The Christian Legal Society would still retain its right of free expression, since it could continue to congregate on campus, express its views, and follow its chosen membership policy. There would be no compelled association. Instead, the Law School would be taking the non-coercive step of refusing to grant a state subsidy to the group.

I argue that the Court should have decided this case as an instance of Hastings exercising state speech through the use of its funds and its recognition of official student groups. Hastings' use of funds should have been seen as an example of state speech that rightly pursued the goal of promoting non-discrimination and the ideal of free and equal citizenship. On my account of value democracy, it would have been not only constitutionally permissible for Hastings to use its expressive capacities to promote a message of non-discrimination; it also would have had a duty to do so as a matter of political morality. It is thus essential that we craft our constitutional jurisprudence regarding the First Amendment to allow the state to pursue its duty of democratic persuasion.

If the state were to continue to fund the Society, it would raise the problem of complicity. The state's financial support for the CLS would make it complicit in the group's message of discrimination. This would be an illegitimate policy, since it would undermine the freedom and equality of gay citizens. It would also violate the public law school's mission of promoting a legal profession that does not discriminate based on sexual orientation, race, or gender. Hastings should be allowed to respect the ideal of free and equal citizenship—and indeed, it has an obligation to respect that ideal—by refusing to subsidize a discriminatory group. I believe that such an approach would be more honest about Hastings' policy, but it would require abandoning the limited public forum requirement of viewpoint neutrality.

The Christian Legal Society might have offered three counter-responses to my approach. First, it might have contended that its ban was on homosexual acts, and not on gay citizens as such. In other words, the CLS could claim that it was not engaged in "status discrimination," or an attempt to diminish the entitlements and rights of individuals based on their membership in an ascriptive identity group, like race, that is beyond their control. According to this line of argument, the Christian Legal Society's membership policy was not a form of status discrimination against gays as a group, but it only excluded citizens who had made the choice to have sex outside of heterosexual marriage. Of course, all instances of homosexual sex fit in that category. But I believe that such an attempted distinction between status and choice of behavior is inconsistent with the ideal of free and equal citizenship, and indeed with the direction of the Supreme Court's jurisprudence, as I noted in chapter 1's discussion of free and equal citizenship. It is not a choice to be gay, any more than it is a choice to be heterosexual. Discrimination against gay citizens, based supposedly on their actions, thus amounts to status discrimination. The Christian Legal Society cannot treat gays as equals while banning them on the basis of their most intimate bonds and relationships.

A second possible counter-response might deny that the Christian Legal Society has a public purpose. On this view, the denial of gays from membership would not deny their equal citizenship, because the organization would only have a private purpose. But such a position, I believe, is belied by the Christian Legal Society's national bylaws. These bylaws speak openly about public life and describe the purpose of the organization as promoting the ideal of the Christian lawyer. The organization's denial of gays into the organization therefore seems to deny the status of the excluded as equals in the public domain of the legal profession. However, even if the Christian Legal Society were to re-define itself as merely having private interests, Hastings would be well within its rights to discontinue funding. It could adopt a policy of funding only organizations with public purposes that are consistent with its mission as a public law school.[12]

The final possible counter-argument is that my view goes beyond refusing to fund the Christian Legal Society's viewpoint, and instead affects their right to associate and assemble. But I believe that this case illustrates the distinction between the entitlement to have one's rights respected, and the right to have one's viewpoint funded. CLS might argue that by refusing to subsidize it, Hastings undermined the group's effective right to assemble on campus. But importantly, Hastings did not deny the group space on campus or even meeting rooms to use. In essence, it did provide some minimal funding and facilities to ensure that the group could exercise its right to free association. But the rights to free association and free speech do not extend to an entitlement to have the organization's message as a whole endorsed or a state subsidy granted to guarantee that it thrives. If the CLS did not receive an official subsidy from Hastings, the group could draw on the resources of its own local fund-raising and from its national organization to continue operating.

Part of what might have triggered a viewpoint-neutral analysis by the Court, employing its limited public forum doctrine, was the intent by the school to distribute funds in a neutral way. Hastings mistakenly stipulated in this case that it intended to create a public forum, and it then argued that its all-comers policy was viewpoint neutral. Within existing case law, democratic persuasion could likely be pursued by universities and colleges if they declared their intention was not to create a public forum, but to promote a message of respect for the freedom and equality of all citizens. In this way, universities could avoid the viewpoint neutrality requirement that the Court applies to the limited public forum. But I would argue that the Supreme Court should reject the viewpoint neutrality requirement itself concerning discriminatory viewpoints when it comes to state funding. This would allow the state and public universities to promote a message of respect for free and equal citizenship when deciding to grant subsidies. While viewpoint neutrality has a place in ensuring that no viewpoint is coercively banned, it would be inappropriate to apply a requirement of viewpoint neutrality to state subsidies for discriminatory groups.[13] One way to do this short of simply abandoning the notion of a limited public forum would be to carve out an exception for discriminatory viewpoints from the neutrality requirement. The Court might recognize that the limited public forum requires the protection of all viewpoints except for those that are discriminatory or hateful in the sense that I have described.[14]

A funding policy of limiting or discontinuing state subsidies to discriminatory or hateful groups would be compatible with the rights of these groups to free speech or association. While it would violate the rights of student groups to coercively ban them, the use of subsidies is significantly different, because it is a non-coercive means for the state to promote equality. It allows groups and individuals to retain their right to express themselves without fear of imprisonment or the use of force. They can continue to meet and speak in public. However, they do not have a right to be subsidized by the state in promoting a message of discrimination.

While my account of value democracy disagrees with the Court's viewpoint neutrality in the limited public forum doctrine, there are other parts of the Court's jurisprudence that are closer to the aims of democratic persuasion. In these cases, the Court often acknowledges that the government should be allowed to promote its own message using state funds. For instance, in *National Endowment for Arts v. Finley*, four artists who had failed to win NEA grants challenged the Endowment's policy of using "content based" criteria in distributing funds.[15] The Court, ruling against the artists, held that the NEA could award grants based on its own standards of artistic merit. The NEA did not need to be neutral about the content of the art that it was funding, so long as "content" refers to artistic or cultural significance.

A harder case would have arisen if the NEA had used not only content-based criteria that discriminated among artistic work by merit, but viewpoint-based criteria. Viewpoint-based criteria refer to political beliefs, such as democratic values or hateful viewpoints, as opposed to more general and non-political content-based criteria, such as artistic skill and originality. In Justice O'Connor's majority opinion, the Court allowed the

NEA to use content-based criteria in awarding grants, but it cautioned that it might have reached a different outcome if the NEA's policy had been viewpoint-based. For example, consider whether the NEA would have been allowed to sponsor viewpoint-based art that celebrated the civil rights movement and criticized racism. Such a policy would have discriminated against racist viewpoints in the grant competition.

Although this policy for distributing NEA funds would not be viewpoint neutral, I believe that it should be allowed. As I have argued, the state has an obligation not only to protect viewpoints from coercion, but also to promote the democratic values that justify rights. One goal of state funding should be to express the democratic value of free and equal citizenship. For example, the state could fund an art program or documentary film that sought to explore the importance of the values of the civil rights movement. But I would oppose funding hate groups, even if their expression were artistically "meritorious." Although D. W. Griffith's *Birth of a Nation* and Leni Riefenstahl's Nazi propaganda film *Triumph of the Will* are often cited for their original and influential cinematography, they express viewpoints that the state should not be complicit in or subsidize. Decisions about state funding should therefore not be viewpoint neutral. Instead, there should be a role for democratic persuasion in funding art that furthers the democratic value of free and equal citizenship, as opposed to subsidizing hateful viewpoints. In short, value democracy suggests that it should be constitutionally permissible for the state to speak in favor of the values of free and equal citizenship when it uses its power to subsidize.

The "state speech" doctrine as it currently exists, however, has a more subtle but equally problematic conception of neutrality at its core. During the George H. W. Bush administration, clinics that received federal funds were banned by the Department of Health and Human Services from telling patients about their right to have an abortion. This ban later became known as the "gag rule." Pro-choice and free speech advocates brought suit against the Department, challenging the gag rule as a coercive restriction on free speech. The Court ruled in *Rust v. Sullivan* that the Department of Health and Human Services' gag rule violated no rights, because the state was using its spending power to directly express its own point of view, in a manner similar to when it orders its own employees to express a message.[16] The Court avoided the viewpoint-neutral requirement of the public forum doctrine by arguing that the clinics and doctors were not part of a public forum, but were speaking on behalf of the state. The Court concluded in this case that the state can condition its use of funds on a non–viewpoint neutral requirement, including the gag rule.

My own framework, with its means-based and substance-based limits on democratic persuasion, serves as an alternative to the Court's jurisprudence. Specifically, although I agree with the Court's contention in *Rust* that the state need not be viewpoint neutral because of its expressive interest, I want to take issue with its conclusion on substantive grounds related to the content of democratic persuasion. Democratic persuasion concerns the state's obligation to promote the values of free and equal citizenship. But in the case of the gag rule, the state expressed itself in a way inconsistent with the most basic democratic values of a legitimate society, violating the substance-based limit. The problem with the gag rule is that it sought to deny information to citizens, not only about their medical options, but also about their legal rights. In a democracy, hindering access to information about legal rights keeps citizens both from being treated as equals and from being treated as free individuals capable of making their own decisions. Withholding such information suggests that some citizens are inferior, since they are treated as not being capable, as the elites in the "know" are, of making decisions about what to do with their rights.

It is important to emphasize here that my concern has to do with the policy of denying information about a right of free citizens. I do not mean to suggest, in upholding this right to information, that the state should take a position in its expressive capacity in order to persuade citizens of one position or another on abortion. The decision of individuals regarding abortion is in the realm of comprehensive conceptions of the good, and thus falls beyond the scope of democratic persuasion.

Value democracy allows the state to take a non–viewpoint neutral approach to state expression and funding. But for instances of state expression and funding to qualify as democratic persuasion, they cannot promote just any value. The state expression and funding must be consistent with a respect for free and equal citizenship, as required by the substance-based limit. The gag rule violated the substance-based limit, and would fail to qualify as democratic persuasion. Since it denied access to information about legal rights, and did not treat citizens as free and equal, the gag rule in *Rust* was an improper use of the state's expressive and funding powers. Just as the state would violate its mandate as a speaker if it were to preach inequality, so too, by denying access to information about legal rights in *Rust*, the state failed to promote the right values. The gag rule example demonstrates that rights against coercion are not the only limits on government action. Importantly, the substance-based limit on democratic persuasion establishes that the content of the state's expression—the reasons it gives for rights—should focus on the promotion of the ideal of free and equal citizenship. Democratic persuasion thus provides a normative standard, in the form of the democratic value of free and equal citizenship, to limit and to evaluate the content of state expression and funding.

The substance-based limit on the state's expressive power contrasts with the prevailing approach of opposing certain instances of state speech on the grounds of viewpoint neutrality. It is often said that some instances of state speech are illegitimate, because they violate the state's obligation not to favor any viewpoint. In *Rust*, and in the two cases I will briefly discuss here, the Court rejects the free speech argument that the state should be neutral, but it then verges on making the opposite claim that the state can say anything. My approach differs from both the Court's approach and that of viewpoint neutrality. Unlike the Court, I suggest that there should be limits on state speech. But unlike the advocates of viewpoint neutrality, I argue that those limits should be based on what is substantively illegitimate for the state to say. When the state speaks, it does not have the entitlement to say anything it wishes. Instead, the state should be subject to a substance-based limit, requiring it to respect the ideal of free and equal citizenship.

One kind of substantive limit on state speech has already been recognized, to an extent, in the Establishment Clause. In my previous discussion of Elizabeth Anderson and Richard Pildes's view of the Establishment Clause, I suggested the idea that the state cannot endorse any one religion in its entirety to be based on the concern that the state should not expressively promote a particular religion.[17] As I noted, this does not mean that the state is prohibited from recognizing religious contributions to the ideals of free and equal citizenship. The state can certainly honor the religious contributions to democratic values of the abolitionist and civil rights movements. But the Establishment Clause does not allow the state to endorse a religion in its entirety. This kind of substantive limit on state speech, however, is at times obscured by the Court's doctrine in other cases where it claims that when the state speaks, it is free to say whatever it wishes.

For instance, in *Pleasant Grove City v. Summum*, the Court considered whether a religious sect had a right to donate a religious monument for display in a public Utah park.[18] Ruling against the sect, the Court held that because displaying a religious monument in a public park would be an instance of state speech, the city could reject the monument. The Court's reasoning for this decision, however, was problematic. Although it admitted that the Establishment Clause serves as a potential limit on state speech, the Court, quoting its previous decision in *Rosenberger v. Rector*, ruled that the state "is entitled to say what it wishes."[19] But the Court's claim ignores the substantive limits that should be recognized on state speech. The justices should have pursued a deeper inquiry in *Summum* to examine if either accepting or rejecting the religious monument would have undercut the equal status inherent in the Constitution. It might have been the case that the city's message was entirely consistent with free and equal citizenship, but the Court neglected to see that when the state speaks, it should be subject to a substance-based limit on what it says. For example, forms of state speech that celebrate racism should be barred on the substantive grounds that they oppose the ideal of free and equal citizenship. Part of an inquiry into these equality-based limits would have been achieved by a more in-depth consideration of the Establishment Clause. But, more generally, I believe, consistent with the substance-based-limit, that state messages that are hostile to the value of equality should be limited. In particular, one potential problem raised by the case is that officials earlier had accepted a monument of the Ten Commandments for the same park. The city's acceptance of this monument and its rejection of the Summum monument risked sending the message that the state favors one religion over another. Value democracy would honor the ideal of equality that underlies the Establishment Clause by prohibiting the state from speaking in a way that is at odds with free and equal citizenship. I explore this ideal of equality in relation to religion in much greater detail in the next chapter.

Value democracy's substantive approach to state speech might also be useful in other areas of the Court's jurisprudence. In *Rumsfeld v. Forum for Academic and Institutional Rights, Inc.*, the Court looked at a federal requirement that private universities accept ROTC on campus as a condition of receiving government funds. The question was whether the requirement, known as the "Solomon Amendment," violated the free speech clause of the First Amendment.[20] The private universities' attorneys argued that the Solomon Amendment was an instance of compelled speech and an "unconstitutional condition" that linked funding to the denial of free speech rights. They claimed that the Amendment would force the schools into expressing an acceptance of the military's "don't ask, don't tell" policy. This policy threatened to discharge homosexual soldiers (but not heterosexual soldiers) if they disclosed their sexual orientation. The Court rejected the arguments of the universities' attorneys, and ruled that the Solomon Amendment did not compel speech or force the universities to say anything. In the Court's view, the Amendment only required universities to allow recruiters on campus.

Value democracy would approach the case differently. The Court should have recognized that military recruitment is an act of state speech. The state speaks when it attempts to persuade college students to join ROTC. But if recruitment is an act of state speech, it must respect value democracy's substance-based limit and be consistent with the value of free and equal citizenship. If part of the message of ROTC includes a defense of the "don't ask, don't tell" policy, the question arises whether this state expression conflicts with democratic values. In particular, we must ask whether the substance of the state's speech, expressed by the "don't ask, don't tell" policy, contradicts the Fourteenth Amendment's Equal Protection Clause.[21] On my view, the policy violated the Constitution's Equal

Protection Clause by denying the equal status of gay citizens. The military recruiters' defense of "don't ask, don't tell" should have been viewed as an illegitimate instance of state speech, in violation of the substance-based limit, much like the Colorado law that denied protection to gay citizens in *Romer v. Evans*, which I discussed in chapter 1.

The substance-based limit thus places an important limit on state speech. State speech is illegitimate if it violates the democratic values of freedom and equality. Critics of my project, however, might worry about the constitutionality of the substance-based limit. Do limits on state speech have a basis in the Constitution? To respond, I begin by noting that there is one limit on state speech that is already acknowledged in constitutional law. The Establishment Clause, as I have noted, prohibits some types of state speech—namely, speech that officially endorses a particular religion as a state religion. One possibility for implementing the substance-based limit in constitutional doctrine would be to expand the Establishment Clause to limit instances of state speech that attack equality. Such an approach is taken by Michael Dorf in a recent law review article.[22] Another way to place the substance-based limit in the context of the Constitution would be to argue that racist state speech, or other state expression that violates the democratic values of free and equal citizenship, fails to meet the rational basis test. In American jurisprudence, all laws that are challenged on the basis of equal protection must be shown to at least have a "rational purpose." It might be argued that state speech that opposes the ideal of free and equal citizenship can fail to meet a standard of rationality, because such speech is based on animus against a particular group. The Court has already struck down certain acts of state legislation for being based on animus. For instance, the Court voided the Colorado plebiscite that discriminated against gays in *Romer v. Evans*. The Court could extend this analysis from state legislation to state speech. It could rule that when state speech violates the value of free and equal citizenship, the speech is based on animus. State speech that is based on animus lacks a rational basis and is unconstitutional. In this way, the Court could ground the substance-based limit on state speech in the Constitution.[23]

The Court's ruling in *Rust* that the state need not be viewpoint neutral when it is sponsoring expression might seem at odds with its claim in *Christian Legal Society* and other public forum cases that the state distribution of funds requires viewpoint neutrality. A common distinction appealed to by the Court to make these rulings seem consistent is that while *Rust* is an example of the state speaking publicly, *Christian Legal Society* and other public forum cases are examples of the state distributing funds to private actors. The Court's distinction rests on an apparent difference in the subject who is speaking. If the state is speaking, it has more leeway to depart from viewpoint neutrality than when it is distributing funds to private actors, who are the speakers.

However, I find any distinction between "state expression" in *Rust* and the state subsidizing "private speech" in *Christian Legal Society* to be dubious. The issue in both cases is whether the government can use its spending power to promote or criticize particular non-neutral values and viewpoints. Indeed, it is quite difficult to discern the difference between the public forum cases and public expression cases solely in terms of the structure of funding. The doctors in *Rust* and the artists in *Finley* were private actors just like the students in *Christian Legal Society*.

Another difference between neutralist public forum cases, such as *Christian Legal Society*, and non-neutralist state expression cases, such as *Finley*, might be based instead on the intent or purpose of the funding. But as I have suggested in my discussion of *Christian Legal Society*, if that is the sole criterion, it is extremely formal. If the state could avoid the viewpoint neutrality requirement merely by stipulating that one of its purposes in distributing funds is to promote free and equal citizenship, it would be easy to overcome by careful wording of the university's intent in its rules for distributing funds. If, however, the viewpoint-neutrality requirement were attached to a deeper understanding of the protection of private speech from public influence, the doctrine should be abandoned when it comes to state expression and funding. Such a doctrine would be at odds with the obligation of the state to pursue democratic persuasion, and it would mistakenly place the neutralist understanding of free speech in the way of the state promoting democratic values. Democratic persuasion suggests that the state should use its subsidy power to promote the values of free and equal citizenship.

Some defenders of the neutralist approach to free speech and government subsidy will claim that I am proposing an "unconstitutional" condition on private speech.[24] This criticism might be interpreted to require that state conditions of funds should not be tied to a group's acceptance of a particular viewpoint. To the extent that this doctrine would require viewpoint-neutral distribution of state funds, I believe it is a mistake. On my view, there is no such thing as "private speech" that is immune from justification or that should be protected from the influence of either other citizens or the state. Free speech entails the right to be protected from coercion, but it does not entail the right of any individual to be free from the promotion of the core values of free and equal citizenship central to the state's legitimacy.[25] The right of free speech does not create an entitlement of any individual or group to be free from criticism when they advance beliefs or an ideology inimical to core democratic values.

In short, both the categories of the "limited public forum" and "sponsored expression" invoke a mistaken conception of neutrality. By contrast,

I have sought to challenge the emphasis on viewpoint neutrality, arguing that state funding should be used to promote the core values of free and equal citizenship and to criticize viewpoints that challenge those values. The power to spend is one of the means for the state to promulgate effectively the reasons that underlie rights. In this respect, the state is not a neutral umpire among competing views, especially when it comes to those views that challenge the very reasons and values that justify rights. Nor are beliefs which are incompatible with the ideal of equal citizenship "private" in the sense that the state has no role in seeking to change them. On the contrary, the state should seek to protect the freedom of expression from coercion while persuading those who hold viewpoints at odds with the state's own core values to change their minds. Particularly when it comes to the promotion of the ideal of equal citizenship, the state should express the very values that underlie freedom of speech in the first place.

III. DEMOCRATIC PERSUASION AND NON-PROFIT STATUS

So far in this chapter, I have argued that state funding and subsidies should be used as part of democratic persuasion. While viewpoint neutrality is appropriate in limiting the state's coercive power, on my view the state should use its spending power to defend democratic values. In particular, state funding should be denied to groups that oppose the ideal of free and equal citizenship. In this section I examine a related question. Should the conferral or withdrawal of non-profit status also be used as a means of democratic persuasion?

On my view, the extension of non-profit status with its tax privileges should be regarded as a type of subsidy. Thus, granting or withdrawing that status and its tax privileges should be considered a legitimate tool of democratic persuasion for the same reasons that apply to state subsidies. It follows that the state should not extend non-profit status to organizations which clearly oppose the ideal of free and equal citizenship, though their rights of freedom of speech and association should be simultaneously protected from coercive interference.

Under federal law, organizations that receive 501(c)(3) status are entitled not only to tax benefits, but also to a kind of public subsidy in the form of tax-deductible contributions. The U.S. government, by making contributions to 501(c)(3) organizations tax-deductible, in effect subsidizes those organizations. It offers what amounts to matching funds to contributions from individuals. When the government grants individuals a deduction, it effectively replaces the money that it would have collected from individual citizens and grants those funds to non-profit organizations. Tax-deductible status therefore provides an important link between the state's spending power and its ability to confer non-profit status. The tax-deductible status for non-profits suggests that the conferral of non-profit status is a type of state subsidy, as the Court has recognized.[26]

The view that non-profit status should be regarded as a kind of subsidy is underscored by the federal tax code, which recognizes non-profit status as a kind of privilege, rather than an entitlement of right. Specifically, non-profits which are not churches are required to show that they provide a "public benefit."[27] As Chief Justice Burger wrote in his majority decision for *Bob Jones University v. United States*: "When the Government grants exemptions or allows deductions all taxpayers are affected; the very fact of the exemption or deduction for the donor means that other taxpayers can be said to be indirect and vicarious 'donors.' Charitable exemptions are justified on the basis that the exempt entity confers a public benefit."[28] I take it that one of the clear necessary conditions for providing a public benefit is that the organization does not seek to oppose or undermine the values of free and equal citizenship. Of course, respect for democratic values is not a sufficient condition for providing a public benefit, since the law does not extend non-profit status to organizations that are established for private benefit, such as an investment club or a family trust.[29]

As in the subsidy case, it is important to point out that the denial of non-profit status for organizations that oppose the values of free and equal citizenship does not entail a denial of their rights. The very reason why a group enjoys rights of free expression and association is what triggers a persuasive response from the state in the denial of non-profit status. These rights are justified by the values of free and equal citizenship. But when groups seek to undermine the values that justify rights, the state best respects democratic rights by protecting the rights of free association and expression from coercive intervention, while using democratic persuasion to defend the reasons for those rights.

In order to demonstrate the way robust rights against coercion might trigger democratic persuasion, I want to begin with a relatively easy case of a hate group, and then extend my analysis to a more controversial issue, regarding the associative rights of the Boy Scouts of America. So far, I have argued that when it comes to their political viewpoints, groups like the Ku Klux Klan should enjoy free speech protections against state coercion. A similar argument applies to the right of free association for these groups. The ability of a group to express its viewpoints is closely connected with its right to limit its own membership to people who agree with that viewpoint. For instance, if the state is to respect the Klan's right of free association, it must not coercively force the organization to take members from different ethnic groups. A forced embrace of the Klan's critics, through compelled association, arguably would undermine its ability to pursue and promote its discriminatory message. This right against compelled association entails a number of other related associative rights. For example, groups including the Ku Klux Klan have associative rights to keep their membership lists private. When groups seek to conduct public marches, they not only have a free speech right to do so, but also an associative right to determine who will march alongside them.[30]

But the very same logic that protects the Ku Klux Klan's freedom to decide who is and who is not in its group also suggests why it should be subject to democratic persuasion. The group's refusal to admit members who are black or Jewish reinforces its opposition to the ideals of free and equal citizenship. Its hateful viewpoint is protected by freedom of association, because citizens should be regarded as having the political autonomy to develop and express their political views. But this same hateful viewpoint should also trigger a persuasive response from the state. The group should not receive any state subsidy, including the tax privileges of non-profit status. Groups devoted to promoting a racist message which directly challenges the ideal of free and equal citizenship cannot be said to pursue the public good or to provide a "public benefit."

I believe the case for protecting the Ku Klux Klan's associational rights while still subjecting them to democratic persuasion is a relatively easy one. I now want to turn to a harder case for the denial of non-profit status. The contemporary law of the freedom of association in the United States has centered on the status of a group that is much more innocuous than the Ku Klux Klan—the Boy Scouts of America. The Supreme Court's decision to hold that freedom of association protects the Boy Scout's right to exclude gay members is perhaps one of the most controversial decisions in recent years.[31]

The case concerned the membership of James Dale, who had spent his boyhood and young adult life in the Boy Scouts of America. He was by all accounts a model scout. In his teenage years Dale was awarded the "Eagle Scout" badge, which is the highest status that a boy scout can achieve in the organization. While in college, Dale continued his involvement in the organization as an assistant Scout Master. However, during his time at Rutgers University, it was revealed in a newspaper article that Dale was gay. The Boy Scouts asked Dale to leave the organization, pursuant to its policy of not allowing openly gay members.

Dale sued the Boy Scouts under New Jersey's anti-discrimination statute, which prohibits a "public accommodation" from discriminating against homosexuals. New Jersey's definition of the public accommodations which are subject to anti-discrimination requirements is quite broad, and included not only the hotels and restaurants that traditionally fall in this category, but also private organizations. The Boy Scouts argued before the Supreme Court that New Jersey's law was unconstitutional as applied to the Boy Scouts, because the law violated the organization's First Amendment rights to freedom of association and freedom of expression.

In its decision, the Supreme Court ruled in favor of the Boy Scouts, arguing that New Jersey's public accommodation law denied the Boy Scouts' right of free association. The central issue for the Court was whether the act of discriminating against Dale was central to the Boy Scouts' message. According to the Boy Scouts, one of their central missions in teaching leadership was to promote the idea of "clean living." They argued that being openly gay was incompatible with clean living, and that barring gays was central to their organization's expressive message. The Court agreed, finding that forcing the Boy Scouts to accept Dale as a member would burden the organization's freedom of expression and association.[32]

Controversy over the decision was present in the Court's dissenting opinions and continues today. Justice Stevens argued in his dissent that the majority's decision undermined the right of the state to pursue the compelling interest of combating discrimination. Andrew Koppelman, in his book *A Right to Discriminate? How the Case of Boy Scouts of America v. James Dale Warped the Law of Free Association*, claims that the Court made a mistake in concluding that the Boy Scout's discriminatory membership policy was essential to expressing a discriminatory message that was central to the organization.[33] Regardless of the arguments when *Dale* was decided, however, I believe that at the present time the Boy Scouts of America has taken on an expressive message of anti-gay sentiment. The Boy Scouts' very willingness to litigate the case publicly for many years suggests that excluding gay members is fundamentally important to the organization. Although this may not have been the case before, parents considering whether to allow their children to join the Boy Scouts must now grapple with the fact of whether they wish to endorse an organization that advocates anti-gay policies.

Given that the Boy Scouts is now so heavily identified with discrimination against gays as a result of its own public battle to defend its right to discriminate, the Boy Scouts of America should be denied the tax-exemption and tax-deductibility privileges of non-profit status. If the Court instead had found that the Boy Scouts was a public accommodation and not an expressive organization, non-profit status would not be an issue. A public accommodation would not be permitted to exclude Dale or anyone else on the basis of sexual orientation. But considering the current case law and the Boy Scouts' continuing to treat discrimination against gay citizens as part of its fundamental message, it can be concluded that the Boy Scouts is an expressive organization that stands opposed to a basic ideal of free and equal citizenship. In short, if the Boy Scouts qualify as an expressive organization that is entitled to rights of free association and expression, it should be subject to the withdrawal of non-profit status with its state-funded privileges of tax exemption and tax deductibility.

I believe the evidence for why the Boy Scouts violate the ideal of free and equal citizenship is made in its own arguments before the Supreme Court. The message of the Boy Scouts toward gay citizens and gay children contradicts the ideal of free and equal citizenship. While the mission of the organization is to teach children about leadership in the society at large, its view seems to be that gay citizens are incapable of such leadership because they refuse to live "cleanly." This amounts to the organization both engaging in and defending a kind of status discrimination that is not just internal to the organization, but relevant to public life more generally.

The Boy Scouts might reply that their message about gays is consistent with the idea that gays are free and equal citizens. But this potential claim is undermined by many of the Boy Scouts' own arguments in the *Dale* case. The organization recognized that Dale had not done anything in his career as a Boy Scout to suggest that he was not a good leader. He had been promoted to Eagle Scout, the highest honor for a Boy Scout. It was only when Dale was discovered to be gay after the publication of a newspaper article that the Boy Scouts deemed him unworthy of exercising leadership and belonging to their organization. The Scouts' reference to homosexuality as the sole reason for rendering an individual unfit to lead strikes me as exactly the same kind of relegation to second-class status that makes distinctions based on race inevitably inconsistent with the ideal of free and equal citizenship.[34] While I have argued that rights of free association should allow the Boy Scouts to select their membership without coercive interference, the fact that the Boy Scouts have taken such a stark position based on status should trigger an active process of democratic persuasion, including the discontinuation of their tax-exempt and tax-deductible non-profit status.[35]

Before I conclude this chapter, it is worth beginning the inquiry into the further issue of whether churches, and not just non-profit groups, should be subject to democratic persuasion. This issue is salient because, unlike other non-profits, churches are not required to demonstrate that they serve a public purpose to receive tax-exempt status.[36] It might then appear that they need not be subject to democratic persuasion when they oppose the democratic ideal of free and equal citizenship. I argue in the next chapter that even religiously based service providers, such as Catholic charities, should be subject to democratic persuasion when they seek to undermine policies that protect the rights of all citizens. But the question is: should the Catholic Church itself, or any church for that matter, be subject to democratic persuasion when its central tenets oppose free and equal citizenship? In extreme cases, should the state-funded privileges of tax exemption and tax deductibility be withdrawn when their religious doctrines conflict with the ideals of free and equal citizenship? As we proceed into this inquiry, it will be essential to identify when church doctrine actually does conflict with the ideals of free and equal citizenship, as opposed to making religious distinctions without implications for citizenship.

I want to begin by acknowledging that it is possible, at least, that a church's central doctrine might be at odds with the ideal of free and equal citizenship. Take, for instance, the Westboro Baptist Church of Topeka, Kansas, which advertises on its website that its central message is that "God hates fags."[37] According to its website, the message that "God hates fags—though elliptical—is a profound theological statement." An examination of Westboro's doctrine, including its explicit message that gay citizens "deserve death," serves to illustrate how a church can be a hate group.

As I argue in the next chapter, religious claims do not immunize citizens from the principle of public relevance or from democratic persuasion. On my view, it would be a mistake to grant an organization like the Westboro Baptist Church tax exemption on the mere grounds that it is religious. Such a church group, like a faith-based group that advances hateful viewpoints, actively opposes the core ideal of civil rights. These civil rights should be extended to straight and gay citizens alike. Given the Court's decision in *Snyder v. Phelps* to protect the free speech rights of the Westboro Church, it is important for the state to clarify that its protection of rights does not imply the state's neutrality or complicity with the church's hateful views.[38] The federal or state government should discontinue tax exemption and tax deductibility for Westboro.

In *Snyder v. Phelps*, the Supreme Court examined the question of whether the Westboro Church's protests at military funerals merited free speech protection. At these funerals, members of the Church held up placards claiming that military deaths are divine punishment for America's tolerance of homosexuality. The protests, however, were held out of the immediate view of the families, and the Court stressed in its opinion that the targeted audience of the demonstration was not the families, but the wider society. In its recent opinion, the Court argued along similar lines as *Virginia v. Black* that this speech is a matter of "public concern" protected by the right of free expression, and not a prohibited threat addressed to the families themselves. Indeed, the Westboro Church was careful enough to frame its views in terms that are sufficiently general to express a viewpoint rather than a threat. The Court's decision stressed the importance of protecting all viewpoints from punishment.[39]

However, if we are to protect the viewpoint of the Westboro Church from coercive sanction, it is equally important to express criticism of its message. Democratic persuasion is particularly important here to ensure that the protection of the Westboro Church's free speech right is not confused with the state condoning or being neutral toward the content of the Church's hateful viewpoint. Indeed, the Court's opinion did condemn the content of Westboro's message. But democratic persuasion should go beyond expression by the Court. The discontinuation of tax-exempt status would make it clear that the government is not complicit in the Westboro Church's viewpoint, and that the discriminatory message is criticized unequivocally. Such a move would combine protection of Westboro Church's right of free speech with democratic persuasion's criticism of a message that is overtly hostile to the ideal of free and equal citizenship.

It is a mistake that the federal law designating the criteria for non-profit status exempts churches from meeting the public benefit requirement. Churches that actively oppose the ideals of free and equal citizenship, such as the Westboro Baptist Church, should not be given tax privileges. This argument might seem quite far-reaching. Indeed, many of the major religions in the world retain practices that might seem at odds with the ideal of free and equal citizenship. For instance, the Catholic Church continues to preach against homosexuality on the grounds that it is sinful. This message might seem to have an affinity with the membership policy of the Boy Scouts of America. In addition, the ban on female priests might seem to violate the ideal of free and equal citizenship. But the question, as I noted throughout this book, is not whether an ideal or expression of an organization is inegalitarian. Rather, the publicly relevant question is whether or not a particular kind of inequality opposes the ideal of free and equal citizenship. When the issue is the potential denial of non-profit status, the state should be reluctant to withdraw that status if there is a good case to be made for the plausible compatibility of a particular theological view and the ideal of free and equal citizenship.

In the case of the Catholic Church, there is a plausible position to be made that its position on female priests does not constitute a clear violation of free and equal citizenship. Unlike the Boy Scouts of America, the Catholic Church does not bar homosexuals from membership. As Andrew Koppelman's argument might suggest, the Church attempts to distinguish between the status of gays within the religion and the Church's disapproval of the act of gay sex.[40] Koppelman therefore argues that the Catholic Church holds a theological basis for distinguishing between gays and non-gays that is not the same as refusing to acknowledge the status of gay citizens as equal citizens. Of course, the Church's position on gay marriage might seem to challenge this view, and to the degree that the Catholic Church engages in public advocacy against gay rights, there is more of a concern that they might violate the ideal of free and equal citizenship. But their internal religious distinction between gay and non-gay parishioners does not seem on its own to violate the ideal of free and equal citizenship.

Similarly, there is an argument to be made that the ban on female priests is not the same as refusing to allow women equal status in society at large. There are historical and theological grounds for denying women the ability to give the sacrament that might not implicate their larger status in society. One way of seeing whether the Catholic Church holds views that are incompatible with the equal citizenship of women is to examine its current attitudes toward public officeholders who are women. The Church does not actively campaign as a matter of policy against either women or gays who seek public office in contemporary American politics. Indeed, it often celebrates Catholic women who attain high political office.

In sum, the question of whether the Catholic Church should receive the tax privileges of non-profit status is not one that can be isolated from public scrutiny. This issue ultimately depends on whether or not the Church's principles are directly opposed to the values of free and equal citizenship. To the extent that the Church does not oppose the equal status of gays and women in society at large, despite its policy on the priesthood, it should not be subject to democratic persuasion. If, however, the Church were to engage in policies that seek to dissuade gays and women from serving in public life, the case would become stronger for discontinuing its state-funded tax privileges. For instance, the more the Church engages in public debate opposing gay rights, the weaker the argument on behalf of their retaining tax privileges would become.

At minimum, I think that the question of whether the Catholic Church's policies are actively opposed to the ideal of free and equal citizenship is ambiguous. It is ambiguous enough to suggest that the church should not be subject to democratic persuasion or the denial of non-profit status. As I suggested previously, the substance-based limit on democratic persuasion restricts it to clear instances in which the ideal of free and equal citizenship is opposed. Similarly, as a means of democratic persuasion, the discontinuation of tax privileges should only occur in cases of clear violations of free and equal citizenship. To the degree, however, that the Church begins to engage in active and current opposition to the fundamental rights of gays or women, this position might change. Moreover, in previous points in history, the Catholic Church might have violated the ideal of free and equal citizenship.

I believe a similar argument can be made about Orthodox Jewish communities that segregate men and women during religious services and refuse to admit women rabbis. These congregations claim to have a theological justification for the separateness of men and women in religious services, and they argue that this justification does not imply that women are less than equals in democratic society. As in the case of the Catholic Church, this theological inequality does not necessarily amount to an inequality of citizenship. To determine whether or not theological inequality implies inequality of citizenship, it is important to examine the role that women play in the wider community. Are they barred from seeking jobs or non-theological leadership positions in society at large? If women have a wider role, as female Orthodox Jews often do in the society at large, this would suggest that the distinction between men and women is a theological rather than political one.

Although I do not believe that either the Catholic Church or Orthodox communities should be subject to democratic persuasion in the form of withdrawing the tax privileges of non-profit status, I also do not want to deny the voice of women, gays, and other members of religious groups who seek to apply the process of reflective revision to their own communities. Indeed, within many of these communities, participants are actively discussing whether certain theological distinctions are at odds with the civic commitment to equality. Women who enjoy equality in the wider society often are leading this charge, challenging whether some of the traditional theological doctrine might be at odds with their general civic status. Within the Catholic Church, gay citizens are beginning to discuss whether the church, like the state, is wrong to deny them the right to marry. This kind of reflective revision is appropriate given the complex nature of the possible tension between theological and civil values. In my view, democratic persuasion is not appropriate in the form of denying non-profit status to the Catholic Church or to the Orthodox community, since they do not dissuade women from participating in the broader democratic society as equal citizens. But I want to be clear that I am not claiming that these groups act in a way that is completely compatible with the ideal of free and equal citizenship. My point is only that this is an ambiguous question which lacks the clarity needed to trigger democratic persuasion in the form of denying non-profit status. At the same time, I take it to be a good thing that the presence of democratic persuasion in the wider culture should trigger reflective revision, as members of these groups ask about the potential incompatibility between distinct gender roles and a commitment to free and equal citizenship.

I have attempted to demonstrate that not all theological inequalities are civic inequalities. At the same time, I must recognize that there might be tensions between theological and civic ideals. In such cases, I grant that there might be cases when a particular church should not receive tax-exempt, tax-deductible non-profit status. In the next chapter, I will discuss the tensions between certain religious conceptions and the ideal of free and equal citizenship more generally. I pay specific attention to the meaning of religious freedom, and suggest that it too is an ideal that requires democratic persuasion to articulate the reasons that justify this right. Religion does not immunize citizens from the reach of either the principle of public relevance or democratic persuasion. I will argue that the case of Bob Jones University is a prime illustration of when a religious organization should not be given the tax privileges of non-profit status, because of its opposition to the ideal of free and equal citizenship.

One objection to my view is that the conferral and withdrawal of non-profit status might be subject to abuse. Instead of using the denial of non-profit status to promote democratic values, some politicians might take power in order to use it for more nefarious purposes. For instance, suppose that legislators propose to deny non-profit status to human rights groups on the grounds that they challenge the policies of the incumbent government. I believe it should be clear by now that democratic persuasion would reject such a move, because of the substance-based limit. Value democracy offers a defense of rights, not a defense of the state as such.

A further response to this concern points out that all theories can potentially be abused. I have made it clear that there are grounds to criticize proposals that would employ the state's expressive and subsidy powers to attack groups that do not actually oppose democratic values. Namely, such proposals should be criticized on the grounds that they are flawed substantively because they misconstrue what it means to oppose democratic values. There is no default position that can avoid such abuse. The status quo, because it is so vague, could also be abused. For example, although there is a requirement in the United States that non-profits provide a "public benefit," this provision might be abused, because it is poorly defined.

On my view, it would make more sense to explicitly define "public benefit" in a way that makes clear that organizations do not qualify for the tax privileges of non-profit status if they oppose the values of free and equal citizenship, as in the case of hate groups or churches like Westboro. This explicit definition of "public benefit" would limit the possible scope for abuse more than the current, vague definition. I propose that the conditions for tax exemption and tax deductibility should be codified more clearly to mean that no group should receive the subsidies of non-profit status if it opposes the ideal that all citizens are to be equal under law. Such groups by definition do not serve a public benefit. Such a definition, codified in law, would have the advantage of being clear and publicly declared in advance. The standard could then be used to rein in potential abuses. Politicians who seek to merely go after their enemies or critics of the current government could be stopped by judges empowered by a statute that clarifies the standards for withdrawing tax-exempt, tax-deductible non-profit status.

Another objection to my argument in this chapter might appeal to the "civil society argument."[41] This argument suggests that the diversity of civil society would increase if tax exemption were granted to associations that oppose free and equal citizenship. As I understand it, the civil society argument implies that greater diversity would give citizens more opportunities to dissent from the government, it might tame extremism, and it might bring about a more stable polity. However, my interpretation of the "public benefit" condition, which requires respect for free and equal citizenship to receive tax exemption, allows for a diverse civil society, because it supports robust protections for the freedoms of association, expression, and religion. Groups that oppose democratic values can still meet, advocate their views, and worship in the manner they choose. What my condition rules out is state subsidies, such as tax exemption and tax deductibility, for associations that are opposed to free and equal citizenship. These associations may still raise money privately and exercise their free speech, association, and religion rights. Given that these groups retain their rights, it is unclear that there would be an effect on the diversity of civil society from the state not granting subsidies to them. Civil society may still very well provide the benefits of diversity.

Even if there were some effects on diversity from not granting tax exemption and tax deductibility to hateful or discriminatory groups, I believe that this consideration would be outweighed by the state's obligation to not be complicit in supporting these groups. It is necessary to clarify that when the state protects groups that are opposed to the values of free and equal citizenship, it is not endorsing these groups, and indeed, it expressly criticizes their discriminatory message. It would be illegitimate for the state to provide grants to, and thus to be complicit in, the activities of associations that seek to undermine free and equal citizenship. Subsidies to hateful or discriminatory groups would be incompatible with the legitimate state's commitment to upholding freedom and equality for all citizens. Since the tax-exemption and tax-deductibility privileges of nonprofit status are forms of subsidy, the state should avoid complicity with hateful or discriminatory groups, and clarify that it criticizes their message, by not providing them with the subsidies of non-profit status.

Another objection to the use of state funding to pursue democratic persuasion might stress, as some economists do, that there is no real difference between the use of incentives and the use of penalties to obtain a goal. They point out that taxes might be freely paid in exchange for the freedom to pursue a certain activity. Therefore, they might challenge, why not use taxes as a means of dissuading citizens from holding certain viewpoints? Many people, however, distinguish between a differential tax, which is widely viewed as a kind of penalty, and a grant or incentive to pursue a particular project. Regardless of whether economists are correct to conflate these two categories, it remains the case that many people would view a differential tax as a coercive limit on their freedom of speech and association.

One thing to note about such a proposal is that it imposes not simply a tax, but a differential tax beyond general taxation in order to dis-incentivize a particular viewpoint. However, it is the aim of value democracy to emphasize to citizens the reasons for rights. Using differential taxes to pursue democratic persuasion would risk undermining this message and is therefore not an appropriate means to pursue democratic persuasion. As I noted earlier, democratic persuasion must convey the message that citizens enjoy the right to dissent from democratic persuasion. My response to the objection is not that the economist is per se wrong to equate taxes and incentives. Rather, it is a mistake to use taxes that are heavier than what other people pay as a means of democratic persuasion because it risks being seen as a sanction. While democratic persuasion criticizes discriminatory viewpoints, it is essential, however, that the state clearly convey that there is a right to dissent. Taxes, rightly or wrongly, are often associated with fines, and a differential tax burden would risk being seen as a coercive sanction on some viewpoints. Democratic persuasion therefore distinguishes between tax privileges that give certain groups the benefit of paying fewer taxes than the general public, and differential tax burdens that force groups to pay greater taxes than the general public. Of course, the discussion here assumes that the organizations are expressive groups and not public accommodations. Value democracy allows for public accommodations like hotels and businesses to be coercively forced by law not to discriminate.

I attempt to respond in this chapter against militant democrats who worry that democratic persuasion is not strong enough to counter illiberal or discriminatory views. I reply that democratic persuasion reaches beyond state expression and includes the use of state subsidy, including non-profit status. However, there is an opposing concern that might be raised, not by militant democrats, but by liberal critics. These liberal critics might claim that while I guarantee free speech for all citizens, I am stacking the deck against those who endorse hateful viewpoints, because I have posited a large role for the state in funding democratic persuasion. However, it would be a misunderstanding to think that the right of individuals to free speech means that they are entitled to be assured that their views will win out in the marketplace of ideas. Individuals do have the right as speakers and listeners to participate in public discussion and to hear all arguments. But there is no entitlement for every argument to succeed. If viewpoint neutrality were applied to state funding, it would imply that hateful viewpoints would be entitled to sufficient support to ensure that they have an equal chance of success as democratic values. Such a requirement would amount to an absurd public policy. The weakest and most inimical views from a democratic perspective would have to receive funding so they could prevail equally in the marketplace of ideas. Such a view would commit us, as a matter of free speech, to bolstering not only hateful viewpoints, but also other fringe ideas to ensure that they could spread in the public forum. But funding views that are inimical to democracy would be an illegitimate state policy. In addition to the interests of citizens as speakers and listeners, the democratic citizenry has an equally fundamental interest that hateful or discriminatory beliefs do not spread in public discourse. The state has an obligation to the citizenry to promote democratic values, ensuring that democratic institutions flourish and that the freedom and equality of all citizens are respected.

I have argued in this section that the use of democratic persuasion is appropriate not only in deciding whether organizations should or should not receive subsidies from the government, but also in discerning whether an organization should receive the tax-exemption and tax-deductibility privileges of non-profit status. Groups that oppose free and equal citizenship should not receive non-profit status, because non-profit status qualifies as a type of subsidy from the government.

IV. Conclusion

At the end of the last chapter, I considered the objection that while democratic persuasion can clarify the reasons for rights, it lacked "bite" in changing the minds of people. In this chapter, however, I have added to the range of means available to democratic persuasion. Specifically, I argued that state subsidies should be denied to those groups that challenge the basic values of free and equal citizenship. In addition, I have argued that the tax-exemption and tax-deductibility privileges of non-profit status are forms of government subsidy, and that the state should not grant them to hate groups and other discriminatory organizations.

The chapter then considered the Court's complicated jurisprudence concerning state subsidy. At times I have stressed the compatibility between my normative concerns and the Court's protection of the right to free expression. I agreed with the Court that discriminatory organizations should have the right of free expression and association. However, I have also been critical of what I regard as the misplaced neutralism in both the Court's "limited public forum" doctrine and its state speech or "sponsored expression" doctrine. My suggestion is that the doctrine of viewpoint neutrality should only be limited to instances of coercion. The Court should uphold the free speech rights of all people's viewpoints, including those of the Ku Klux Klan and Westboro Church when they are not threatening individuals or inciting immediate violence. But if the Court extends the doctrine of neutrality to state subsidy, it risks muting the possibilities of the democratic state to express the reasons for rights and to persuade citizens to adopt them. Indeed, if the state were to fund discriminatory groups that oppose the very reasons why we protect rights in the first place, the state would risk complicity with hateful viewpoints and thus undermine its own legitimacy. To avoid this danger, the state should withdraw subsidies and tax-exempt, tax-deductible status for discriminatory organizations that oppose free and equal citizenship.

In concluding this chapter, I want to note a distinction between the use of state funds to promote the values of free and equal citizenship directly and the use of state funds to protect inverted rights. Rights like freedom of speech are "inverted" when they are used to express messages, such as discrimination, that are at odds with the democratic values that justify those rights. The protection of the rights of speakers and listeners to say and hear all viewpoints costs money. For instance, if the Klan wishes to hold a public rally, an expensive police presence might be required to ensure that there is no violence. As Stephen Holmes and Cass Sunstein point out in their book, *The Cost of Rights*, rights require resources to secure.[42] But when the state devotes funding to protecting an inverted right, like free expression, it is central that the state make it clear that it is not funding the messages of the organizations that use the right. In the case of a Klan rally, the state is funding the police force to protect the rights of the Klan and of the citizens who might stage a counter-protest. But the state is not endorsing the message of the Klan.

By contrast, my focus in this chapter was on explaining why the state should fund and endorse particular viewpoints to promote the ideals of free and equal citizenship. In these cases, the state does not fund all parties equally without regard to their views. It rightly seeks to advance the democratic values that states are required to uphold if they are to be legitimate. It also funds the criticism of groups protected by rights of free speech and association. Democratic persuasion, including the use of grants and the tax privileges of non-profit status, helps to clarify that the state's funding of rights of free expression for all parties does not imply neutrality to the messages expressed using these rights.

I now turn to a distinctly hard case for value democracy and the notion of democratic persuasion. Namely, should the state pursue democratic persuasion when the discriminatory organization is a religious one? When religious comprehensive conceptions conflict with an ideal of equal citizenship, it is widely thought that rights of religious freedom, and not only free speech, are implicated. The problem with denying funds or tax-exempt status to the Westboro Church, the Christian Legal Society, or even the Boy Scouts of America might lie not in a violation of their rights of free speech, but in their entitlement to religious freedom, specifically, the constitutional right of free exercise. In the next chapter, I take up this challenge, arguing that value democracy requires not only a reformulation of the way we think about free speech, but also of religious freedom itself.

CHAPTER FIVE

Religious Freedom and the Reasons for Rights

I. INTRODUCTION

IN CHAPTERS 2 AND 3, I argued that views at odds with the ideals of free and equal citizenship, even when expressed in the family and in civil society, should be subject both to reflective revision by citizens and to democratic persuasion by the state. On my account, such beliefs are not cordoned off into a "private" realm where public values do not apply. But what are the implications of value democracy for inegalitarian beliefs that are religious in nature? Does a concern to protect religious freedom mean that these beliefs should never be criticized by the state? In short, should democratic persuasion refrain from applying to religious beliefs, even when those religious beliefs oppose the ideal of free and equal citizenship?

One argument for the position that the state's expressive capacities should never be used to criticize religious beliefs appeals to religious freedom apart from any claims of freedom of expression. Defenders of religious freedom often seek to protect existing religious beliefs from the influence of the state. They therefore tend to adopt a "static" conception of religious freedom: they believe that the current beliefs and practices of any given religion merit protection, because religion is said to be a "special" type of belief that deals with the deepest matters of conscience. On a static conception, state influences that lead to changes in these beliefs are at least presumptive violations of religious freedom. The "accommodationist" account of Michael McConnell is a prominent example of the static conception.[1] McConnell seeks to protect existing religious beliefs from the influence of state policy, regardless of whether change is sought intentionally or unintentionally by the state. Religious beliefs in general, he argues, have a special weight in the public forum because they are linked to the value of religion itself. For theorists who hold static conceptions of religious freedom, even unintentional burdens by the state on religious beliefs are problematic, while intentional attempts at transforming these beliefs are ruled out entirely.

The static view is often assumed, not only in constitutional jurisprudence, but also in normative accounts of religious freedom. For example, it is seen as being required by the account of legitimacy offered in John Rawls' theory of political liberalism. Many theorists argue that political liberalism should be concerned with preserving existing religious beliefs when it forms an overlapping consensus between reasonable comprehensive views. Martha Nussbaum tends to the static view when she interprets political liberalism as requiring extensive accommodation of existing religious beliefs.[2] The static view is also assumed in leading accounts of religious freedom that fall outside the political liberal framework.[3] Fundamental to these accounts is the contention that the state should, in addition to respecting religious practices, refrain from interfering at all with religious belief, intentionally or otherwise.

In this chapter, I argue that religious beliefs should not be exempt from the principle of public relevance. When religious beliefs oppose the core values of free and equal citizenship, democratic persuasion is justified in order to transform these beliefs. I appeal to the ideal of religious freedom itself to counter the worry that this feature makes value democracy an anti-religious, secular account. Here I take the arguments underpinning my account of free expression, described in the last two chapters, and extend them to the issue of religious freedom. The right of religious freedom is based on the value of free and equal citizenship. As in the case of freedom of expression, when religious beliefs conflict with free and equal citizenship, the religious beliefs should be protected from coercive intervention by the state. This protection is meant to respect the freedom of citizens to choose their religious beliefs without state coercion. But the state also has the obligation to promulgate its reasons for respecting religious freedom. This calls for democratic persuasion in an attempt to change the minds of citizens who oppose the values that justify religious freedom itself. Religious freedom, then, entails both a protection of religion against coercive transformation and a duty for the state to promulgate the reasons for the right of religious freedom. The logic that led us to propose a transformative theory in our examination of freedom of expression therefore suggests the importance of a transformative account of value democracy when religious beliefs challenge the core values of democracy.

Drawing on the arguments of the previous chapter, I suggest that when the state seeks to transform hateful or discriminatory religious beliefs, it should respect both the means-based and substance-based limits on democratic persuasion. The substance-based limit, as readers will recall, suggests that value democracy should promote only the shared values of free and equal citizenship and avoid the promotion of a comprehensive religious belief. The substance-based limit helps to ensure that the transformation of religion is not the same as the displacement of religion. The means limit stipulates that democratic persuasion should rely on the state's expressive and subsidy capacities, and not its coercive capacities.

My argument proceeds in three stages. First, I argue that religious freedom is a principled commitment that requires the transformation of hateful or discriminatory religious viewpoints. Second, I place this transformative account in the context of a wider theory of value democracy. I claim that this transformative account does not require an all-or-nothing choice between a commitment to value democracy or to religion. Finally, I emphasize the compatibility of my transformative account of religious freedom with basic rights, such as freedom of association.

My emphasis in this chapter, as it has been throughout this book, is on why certain rights against state coercion are rightly complemented by a persuasive state role in promoting the reasons for rights. This role is particularly important in clarifying why "inverted rights," as I called them in chapter 3, need to be clarified by the state in its expressive capacities. An inverted right protects against coercive beliefs and practices, even when they are at odds with the reasons for rights. But it is also essential that the state use its expressive capacity to transform beliefs and practices that oppose free and equal citizenship. I concentrate specifically on generating an account of the free exercise of religion, in contrast to an account of rights against establishment, because the right of freedom of religion is inverted, and therefore gives rise to another incarnation of the paradox of rights. I note too that my aim throughout this book has been to develop value democracy in dialogue with existing practices, including Supreme Court doctrine. But I do not defer to that doctrine as always being correct. At times I will reinterpret it and suggest how it should be understood or changed within the context of value democracy. My project is one of normative political theory and not solely one of constitutional interpretation.

II. Religion v. Religious Freedom: The *Lukumi* Principle

On a static analysis of religious freedom, such as that suggested by accommodationist thinkers, the first concern should be whether laws intentionally or unintentionally burden religious practices. On this view, an account of religious freedom must be sensitive not only to the dangers of the state's directly attacking religious belief, but also to unintended effects of policy on religious exercise. Accommodationists assume that religious freedom is endangered whenever existing religious beliefs are burdened or changed.[4] Accommodationist thinking figured strongly in the Supreme Court's jurisprudence prior to *Employment Division v. Smith* in 1990.[5] On the pre-*Smith* standard, any time a neutral law, which was passed without any intent to discriminate, adversely affected religious belief or practice, the Supreme Court would presume that the affected parties were entitled to exemption. Employing a strict scrutiny test, the Court ruled that non-exemption would only be justified if the state could demonstrate that it had a compelling interest in non-exemption and that it had "narrowly tailored" its means of achieving that interest. The Supreme Court rejected the pre-*Smith* standard in *Employment Division v. Smith*, claiming that it was unworkable.

I want to continue to examine the accommodationist approach to religious freedom, not as a defense of a particular Supreme Court doctrine, but more generally, as a way to understand religious freedom. In particular, I suggest that it is a mistake to think that any time a religious view is indirectly affected by state policy, there is a problem from the standpoint of religious freedom. Indeed, I will argue that intentional attempts to transform certain illiberal religious doctrines are an essential part of democratic persuasion. The fact that a discriminatory or hateful religious view is part of a broader theology does not immunize it from democratic persuasion. The aim of democratic persuasion, in attempting to transform hateful or discriminatory religious views, is to realize the ideal of religious freedom and its underlying values.

A fundamental flaw in static views, which associate religious freedom with the preservation of existing religious beliefs, is that they cannot account for the potential tension between these beliefs and the protection of religious freedom. Consider the Court's decision to strike down municipal legislation prohibiting animal sacrifice in *Church of the Lukumi Babalu Aye v. City of Hialeah*.[6] In this case, the city of Hialeah, Florida, had intentionally targeted the Santeria religious practice of sacrificing live animals. The legislation was designed to single out animal "sacrifice" in particular for criminal sanction, although similar forms of animal slaughter, such as kosher methods, were permitted for food processing. A unanimous Court held that the Hialeah legislation could not be explained on any basis other than animus toward the Santeria religion. While the city's legislation might seem to be concerned with animal welfare, it did not outlaw other forms of killing animals that may have been slow or painful. According to Justice Scalia's opinion, it is the term "sacrifice" that is most telling of the legislation's intent to discriminate against the Santeria. On my view, then, the Supreme Court's decision to strike down the councilmen's law countered a potential move by the town of Hialeah into the rights-violating Invasive State. The Court prevented Hialeah from disrespecting the rights of the Santeria members. But the Court also sent a message through its expressive capacity that criticized the discriminatory beliefs of the Councilmen. This message opposed the potential move of the town leaders toward the discriminatory Hateful Society.

I suggest that we study this decision because it is a relatively uncontroversial starting point for thinking about religious freedom, as revealed by the unanimous agreement of the Court. I want to take the case as a starting point, however, to develop my more controversial application of democratic persuasion to cases of religious freedom. I also wish to use this case because it is commonly thought to be a paradigmatic example of the static model of religious freedom, which prohibits the state from criticizing religious beliefs. However, I hope to use the *Lukumi* case as an example of why religious freedom at times requires democratic persuasion. My aim is not to oppose the accommodationists' claim that religious freedom supports some exemptions to general laws. Instead, I examine the philosophical inadequacy of an accommodationist approach when issues of equal citizenship are implicated.

Since the ordinance at issue in *Lukumi* hindered religious practices, a static analysis would likely suggest that it should be struck down. Not only did the Hialeah city councilmen who passed the law limit the religious practice of animal sacrifice, but they apparently did so with the intent of burdening the Santeria religion specifically. The flaws and limits of the static approach, however, can be found by looking at the transcript of the meeting in which the city as a whole discussed the ordinance. The transcript, quoted in Justice Kennedy's majority opinion, reveals that the ordinance itself was religiously motivated. One councilman justified his opposition to the practice of animal sacrifice by stating, "I don't believe the Bible allows that." The chaplain of the Hialeah police department variously described Santeria practices as "an abomination to the Lord" and the worship of "demons."[7] A static conception of religious liberty overlooks the fact that, whatever the Court's decision in *Lukumi*, there would have been an adverse effect on some religion. The Santeria practitioners would have been adversely affected if the law had been allowed to stand. On the other hand, striking down the law would apparently burden the religious views of the councilmen and others, who believed that it is a Christian moral duty to ban animal sacrifice. From the standpoint of the councilmen, their religious beliefs require banning by law Santeria animal sacrifices.

In striking down the ordinance, the Court not only protected the Santeria religion from illiberal, coercive legislation, but it also served to criticize the illiberal beliefs behind the legislation. The religious motivation of these beliefs did not immunize them from criticism. On my account, the Court's decision to strike down this law was an important example of democratic persuasion. The Court expressed the message that the particular views of the councilmen that led them to pass the ordinance, regardless of whether they were religious or not, should be criticized for violating the ideal of free and equal citizenship in value democracy. Ultimately, I want to argue that the Court's message to the councilmen can serve as a basis for justifying democratic persuasion in regard to religious views that reject the core values of democracy. But before I build to that point, it is important to see why the Supreme Court criticizes discriminatory religious views, such as the councilmen's, even as it upholds the ideal of religious freedom. The Court's criticism of discriminatory religious views is often missed by the accommodationists and their static view.

Rights of religious freedom and free exercise, such as those protected in *Lukumi*, are structured in a way so that their criticism of discriminatory religious views might be overlooked. In the previous chapter, I suggested why certain rights of the freedom of expression are inverted, in that they hide the reasons for protecting a right by appearing to condone those behaviors that are protected. In this case, the inverted nature of free exercise is a bit more subtle, but it is also present. Specifically, in protecting the members of the Santeria religion, the Court might seem to say that it is neutral and has no opinion about religious views. But, as I have argued, it is not acting in a neutral way in regard to religious reasons. The Court is protecting the religious freedom of the Santeria against a discriminatory religious doctrine promoted by the councilmen. Far from having no opinion about all religious beliefs, the Court is protecting one set of religious beliefs and criticizing another.

We are thus confronted by a seeming paradox of religious freedom, similar to the paradox of rights that we discussed earlier in the book. It is usually understood that religious freedom protects certain religious practices and beliefs. But some of these religious practices and beliefs are at odds with freedom of religion itself. According to value democracy, discriminatory beliefs and practices are rightly criticized by the legitimate state. In particular, the councilmen's religious "practice" of suppressing the Santeria religion in the name of religion is rightly subject to transformation through democratic persuasion. Specifically, the case of the Hialeah ordinance suggests that those who seek to use the power of the state to restrict a religious belief or practice, even when motivated by their own religious beliefs, should be criticized and prevented from violating the rights of other citizens. Of course, when a law such as the Hialeah ordinance is struck down on First Amendment free exercise grounds, those who passed the law are not sanctioned through criminal law. But the Court's decision should be interpreted, on my view, to legally prohibit government officials from enacting policies that undermine religious freedom. The Court's decision also sends a message that the beliefs behind discriminatory statutes, even if religious in nature, are incompatible with religious freedom. Democratic persuasion draws on the insight of the Court that even religious motivations for unjust laws are invalid and should be challenged by the state in its expressive capacity.

The Hialeah example suggests that an account of religious freedom must be able to distinguish between two sorts of existing religious beliefs: first, those that are compatible with the ideal of religious freedom and the values of free and equal citizenship that underlie that freedom, and second, those beliefs that are inconsistent with the ideal of religious freedom—such as the views of the councilmen who sought to ban Santeria religious practices. Unlike the views of the councilmen, the Santeria practice of animal sacrifice fell in the first category because they were compatible with religious freedom and the ideals of free and equal citizenship more generally. The views of the councilmen, by contrast, fell in the second category, since they sought to impose their interpretation of Christian beliefs on the Santeria. The ordinance that they passed violated an important component of the right of free and equal citizens to determine their own religious beliefs. The Court's invalidation of the Hialeah ordinance sent the message to the law's supporters, as well as to citizens more generally, that the councilmen's reasoning failed to comport with the ideal of religious freedom. The Hialeah example reveals how a principle of religious freedom might itself conflict with existing religious beliefs. In the face of such conflicts, a principle of religious freedom is transformative with respect to religion.

I contend that *Lukumi* highlights why an account of religious freedom might require the transformation of existing religious beliefs through democratic persuasion. Toward the end of his opinion, Justice Kennedy writes,

> The Free Exercise Clause commits government itself to religious tolerance, and upon even slight suspicion that proposals for state intervention stem from animosity to religion or distrust of its practices, all officials must pause to remember their own high duty to the Constitution and to the rights it secures.[8]

The fundamental question, which Justice Kennedy does not address, is what we should do when "animosity to religion" is itself based on religion. I propose, according to what I call the *Lukumi* principle, that the commitment to "religious tolerance" is twofold. First, it entails the protection of the right to express religious beliefs and to practice one's religion free from coercive sanction, even when that religion espouses principles at odds with the ideal of free and equal citizenship. Second, the *Lukumi* principle entails that the state should explain why the democratic values underlying religious freedom are incompatible with religious beliefs that contradict the values of free and equal citizenship. Importantly, the phrase "animosity . . . or distrust" as it is used in Justice Kennedy's opinion cannot refer only to intentional hatred. Even if attempts to coercively limit religious practice are based in the love or altruism that might be said to come with a desire to convert others to a "true" religion, these attempts still must be rejected as incompatible with religious freedom. The state therefore rightly criticizes religion when religious views conflict with the principle of religious tolerance itself. According to the *Lukumi* principle, the state should use democratic persuasion in an attempt to change those religious views that conflict with free and equal citizenship. At the same time, it must protect the right to hold these views. For this reason, the *Lukumi* principle rules out coercive sanctions or bans on religious views.

I want to be clear about precisely what kinds of motivating beliefs are rightly subject to criticism by the state. The councilmen in *Lukumi* believed that their general set of religious beliefs supported the ordinance, but it is not their general set of beliefs that should be criticized. Some of their beliefs can be distinguished from the desire to outlaw the religious practices of others. For instance, as I elaborate in the next section, a religious belief in God is compatible with the requirements of the *Lukumi* principle. The beliefs that should be criticized are the specific ones that motivated the councilmen's attempt to legally prohibit Santeria. The councilmen's belief that their religion required legally sanctioning the Santeria religion is incompatible with the ideal of free and equal citizenship, and is rightly subject to democratic persuasion.

Some might object that I am mistaken in discussing the beliefs of the Hialeah law's proponents rather than restricting my concern to criticizing their actions after the fact. One could argue that the threat to religious freedom was not the beliefs of the proponents of the law per se, but rather the fact that they issued an ordinance restricting the practice of another religion. On this view, religious freedom does not concern beliefs at all; instead, it concerns the limits on the kinds of actions lawmakers can take or the laws that they can pass. I think it is a mistake, however, to separate belief and action in this way. Although the Court is concerned to protect rights against certain kinds of state action, in its opinions and reasoning it also addresses the beliefs and principles that are used by citizens to justify laws. When it strikes down illegitimate laws, the Court does so often because the reasons and beliefs for such laws violate public principles that are central to the state's legitimacy. These beliefs are not only relevant after a discriminatory law has been passed. If the Hialeah councilmen were unsuccessful in passing the ordinance at issue, their flawed beliefs about coercion would still rightly have been subject to public scrutiny.

Importantly, the Court allows in some instances that although the actual motivation for a law might be problematic because it is inconsistent with a "rational basis," a legitimate rationale might be available for the law. Imagine for instance that someone grounded civil rights legislation in the desire to see a race war break out. Although that motivation would be clearly illegitimate, other reasons for the law consistent with public values are available and so such legislation should not be struck down. But in the *Lukumi* case, there was no such rationale available for the law. As I suggested, the claim that the law was motivated only by a concern about animal rights is undermined by its exclusive focus on Santeria practices.

The Court's "animus" doctrine serves to illustrate why the beliefs that motivate law, and not just the actions of the law, are publicly relevant. According to the animus doctrine, which I introduced in chapter 1, laws that limit the rights of gay citizens are based on a set of beliefs that have no place as the basis for legislation. For instance, in *Romer v. Evans*, the Court struck down a plebiscite that restricted gay rights, ruling that the only possible motivation for the law was discriminatory.[9] Although the doctrine the Court employs here is one of "animus," which is sometimes defined as "hatred," it is clear that there are some reasons for such laws aside from pure hatred. Indeed, laws that restrict gay rights are often based on religious doctrines which condemn homosexuality, and therefore appeal to a certain kind of religious reason. It is a mistake, therefore, to claim that the only motivations that are inappropriate for legislation are pure hatred. Rather, the animus doctrine employed in *Lukumi* suggests that certain reasons, religious or not, have no place in the public sphere. In the gay rights cases, as well as in *Lukumi*, the Court not only strikes down laws, it also criticizes the discriminatory beliefs that motivated the legislation. These discriminatory beliefs are incompatible with the ideal of equal citizenship. Even if the beliefs are religious in nature, they are still rightly subject to democratic persuasion. The state, in its persuasive capacity, should attempt to convince citizens that the discriminatory reasons have no place in public discourse.

The Court protects religious freedom both by striking down laws that violate rights, and by seeking to persuade citizens to abandon the discriminatory reasons that motivate laws violating rights. The Court should criticize these hateful or discriminatory reasons, even when they are religious in motivation. The Supreme Court thus acts as an exemplar of public reason in two senses that are relevant to discussions about religious belief and religious freedom. These two senses echo the role that I described for the Court in chapter 3's discussion of free speech.[10] First, the Court upholds democratic values by striking down unconstitutional laws, such as those that constrain the practice of one religion for discriminatory reasons that violate free and equal citizenship. The Court acted in this way in *Lukumi* by striking down a law that discriminated against the Santeria. Second, the Court acts as a model for the wider citizenry, including public officials, when it explains why discriminatory laws are illegitimate and when it speaks in defense of the values of free and equal citizenship. The Court's audience includes not only the parties to the case, but also all citizens who participate in politics.

In *Lukumi* specifically, the primary purpose of the Court's decision was to strike down a law violating religious freedom. But it did more than this. The decision also criticized the reasons given by the law's proponents, and it rebuked them for violating their duty to respect religious freedom. The religious nature of the reasons behind the law did not immunize them from scrutiny. Nor were the law's proponents shielded from criticism by their right of free speech. Freedom of expression protects their right to express their discriminatory views, but it does not rule out criticism of those views. For example, the Court in *Lukumi* expressed a principled disapproval of the kind of religious reasoning used by the Hialeah councilmen in their attempt to impose religious beliefs on others. The Court, far from being neutral or silent, directly criticized the views of the Hialeah law's proponents. This decision is relevant for all those who would attempt to use similar reasoning to pass equivalent laws in other locales.

It is especially important that decisions such as *Lukumi* serve as an example for the wider citizenry, given that democratic citizens have the power to vote for representatives and even, at times, directly for legislation. The Court's opinions can warn citizens about the pitfalls of passing unconstitutional laws that would impose one set of religious beliefs on fellow citizens. However, given that most Supreme Court opinions are not widely read, the ruling in *Lukumi* is not itself sufficient to promulgate the principle established in it. Wider publicity of the Court's decision and promotion of the principle underlying *Lukumi* are necessary if its example is to transform citizens' thinking. A variety of institutions within the legitimate state should take on this task of publicity and promotion. While it is commonly recognized that the content of rights should be widely promulgated, I want to emphasize why it is also important to promote the reasons for rights. These reasons include the *Lukumi* principle and the more general ideal of equal citizenship that underlies rights to religious freedom. The responsibility for promulgating the reasons for rights should not fall only on the Supreme Court or any other single state actor. Rather, the promulgation of the reasons that underlie rights is a diffuse duty incumbent on all state actors and citizens.

One worry about democratic persuasion in regard to religious belief might be that it would fail to respect the core idea that citizens are entitled to retain their own religious beliefs as they see fit. Accommodationists might argue that any attempt to transform belief conflicts with this entitlement of citizens. But the accommodationists overlook the two distinct limits on democratic persuasion that preserve religious freedom. As I suggested in the previous chapter, the first, means-based limit on democratic persuasion circumscribes the method through which transformation should be attempted. The second, substance-based limit narrows the range of beliefs that may be subject to transformation.

The means-based limit requires that the state not pursue transformation of citizens' views through any method that would violate fundamental rights, such as freedom of expression, conscience, and association. For example, the state cannot prohibit meetings of the Anti-Santería Society

or threaten criminal sanctions against the Hialeah councilmen for holding
and expressing beliefs that conflict with the *Lukumi* principle. However,
a public articulation of why the councilmen's views are inconsistent with
religious freedom would not violate their rights, even if this point were
articulated by state officials. The *Lukumi* principle should be defended
by state officials as well as by citizens participating in democratic debate.
Ideally, citizens and their representatives will successfully defend the *Lukumi* principle such that laws that would violate it will not come before
the Court. As I have argued elsewhere, it is better for public principles
to be defended through majoritarian processes than through judicial review.[11] It is only as a last resort, when lawmakers and citizens fail to heed
this duty, that they are rightly rebuked by the courts.

On the view developed in this book, the state can respect the "means-
based" limit by confining its attempts at transformation or promotion to
its expressive rather than its coercive capacities. For example, public officials and citizens may make arguments that defend the *Lukumi* principle
when engaged in public discussion, even in the face of religious opposition. As I add in the next section, there is also a role for educators to teach
the importance of religious toleration, even if some parents hold religious
objections. The right to hold and express a belief at odds with the ideal of
equal citizenship does not entail a right to hold it unchallenged.

I have taken the position that mere reasoning by the state to its citizens
is not tantamount to coercion. Following Mill, I have claimed that a right
to free speech is not a right to be shielded from discussion. If citizens are
successful in persuading each other through reason, and their views are
transformed, this is not evidence that they have been coerced. To the contrary, we tend to regard such "transformations" as freely chosen. One need
not be a full-blown Kantian to accept as much. When we move from the
question of individual persuasion to state persuasion, we should observe
that the state has a particular interest in advancing principles, such as the
ideal of religious freedom articulated in *Lukumi*, that are essential to its
own legitimacy. It is also essential that the state use as much as possible
the means of reasoning to defend its most fundamental principles. Like
the Supreme Court in *Lukumi*, state officials should reason by means of an
appeal to public principles.

It might be objected that because of the state's massive power, its own
expression can be in a sense overwhelming. If the only viewpoint that
citizens were able to hear on the subject of religious toleration was the one
articulated by the state, state expression might be tantamount to propaganda. However, this point only shows that the state's voice must allow a
diversity of opinion in the polity at large. The state should therefore work
to protect the free speech rights of citizens. Another objection might emphasize the fact that particular state officials will not always advance the

Lukumi principle—indeed, they might contradict it. Yet this is no more an argument against a role for state expression than the fact that state officials sometimes enact unprincipled law would be an argument against principled limits on state action. In sum, the means-based limit emphasizes the importance of reasoning on behalf of the principles of the legitimate state.

The second limitation on attempts at transformation, which I have called the "substance-based" limit, narrows the range of beliefs that the state is properly concerned to transform. The state can only criticize those religious beliefs that violate the ideal of free and equal citizenship. There are a variety of religious beliefs that might appear to violate the *Lukumi* principle, but which need not affect our capacity to see each other as free and equal. For instance, one might believe that all non-Christians are condemned to hell, but also think that theistic reasoning has no role in lawmaking because sinners cannot be saved through legislation. Since this view says nothing about which beliefs should be imposed on others, it is not publicly relevant. The need for transformation arises only in regard to those views that conflict with the ideal of free and equal citizenship.

The substance-based limit suggests that only those beliefs that most blatantly oppose the principles of equal citizenship are rightly subject to transformation on the distinct grounds of democratic persuasion.[12] For instance, I acknowledged earlier that reasonable people might disagree about the implications of equal citizenship for issues such as affirmative action, and that no position on this issue should be subject to transformation. Rather, it is those beliefs, religious and otherwise, that are openly hostile to or implausibly consistent with the values of equal citizenship that the state should seek to transform.

The means-based and substance-based limits offer some traditional privacy protections. I have left immune from democratic persuasion many beliefs about the internal structure of the family and civil society. For instance, the government's scrutinizing my dinner guest list would be a clear misapplication of the need to promote the *Lukumi* principle. Nor should the state spy on citizens in an attempt to determine whether they hold beliefs that conflict with the ideal of free and equal citizenship. Such a practice would violate the means-based limit by employing coercive, not expressive, methods. It would also violate the substance-based limit, because it unjustifiably targets citizens who have not demonstrated that they oppose democratic values.[13] As my discussion of *Bob Jones University v. United States* will illustrate, however, beliefs about internal affairs are not always immune from public scrutiny.[14]

It might be objected that, even if we accept the authority of the state to criticize hateful or discriminatory beliefs, this need not commit us to a purposeful transformation of religious belief per se. One could draw on

Rawls' distinction between neutrality of effect and neutrality of intent toward religion to argue that the aim of state action should be to challenge discriminatory beliefs. On this account, we should think of the transformation of religious beliefs as an acceptable but unintended consequence of challenging discriminatory beliefs that are at odds with the ideal of free and equal citizenship.[15] But this doctrine ignores the fact that some discriminatory beliefs are explicitly religious. For instance, the Hialeah councilmen's arguments are couched entirely in terms of the need to save practitioners of Santeria from a false religion. When one councilman said that he was "totally against the sacrificing of animals" but that kosher slaughter was acceptable because it had a "real purpose," he was expressing a religious belief that denied the equality of Santeria's adherents in deserving rights of freedom of religion. The city's police department chaplain, too, contradicted the ideal of free and equal citizenship when he made a leap from a statement that is protected by the *Lukumi* principle ("We need to be helping people and sharing with them the truth that is found in Jesus Christ") to a statement that violates the principle ("I would exhort you . . . not to permit this Church to exist").[16]

Perhaps the clearest example of a religious belief at odds with the ideal of equal citizenship comes from the Westboro Baptist Church, discussed in the previous chapter. On my view, it is not possible to divide the church's fundamental religious tenets from its commitment to hatred against gays. Indeed, the church's website pronounces its fundamental commitment to the idea that "God hates fags." In a Kansas State Supreme Court case, a statutory question arose as to whether the Westboro Church should receive a tax exemption for a truck it used to transport its members to protests. The question was whether the state agency that granted tax exemptions was correct to claim that Westboro's protest activities were secular and subject to taxation. Westboro replied that the activities were religious, and that the church was entitled to tax exemption because under the Kansas tax code all religious activities are tax exempt.

In its holding, the Kansas Court pointed to evidence suggesting that less than half of the signs carried by Westboro members in the protest mentioned a deity. The Court then concluded that the activity was indeed secular.[17] The opinion includes a laudable discussion of the free exercise clause and an argument that non-profit status is not required of churches engaged in secular activities. But I believe it is a mistake to rest this argument about tax exemption on categorizing activities that conflict with the ideal of free and equal citizenship as secular. Contrary to the Kansas Court, Westboro's message is fundamentally religious. The church is expressing the religious message that it is against God's will for the U.S. government to protect gay rights. This is a political view, but one that is thoroughly religious in its content. Indeed, the religious content is so core to Westboro's message that they emphasize it in the web address of their church. On my view, the religious nature of the church's hateful viewpoint does not make it immune from public justification or democratic persuasion. Religious freedom protects the right to hold beliefs free from government coercion, but it does not imply the right to hold these beliefs unchallenged. Democratic persuasion should aim to transform religious views when they oppose the ideal of free and equal citizenship.

There is, in short, no way of getting around the fact that attempting to transform a discriminatory belief is sometimes tantamount to attempting to intentionally transform a religious belief.[18] Indeed, Rawls maintains, despite his claim of "neutrality of intent" toward religious doctrines, that he hopes unreasonable religions will become reasonable over time. But I have argued that the account of transformation should not, as Rawls suggests, be restricted to a mere "hope" that it will occur.[19] Promoting the transformation of hateful or discriminatory religious views is rather a commitment that is grounded in the idea of religious freedom itself.

I take the *Lukumi* principle to suggest that democratic persuasion should not shy away from instances of transformation that involve religious belief. Just as the family in civil society does not immunize so-called private belief from democratic persuasion, neither should the fact that a belief is religious imply that it is off-limits to the state acting in its expressive capacity, subject to the means-based and substance-based limits. Thus, the *Lukumi* principle indicates that religious beliefs, like the family, can be publicly relevant. Ideally, citizens would not only apply a conception of religious freedom in examining their broader religious views, but they would also ask if their religious views are at odds with an ideal of free and equal citizenship. It is this value of free and equal citizenship that I believe underlies the more specific commitment to religious freedom. Citizens should recognize their duty to examine their religious beliefs through a process of reflective revision, checking to see if their beliefs conflict with an ideal of equal citizenship. But when citizens fail to engage in reflective revision on their own, the state has a role in seeking to persuade them to endorse an ideal of equal citizenship.

I have explained why reflective revision and democratic persuasion apply to discriminatory or hateful religious beliefs. But there is reason to have some reticence, even beyond the two limits of democratic persuasion, when the state seeks to transform religious belief. Namely, given the history of religious bigotry throughout the world and the United States, there is a danger that an attempt to transform religious belief might become corrupted and fail to fulfill the aim of promoting equal citizenship and respecting religious freedom. The state's claim to endorse an ideal of equal citizenship may in fact mask a view that is motivated by bigotry. For example, one worry that has commonly been expressed about the French conception of equality and the country's attempt to ban both the burqa and headscarf is that a concern for egalitarian values is being misused as a cover for religious bigotry. President Sarkozy's attempt to ban the burqa in France using coercive law clearly violates the means-based limit. But his motivations also seem to appeal to French suspicion of Muslims, and his assertions of his feminist credentials appear suspect at best. The timing of the proposal and his attempt to carry it out in a manner that appeals to anti-Muslim sentiment raise the worry that this kind of persuasion is not only coercive, but that it is based on bigotry and not a defense of equality. Similarly, the debate over the French headscarf in schools is ostensibly about equality, but it is unclear that the headscarf itself is at odds with a notion of equality. As many have suggested, it might be interpreted as a symbol of resistance and non-subordination to the dominant French culture. The controversy over the headscarf, like the one over the burqa, raises a concern that the French state is not protecting equality but promoting bigotry, in violation of the substance-based limit on democratic persuasion.[20]

Although democratic persuasion is sometimes aimed at religious belief, it is important to note it can also criticize the animus that is directed against minority religions. As in the case of Santeria, Muslim communities have recently been the target of proposed policies that violate their religious freedom and entitlement to be treated as free and equal. It is important not only for the courts to block such laws, but that citizens speak out against discriminatory laws before they are enacted. One recent example of democratic persuasion that criticized religious animus took place regarding the so-called Ground Zero Mosque. An Imam, who led a mosque near the former World Trade Center in New York, planned to build "Cordoba House," an Islamic center dedicated to interfaith understanding and community events. Anti-Muslim accusations erupted, accusing the planned center of being a "victory mosque" that celebrated the destruction of the World Trade Center by Islamic extremists. There was no evidence to show that this was the intent of the center, and by all accounts the Imam held moderate views.

Some opponents sought to prevent the center from being built by proposing that the site be declared a historic landmark. Such a move to block the building of the center would have been a clear violation of the free exercise clause. As in the *Lukumi* case, the proposal sought to target a particular religion. There was no sense that any other religion proposing a holy site near Ground Zero would have been opposed. At this stage, Mayor Bloomberg spoke in defense of religious freedom, and criticized the wave of anti-Muslim religious animus surrounding the Cordoba Center. Mayor Bloomberg's expression was a clear example of democratic persuasion. He rebuked the opponents of the center for failing to internalize the meaning of the right to religious freedom and free exercise. Even if anti-Muslim animus were based on religious beliefs, it should be criticized. Mayor Bloomberg's criticism of anti-Muslim animus stands as a reminder that rights require not only the protection of religious minorities, but also the expression of the reasons for rights, which are based on free and equal citizenship and exclude religious animus. Mayor Bloomberg's criticism of anti-Muslim animus is precisely the kind of democratic persuasion that is required by value democracy. Indeed, Bloomberg's example suggests a way to address the case of Geert Wilders, which I discussed at the beginning of the book. Wilders' anti-Muslim rhetoric should not be coercively banned, but the state and its citizens should refuse to enact his views into law. The state and its citizens should also engage in democratic persuasion, publicly criticizing Wilders' discriminatory beliefs.

The ideal of religious freedom itself, as well as the ideal of equal citizenship, should be articulated and defended by the state. When the ideal of equal citizenship is directly threatened, the state should seek transformation through persuasion. In the next section, I will turn to some of these instances and explore the relationship between democratic persuasion and religious pluralism.

III. Dialectics of Religious Transformation

In this section, I suggest how the transformation of discriminatory religious beliefs could be achieved, and I explain why such transformation does not constitute an attack on religious freedom itself. Susan Okin, whose work on multiculturalism also stresses the importance of transformation, concedes that the promotion of free and equal citizenship might cause some cultures—and, we can gather, some religions—to become "extinct."[21] A challenge to my view of democratic persuasion might assert that, like Okin, I risk extinguishing religion. Does my view that the state should seek to transform discriminatory or hateful religious beliefs force a choice between the secular and the religious?

I respond to the concern about religious extinction by emphasizing why the transformative theory does not entail an all-or-nothing choice between religious freedom and the continued existence of religious beliefs. There are two reasons why my account respects religion. First, the relevant type of transformation is dialectical in that it suggests a synthesis between democratic values and religious views. At times this synthesis might occur when religious traditions help to clarify the very meaning of these values. Second, the type of transformation that is called for by value democracy cannot be forced on any religious groups. Although religious freedom ideally results in dialectical transformation, I emphasize that it also protects religious groups that choose to resist transformation. I therefore use "dialectic" in its traditional sense: to mean only that religious beliefs and the ideal of free and equal citizenship can result in new and varied combinations or "syntheses."[22]

Before I elaborate on the kind of dialectic that will ensue when democratic persuasion results in the transformation of a religious view, it is helpful to return to the idea of reflective revision. While democratic persuasion is by its nature a public kind of dialectic, reflective revision suggests how a dialectic might follow from individuals' own attempt to apply values of equal citizenship to their own religious beliefs. For instance, individuals who hold religious beliefs which deny the possibility of equal citizenship for non-believers might engage in reflective revision, reevaluating the aspects of their religious beliefs that are incompatible with free and equal citizenship.

But abandoning the discriminatory or hateful aspects of religious doctrine is not tantamount to abandoning religious belief itself. The attempt to incorporate and make consistent one's religious beliefs with an ideal of equal citizenship will result in the change of a religious doctrine, but change is not equivalent to destruction. For instance, certain Protestant denominations were once associated with the notion that "true Christian belief" should be imposed upon others. But with time, these denominations incorporated the idea of religious toleration, and eventually, toleration of non-believers. In this way, Protestant denominations transformed to incorporate an approximation of the *Lukumi* principle and a respect for citizens as free and equal. Yet the denominations are still recognizably Protestant.[23] To take another example, when the Church of Latter Day Saints agreed to begin admitting African Americans to full membership after years of discrimination, this change did not affect the church's continuation or its commitment to its core religious doctrines. Similarly, democratic persuasion might consist of citizens or the state seeking to convince individuals to change aspects of their religious beliefs that conflict with a democratic commitment to free and equal citizenship. While this might result in a change of religious belief, it does not involve persuading citizens to abandon religion entirely.

Ideally, religious beliefs would reinforce the democratic values of free and equal citizenship. In such instances, religious conceptions and the fundamental commitments necessary for democratic legitimacy would be in harmony, and there would be no need for the transformation of religious beliefs. Such an idealized view pervades much of the discussion about the role of religion in contemporary political theory. For instance, John Rawls and Amy Gutmann cite Martin Luther King Jr.'s arguments against segregation as an example of how religious identity can enhance the democratic values of freedom and equality. Gutmann writes that King's "civic genius was his ability to move between religious and secular sources of the same political argument in the course of communicating to his fellow citizens, showing that the religious identities of believers can be a powerful public force in support of democratic justice."[24] King's distinctive contribution appealed to Christian morality to promote norms of equal citizenship.[25]

Although King serves as an example of an ideal synthesis of equal status and religious values, in other cases, particular religious views might come into conflict with democratic values, including religious freedom itself. In such cases, the *Lukumi* principle should be invoked. The *Lukumi* principle gives the state the obligation to criticize religious beliefs that oppose the ideal of religious freedom—for example, because they demand the imposition of their views on non-believers. The *Lukumi* principle is a democratic one that is not based on any comprehensive doctrine. It is grounded instead in an attempt to think about the kind of religious freedom that should be protected in a society of free and equal citizens. By extension, when particular religious beliefs oppose democratic values more generally, the state should seek to transform those existing beliefs in defense of free and equal citizenship. Thus, while my theory retains a commitment to democratic values and avoids appeal to comprehensive conceptions, it rejects the static claim that would prevent any existing religious view from being criticized, no matter how hateful or discriminatory it might be. My theory acknowledges, however, that some religious views, such as King's, do support free and equal citizenship.

Having argued that the ideal of free and equal citizenship commits the state to seek the dialectical transformation of religion, I turn now to the contention that my view constitutes an "attack" on religion. Does the commitment to democratic values of legitimacy, such as religious freedom and the concern to treat citizens as equals, require that we ask those who hold religious views incompatible with those values to abandon religion itself? In short, is democratic persuasion an attempt to convince people to forsake religion?

Some liberal political theorists in the Rawlsian tradition, such as Stephen Macedo and Rob Reich, have highlighted what they see as the potential conflict between religion and democratic values. Reich, for instance, argues that citizens must be committed to the individual rights of children and that the "state must take its own side" when these rights conflict with the norms of identity groups.[26] Reich believes that this conflict might sometimes be unbridgeable. Similarly, Macedo emphasizes why conflicts in education policy between religious views and commitments to free and equal citizenship might be irresolvable through deliberation. He argues that the case of *Mozert v. Hawkins County Board of Education*[27] pits the democratic value of respect for a variety of cultures against a religious worldview that would exclude even knowledge of these cultures.[28] Since respect requires at least basic knowledge of other cultures, the conflict between the religious viewpoint and the values of free and equal citizenship is intractable in this case.

Although these liberal theorists might acknowledge that we should seek to avoid these confrontations through innovative policy, they help to elucidate the fact that, in some instances, there will not be an easy policy solution to conflicts between religious beliefs and the commitment to equal status. Even if we concede that Macedo and Reich are correct that conflicts between norms of legitimacy and some comprehensive conceptions are inevitable, however, such conflicts do not require that we sacrifice religious beliefs altogether when we attempt to transform them to become compatible with democratic values. The partial tension between comprehensive doctrines of some identity groups and democratic values such as religious freedom or equal respect does not mean those doctrines must be rejected entirely. Democratic values can be endorsed by and derived from a variety of comprehensive conceptions of the good, both religious and secular. The standard of legitimacy may thus require the transformation of identity, but it does not demand the abandonment of identity. Again, the model here is not all-or-nothing, but dialectical. The value of equal status might interact with religious norms to produce changes in identities that make them compatible with democratic values, while still allowing the religion to continue and even flourish.

Consider, for instance, the story told by Anne Fadiman in her book, *The Spirit Catches You and You Fall Down*, in which a Hmong family's religious values led them to reject medical care for their daughter's epilepsy.[29] If we are committed to the individual rights of the child, it might be thought that we need to reject an identity featuring unbridgeable conflicts with the principles of free and equal citizenship. A key point, however, is that although the state might require that medical treatment for a minor be imposed on a religious community against its wishes, the members of the community might, over time, grow to accept such a requirement without abandoning their religious identity. Ideally, they would learn to accept this specific policy based on their considered acceptance of the democratic principle that decisions about medical care must incorporate a concern to care for their children. Religious identity itself might change to accommodate modern medicine in such a case, but it is important to note that religious groups would not be required to abandon their beliefs. Even if some change in identity were necessary, only very conservative notions of culture (e.g., Devlin's) equate any change in a culture with its destruction.[30] Religious identities might be transformed by democratic persuasion, which results in a dialectic between an ideal of free and equal citizenship and religious beliefs without the abandonment of religion per se.

Indeed, if we examine two of the most famously contested cases that pitted the freedom of religious belief against norms of equal status, we can see that these beliefs were changed rather than abandoned. I begin with the case of *Bob Jones University v. United States*.[31] Bob Jones University is an evangelical Christian school in Greenville, South Carolina, that once banned interracial dating and enforced other racially discriminatory policies. The university's administrators considered these racially discriminatory policies to be grounded in the institution's understanding of the Bible. When the IRS instituted a new policy that discontinued tax-exempt status for groups that discriminated based on race, it revoked Bob Jones's non-profit status. Defenders of the static view, who espouse the principle of accommodation, might suggest that Bob Jones should have been given an exemption from the policy because its discriminatory policies were based in religion.

I want to first suggest why the IRS action against Bob Jones is an example of the kind of transformation that I have defended. Because this is a harder case than that of *Lukumi*, it will help to deepen and clarify my argument for the *Lukumi* principle. Some might contend that, unlike the town council's ordinance in *Lukumi*, which clearly involved state action, Bob Jones's policy involved only a private belief. It could be argued that even if these policies were morally objectionable, they were not grounded in a belief that the political rights or equal citizenship of others outside the university should be undermined. On this view, we might see Bob Jones's policy as merely an internal matter of campus organization that is irrelevant to beliefs about public policy.

A closer look at the facts, however, gives one indication of why Bob Jones's policy cannot be distinguished from public advocacy of beliefs that oppose the ideals of free and equal citizenship. Namely, the school explicitly extended its policies to punish students who were members of groups that advocated interracial marriage in the wider society.[32] This broad provision prohibited students, not only from expressing support for interracial marriage while on campus, but from even holding membership in a public organization such as the NAACP. Such a position violates at least one core right of equal citizenship: the right of interracial marriage, protected by the Supreme Court in *Loving v. Virginia*.[33]

This would be a harder case if Bob Jones's policies did not include such an explicit provision against public support of interracial marriage. It might be logically possible for a school like Bob Jones to have an internal policy that prohibited interracial dating and marriage but that said nothing about whether the university was opposed to the legality of interracial relationships in the wider society. Absent some explicit clarification, this policy would likely be perceived by students to express disapproval of the legal recognition of interracial relationships even outside its campus. Given Bob Jones's status as an educational institution and its concern to instill moral values, few students might distinguish an ostensibly internal message about race relations from a wider claim about the status of blacks and whites as equal citizens.

However, an inquiry into students' perceptions about the wider implications of the policy would not be determinative on this issue. A more conclusive inquiry should ask whether Jones could have some principled reason for believing its prohibition on interracial dating was compatible with an endorsement of the legality of interracial marriage. Such a principle would have to avoid any appeal to worries about so-called miscegenation in the larger society—worries that are incompatible with the ideal of free and equal citizenship. For instance, a Presbyterian institution might prohibit interfaith marriage among its students out of a concern to preserve its own community of faith without suggesting any implications about the acceptability of interfaith marriage in the wider society. I doubt that an institution like Bob Jones has any such justification available. In sum, what makes Bob Jones's policy subject to transformation is its direct affront to the ideal of equal citizenship. The university does not merely object to a law, or even a basic right, but rather, because its racist policy directly challenges the very ideal of equal citizenship.

It is important to note the significant difference between the kind of pressure an institution like Bob Jones experiences in the possible loss of non-profit status and the kind of pressure citizens might feel in the face of purely expressive state action. Bob Jones faced financial pressure to change its views. Despite this pressure, it is still justifiable as part of the state obligation to promote the values of free and equal citizenship. Non-profit status is a state-sponsored subsidy, granting the benefits of tax-deduction and tax-exemption, as I argued in chapter 4. This subsidy should be linked at minimum to an institution's willingness not to undermine the ideal of free and equal citizenship. On my view, institutions granted this advantage do not have to actively promote democratic values, but they do have to be willing not to undercut them. There is a difference, however, between institutions that should be charged, at minimum, with not undermining public values and an individual household. While the tax benefits enjoyed by a university can be linked to its obligation not to undermine public values, citizens are not to be assigned a tax status based on their beliefs about free and equal citizenship. There are no "non-profit families" who pay less money in income tax because they have certain public-minded commitments. Any attempt to assign such status based on the content of one's belief or for any other purpose would likely be punitive and thus violate the means-based limit. But denying entry into the world of non-profits is different. We do assign tax advantages based on a set of required public purposes of such groups. It no more punishes Bob Jones University to withdraw that status if they refuse to respect democratic values than it would to deny non-profit status to a group that had just been founded but failed to identify a public purpose in its application for non-profit status. Bob Jones might reply that its continued existence might seem to depend on its non-profit tax status. However, the intuition might push in the other direction if we ask whether an institution with these views has a right to be founded in the first place. In sum, although the pressure from the IRS is more intense than mere reasoning, the option to resist or ignore transformation, on my view, means that its rights were not violated.

In 2000, seventeen years after the Supreme Court ruled against the school, the president of Bob Jones University appeared on television to announce that the school was lifting its policy against interracial dating. A page now exists on the school's website with a statement that expresses regret for having "allowed institutional policies to remain in place that were racially hurtful."[34] Despite the university administration's rhetoric about how its discriminatory policies were based in fundamental religious beliefs, it is far from clear that Jones is a less religious institution because it now permits interracial dating. For example, these changes have not prevented the school from enforcing a religiously based strict code of sexual conduct.

Regardless of the reasons why Bob Jones decided to change its policies, its transformation did not involve an all-or-nothing change.[35] As was the case when Bob Jones began to admit black students, the decision to end the racially discriminatory policies in question did not require the abandonment of its religious belief altogether. Even if we concede that Bob Jones's particular commitment to racially exclusive policies was genuinely religious and that the state intended to transform this religious belief, the university remains undeniably a religious institution, despite its changing these particular views concerning interracial marriage.

So far, I have largely focused on the ways that conflicts between commitments to equal citizenship and religious identity can result in the transformation of particular group identities. At times, identity groups themselves can help clarify a society's understanding of public values, such as equal status. The case of *Mozert* cited by Macedo, for instance, could easily be seen as "all-or-nothing." In that case, a mother objected to her child's being subject to curriculum that included a textbook that taught non-biblical literature and presented information about other cultures. The court in *Mozert* refused to grant a free-exercise objection. The case is thus a classic instance of religious belief being pitted against public values, such as respect for and knowledge of other cultures. But the story does not end there. The litigant who brought the case continued to engage in public debate and has arguably come to hold a view, as a result of democratic persuasion, that is compatible with respect for free and equal citizenship. A detailed look at the mother's views reveals that her new position is not that the textbook objectionably included non-Christian perspectives, but that the curriculum failed to emphasize that women who choose to stay home to raise a family also have a legitimate conception of the good, which the state ought to recognize.[36]

I take this case to illustrate two points: religious perspectives can change to become more publicly justifiable, and religious perspectives themselves can generate and clarify public values. The claimant's revised view was right that the perspectives of homemakers should be included, and the textbook's exclusion of this viewpoint may have resulted from a position that was not publicly justifiable because it was excessively secularist. One way of understanding this dialectic is to see it as an argument against forcing a choice between religion and public values. But I think this case demonstrates the opposite. The dialectic emerged precisely because the court forced the claimant to choose between public values and the discrete aspects of her religious beliefs that conflicted with those values. Her beliefs both became more reasonable and resulted in a position that educated the public at large.[37]

I now want to address one final challenge to my view about the relation between value democracy and religion. I have thus far sought to demonstrate that a religious viewpoint's transformation does not entail its destruction. The evidence for this is that there are cases when religious viewpoints were able to change and yet survive. But despite these specific instances of dialectical change, one might counter that part of the essence of religion is its insularity from public culture and principles. On this view, a religious doctrine could not, without destroying its religious character, be open to change by appeal to the democratic value of free and equal citizenship. Suppose, for instance, that a citizen of Hialeah derived her commitment to outlawing the practice of Santeria from a particular passage in the Bible prohibiting idolatrous sacrifice. If this citizen's religious views required a literal reading of the entire biblical text, she could not abandon a discrete commitment to outlawing idolatrous sacrifice without denying biblical literalism itself and therefore her entire comprehensive religious view.

Here, I believe, I must bite some bullets. If defenders of religion insist on defining it by its insularity, I respond that my view is clearly incompatible with some religions. As I have argued, however, many religions are decidedly not marked by insularity and discrimination. Such religious views not only are entirely consistent with the principles of free and equal citizenship, but they also support them from within. I believe, moreover, that the static nature of such an insular account of religion ignores the reality that religions have survived for centuries precisely because they are able to evolve—not only to fit changing cultural contexts, but also to incorporate fundamental values, such as those that I have suggested form the basis of a free society.[38]

IV. The Right to Resist Religious Transformation and the Freedom of Association

I have suggested an alternative to static conceptions of religious freedom. On my view, the state should promote principles of free and equal citizenship even in the face of religious doctrines that oppose them. Because of the substance-based limit on transformation, some groups whose internal policies make them appear hostile to these principles might not be subject to transformation, as long as they do not seek to impose their religious beliefs on others with the force of law. However, if we also adhere to what I have called the means-based limit, even those groups that do seek to impose their religious beliefs on others by law—thus showing an active hostility to the ideal of free and equal citizenship—retain certain rights to resist transformation. State expression and financial inducements should stop short of coercion. If we are to avoid slipping into the excesses of the Invasive State, value democracy's commitments to the freedoms of expression, association, and conscience require that the state not use force to change religious viewpoints. Of course, the state should not view religious belief as justification for violent crimes, and it rightly punishes even those who give religious reasons for violence. But policies involving coercive sanction cannot serve as the means of transforming discrimination beliefs. To ensure respect for the means-based limit, an account of religious transformation must endorse a robust conception of freedom of association.

The right to freedom of association entails what might be called a series of rights to resist democratic persuasion. For instance, it is essential that even hateful or discriminatory religious associations not be forced to publicize their membership lists or the content of their meetings. Subject to the reasonable limitations that accompany any rights, the rights to exist and to congregate should be granted to even deeply discriminatory groups that oppose free and equal citizenship. Private associations that receive no public subsidy also have a fundamental right to decide on their own membership.[39] This right is particularly important when membership is connected to a group's expressive purpose.[40] For instance, I take it to be a right of religious groups to exclude nonbelievers. Often, these rights protect matters of internal membership and organization, matters that do not necessarily violate the political ideals of free and equal citizenship. However, even for groups with views clearly opposed to these ideals, the rights of association must be protected. I therefore stress in this section why, alongside the state's role in promoting public values of equal citizenship through its expressive capacity and its role as an effective subsidizer of non-profits, there exists a right for groups or individuals to resist transformation. This exit option complements my claim that the state should limit the means of transformation to reasoning and financial inducement.

To clarify this idea, consider Bob Jones University. When faced with a choice between tax-exempt status and racial discrimination, it initially chose the latter, although it would later be persuaded that it had made a mistake in opposing interracial marriage. The university retained its right to promote values antithetical to free and equal citizenship. However, permitting the continued existence of the university does not imply that it should have been "left alone," in the sense of never being criticized for its policy of expelling students who married interracially. Institutions that retain racially exclusive policies, like Bob Jones University initially did, should be subject to democratic persuasion by citizens and representatives of the state. Yet the institutions' rights to freedom of association and expression require that they not be forcibly shut down. For this position to work, of course, it is important not to regard the concern to protect such a university's rights as an endorsement of its values.[41]

An actual case involving a religious institution's decision to resist democratic persuasion concerns a recent controversy in Boston over gay adoption and the Catholic Church. In March 2006, Catholic Charities of Boston, which had long been a non-profit entity licensed to facilitate adoptions, shut down its adoption services rather than comply with a state law requiring adoption agencies not to discriminate against gay families.[42]

While it might seem that this is an unacceptable instance of the state coercively preventing a religious organization from participating in charity work, a closer examination of the situation reveals otherwise. As I suggested earlier in my discussion of Bob Jones, Catholic Charities certainly must have felt more pressure than it would have if Massachusetts had merely criticized the group's refusal to facilitate gay adoptions. But the state's action is not objectionable in the way that it would have been if there had been an outright prohibition on Catholic Charities' ability to operate. The issue here concerns Catholic Charities' financial relationship to the state, since the group was receiving the tax privileges of non-profit status. In addition, the group directly received funds from the state for each adoption it carried out. The question of whether to force the organization to respect gay couples' right to adopt, then, should be evaluated with regard to the state's role as a potential subsidizer, given that the organization directly receives state funds. For this reason, the state may permissibly seek to transform discriminatory religious beliefs. In no way was Catholic Charities compelled to participate in a state program funding adoption. If Massachusetts were to allow private adoption, Catholic

Charities would be able to resume its adoption program, but not as a non-profit licensee eligible for federal funds.[43]

We can illustrate this important point simply by imagining a hypothetical state discontinuing a subsidy to a faith-based adoption agency because of the agency's noncompliance with an anti-discrimination law against gays. The state still allows the agency to operate, but it provides no subsidy. In such a case, the state as spender decides not to actively support a religious policy that is fundamentally at odds with the state's commitment to equal status for gay citizens.[44] At the same time, the adoption agency and its associated church are not forced to give up their religious beliefs about the immorality of homosexuality or the importance of charity work. The state is thus able to express its commitment to equal status and its disapproval of the church's actions without resorting to the kind of coercion that would come with an outright ban on adoption services that do not facilitate gay adoption.

In sum, if religious groups that hold discriminatory views wish to resist democratic persuasion, they should be allowed to do so as a matter of law. These rights to resist, however, do not imply that the state accepts these discriminatory views. Rather, the state should clarify its position by criticizing discriminatory views for opposing the democratic values of free and equal citizenship.

V. Conclusion

In this chapter, I suggested why static conceptions of religion neglect the fact that a commitment to religious freedom itself requires transformation of some religious beliefs. Religions, on my view, are not relegated to a private space that is entirely exempt from public values. On the contrary, the "*Lukumi* principle" I have proposed claims that when conflicts emerge between existing religious views and the value of free and equal citizenship, the state should work to transform religious belief. I argued that such transformation must respect both a "means-based" and a "substance-based" limit. The state should seek transformation through persuasion, not coercion, and it should attempt to change only those discriminatory or hateful beliefs that oppose the democratic values of free and equal citizenship. In recognizing these limits, value democracy can promote its own principles while respecting the rights of all citizens. My approach therefore grounds a transformative theory of religious freedom in the protection and promulgation of the reasons that underlie rights, including rights of religious freedom.[45]

Value Democracy at Home and Abroad

I BEGAN THIS BOOK by exploring two dystopias that symbolize the fears of two major theories about the relation between rights and equality. The dystopia of the Invasive State evokes the liberal fear of a government that seeks to promote equality at any expense, with no respect for the boundary between the public and the private. The Invasive State would spy on the family and civil society, intervening whenever it would be necessary to protect an ideal of equality. At the opposite extreme, the dystopia of the Hateful Society would allow discriminatory viewpoints and deeply inegalitarian practices to thrive in a culture of rights. To avoid the Hateful Society, some feminist thinkers and militant democrats believe that some basic liberties need to be sacrificed to promote equality.

But I argued that value democracy offers a third alternative, which avoids these two dystopias and their flawed understanding of the relation between rights and equality. Value democracy recognizes that civil society and the family might contain practices and beliefs that oppose the fundamental democratic values of free and equal citizenship. We should therefore reject the claim of some liberals that these spheres are publicly irrelevant and immune from justification. Instead, I proposed a "principle of public relevance," suggesting that when beliefs oppose the values of free and equal citizenship, individuals have a duty to change their beliefs to make them compatible with democratic values. This change can occur in two ways. First, individuals can engage in "reflective revision," examining their own beliefs and practices, and changing them to be compatible with free and equal citizenship. Reflective revision is a way to realize the principle of public relevance through individual action regarding one's own beliefs. Although it might be thought that discriminatory beliefs in the family and civil society are publicly irrelevant, and cordoned off by rights to privacy, free speech, and free association, I argued in chapter 2 that the values of free and equal citizenship should lead us to rethink how we conceive of privacy. Some beliefs and practices may be protected by rights, but still be publicly relevant. I thus proposed a conception of "publicly justifiable privacy." It claims that the right to hold and express discriminatory beliefs and practices in the family and civil society should be protected from coercive state bans. But publicly justifiable privacy also regards those beliefs and practices as publicly relevant, in that citizens have a duty of reflective revision to change their beliefs and practices to be compatible with free and equal citizenship. I gave arguments from democratic congruence, stability, interconnection, and public trust to explain why discriminatory beliefs in the family and civil society should be revised. If these beliefs are not revised, they will undermine respect for the freedom and equality of citizens throughout society.

But this account gave rise to a problem: what if individuals refused to engage in reflective revision? Given that rights protect beliefs and practices within the family and civil society, what can be done to avoid the Hateful Society, where discriminatory values spread unopposed? Simply protecting the right to express hateful beliefs without criticizing them, I argued, would make the state complicit in those beliefs, and might even give the appearance of the state condoning them. But banning discriminatory or hateful beliefs would violate rights, falling into the trap of the Invasive State. In response, I proposed a conception of "democratic persuasion" in chapter 3. Democratic persuasion is the second way that individual beliefs can change to be consistent with free and equal citizenship. If citizens fail to reflectively revise their discriminatory beliefs, the state and other citizens have a duty to engage in democratic persuasion: they should criticize discriminatory beliefs, and convince those who hold them to adopt instead the values of free and equal citizenship as their own. Democratic persuasion is the implication of the principle of public relevance for state and citizen actions regarding discriminatory beliefs held by other citizens. As chapter 3 explains, democratic persuasion respects rights and avoids the Invasive State, because it is non-coercive and relies on the state's expressive capacity. But democratic persuasion can also help us to avoid the Hateful Society, because it allows a way for liberal democracy to criticize discriminatory and hateful beliefs in the family and civil society.

In chapter 4, I expanded this notion to include state subsidy. I argued that it does not violate the rights of freedom of association or speech for the state to advance the values of free and equal citizenship by using its power to confer or discontinue the subsidies of tax exemption and tax deductibility that accompany non-profit status. I suggested a way of understanding the use of state subsidy that respects the right to free speech and challenges the Supreme Court's current viewpoint neutrality doctrine in funding. I applied the argument to the cases of two groups that discriminate against gays, the Westboro Baptist Church and the Boy Scouts of America. I argued both that their rights of free expression and association should be protected, and that they should not receive state subsidy in the form of tax-exempt, non-profit status. Finally, in chapter 5, I asked the question of whether democratic persuasion could apply to discriminatory religious views. I argued that democratic persuasion is compatible with religious freedom, which itself rests on an ideal of free and equal citizenship that is independent of any religious conception. The attempt to transform inegalitarian religious beliefs does not violate religious liberty, but is instead a way to promote in the wider culture the reasons and democratic values that justify religious liberty itself.

As I have noted, it is sometimes said that a liberal is a person "who cannot take his own side in an argument." This famous quote paints liberalism as a theory of neutralism, which is incapable of defending its own fundamental values. One advantage of traditional liberal theory is that it protects rights against coercion, but I have suggested that for any theory of rights to take its own side, it must promulgate the reasons for rights. Democratic persuasion is a way for liberal theories to offer a robust protection of rights while defending the fundamental values of freedom and equality. Previous liberal theories, because of their excessive focus on coercion, have found it difficult to reconcile freedom and equality. It has seemed that we are faced with a dilemma: to choose either the dystopia of the Invasive State to protect equality or the dystopia of the Hateful Society to protect freedom. By opening the argument in political theory beyond coercion, and by developing the idea of non-coercive democratic persuasion, I believe I have begun to suggest how a third alternative can be realized. The liberal democratic state should both offer robust rights protections and promote the values of free and equal citizenship that justify rights.

Now that I have summed up the argument of the book, I want in conclusion to examine some possible further implications of democratic persuasion that might be a source for further study. The first implication is that the book's view might serve as a model for other states that seek an alternative to the two dominant approaches to free speech. On the one hand, prohibitionists want to coercively outlaw hateful viewpoints and political viewpoints that challenge democracy. On the other hand, neutralists would protect free speech, but they would be silent in response to hateful viewpoints. Some have posed the choice as one between European- and U.S.-based approaches to the topic. But I believe that democratic persuasion, with its combination of viewpoint neutrality in regard to coercion and its robust expression of free and equal citizenship, could serve as a third alternative to these two dominant approaches to free speech. This third approach allows free speech advocates to retain the protections against coercion found in rights of free expression. But democratic persuasion also gives voice to the fundamental value of free and equal citizenship that underlies free speech. It addresses the egalitarian concerns of militant democrats and feminists discussed in chapter 1.

For instance, a recent inquiry into Latin American approaches to hate speech suggests problems with both of the prohibitionist and free expression models. According to Tanya Hernandez, an attempted criminal prosecution under Brazil's prohibitionist hate speech legislation was met with considerable opposition.[1] Yet Hernandez argues that doing nothing would fail to challenge a dangerous and continuing legacy of racism in Brazil that has its roots in slavery. Democratic persuasion, however, could serve as a third model for Brazil and other Latin American countries, avoiding the problems of coercion, while still combating the legacy of racism.

A second implication of the book's view is that it can also serve as a model for understanding how to promote ideals of equality in international law without violating the rights of individuals or the rights of states. Indeed, democratic persuasion already has a prominent role in international law. Because there is no international state that can threaten coercion, international law often relies on mechanisms of persuasion in order to further its goals. This is an ambitious topic that should be developed in another place, but I want here to at least make some suggestions about the possible international implications of democratic persuasion.

Statements and speeches by leaders committed to principles of free and equal citizenship are the most visible examples of applying democratic persuasion in the international realm. These speeches are one way to establish that the values of free and equal citizenship have global reach. For example, in the midst of the democratic movements sweeping the Middle East, attention has been focused on the words of leaders from democratic states. Expressions of support for pro-democracy movements clearly have meaning and value for democratic reformers.

For example, in 2009, many Iranians took to the streets to protest the results of a contested election—which was thought to be fraudulent—and to demand a more robust set of democratic rights. Some world leaders expressed support for the protestors, but were concerned about being perceived as meddling in the internal affairs of Iran. President Obama, who said that he was "appalled and outraged" by the violence inflicted upon the protestors, warned, "Some of the comments that I've made [are] being mistranslated in Iran, suggesting that I'm telling rioters to go out and riot some more. There are reports suggesting that the C.I.A. is behind all this."[2] His comments reflect the danger that persuasion on behalf of democratic principles can be manipulated by the criticized governments to raise concerns about their own sovereignty. But it is essential in theorizing about the international reach of a robust set of human rights that we not allow our theories to be driven by concerns about coercion. Merely speaking on behalf of human rights, or affirming solidarity with protestors on behalf of these rights, does not violate rights of state sovereignty. As President Obama indicated when he underscored the entitlement to free speech and other rights associated with democracy, a primary implication of human rights is an obligation to stress their global reach. Such a purely expressive defense affirms the importance of rights while respecting sovereignty.

Democratic persuasion, far from being out of place at the global level, is at the heart of much international human rights law. For instance, the Convention on the Elimination of All Forms of Discrimination Against Women (CEDAW) purposely adopts a persuasive, and not a coercive, approach to human rights. This persuasive and non-coercive approach is especially important, given the treaty's concern with addressing inequality in families throughout the world. If inequality in the family were challenged through coercive measures, this would trigger concerns not only about sovereignty rights, but also about privacy rights. But because CEDAW employs only expressive capacities, it exemplifies democratic persuasion in the international realm.

Adopted by the United Nations General Assembly in 1979, CEDAW binds ratifying states to a commitment to secure the rights of women, including reproductive rights, economic rights, and political rights.[3] The convention has been ratified, with certain reservations, by almost every UN member-state. The notable exceptions include Iran, Sudan, Somalia, and the United States.[4]

CEDAW is a prime example of democratic persuasion in defense of human rights. Signing the treaty is one way for states to use their expressive capacities abroad. The convention is broad in scope, criticizing a wide array of state policies, such as employment discrimination, for violating the rights of women. The treaty argues that not only governments, but also families should respect the equality of women. The remedy that it suggests for non-compliance with these ideals is not found in the threat of force. It is found in the exposure of international reports. The reports made by states to the United Nations Committee on the Elimination of Discrimination against Women and the ensuing dialogue both aptly illustrate how families can be transformed by international norms without violating sovereignty rights against coercive intervention. The CEDAW reports have addressed state action, such as legally ensuring women equal access to education, but they have also concerned civil society, such as encouraging women to enter various professions despite religious prohibitions or dissuasion by their families. The reports issued by CEDAW are examples of how international norms of equality might be brought into direct contact with individual women.

Some might object to these guarantees on the grounds that they violate the practices and beliefs of some religious groups. For instance, these groups might contend that women should not be allowed to work, contrary to Article 11 of CEDAW.[5] But a future project might argue that the arguments I made in the previous chapters about the domestic sphere and about religion apply internationally. I argued in the last chapter, for instance, that some freestanding commitments to the ideals of free and equal citizenship will potentially conflict with certain religious beliefs. However, states can simultaneously respect the rights of citizens and promote the values of free and equal citizenship by relying on their expressive, and not coercive, capacities. Internationally, reports linked to human rights treaties, including CEDAW, also serve as a persuasive mechanism for promoting equal citizenship—in this case as it concerns the status of women. For example, CEDAW requires rights of women to have the choice to work and a right of girls to an education. While women might make a choice not to work, I take it that when they have no option to choose whether to work, their independence is undermined to such a degree that they cannot be thought of as free or as equal. Education for girls serves as a precondition to free and equal citizenship, as I argued in chapter 2. When states do not respect the rights of women to work and to be educated, their government should be subject to global democratic persuasion.

The treaty also clarifies how democratic persuasion at an international level might counteract inequalities in the so-called private sphere of the family and civil society. While rights to privacy and free speech and association rightly protect private associations and the family from coercive intervention, they do not make these institutions immune from the need for public justification, and in some instances, from public criticism. CEDAW makes it clear at a global level how democratic persuasion might address inequalities in the private realm without violating privacy or sovereignty rights. The treaty not only reaches into the domestic practices of states, but also serves to promote the values of free and equal citizenship in the family and civil society. The treaty therefore shows how these values might have a global reach through democratic persuasion, without violating either sovereignty or privacy rights. My emphasis in this book has been on democratic persuasion within states, but in this conclusion I have thought it worth pointing to a possible extension of my theory to relations between states.

Both domestic and international accounts of political theory often focus on coercion, and with good reason. Coercion is the act of forcing persons to act against their own will. Any use of it should be done with an attention to fundamental issues of justification. But while rights often limit coercion, we should also begin to theorize about the multiple other tools available to the state. Persuasion offers a way of articulating why we protect rights. It clarifies the state's fundamental values, especially free and equal citizenship, in a way that neutralists have failed to do. Such a project is important in avoiding complicity in hateful viewpoints that are protected by rights, but are at odds with the core liberal democratic values of free and equal citizenship. Democratic persuasion is also important in defending democracy itself from being undermined. I have argued that a legitimate state will have not only laws that protect rights, but also widespread endorsement among citizens of the reasons for rights and the principles of democracy. In response to the critics who challenge democracy's core values, the state must have a principled and persuasive reply that defends free and equal citizenship.

Notes

· · · · · · ·

INTRODUCTION

1. Associated Press, "Neo-Nazi Group Resurfaces, Citing Obama," *New York Times* (April 26, 2009), A19, and David Holthouse, "The Year in Hate, 2008," *Southern Poverty Law Center Intelligence Report* 133, special issue, spring 2009, http://www.splcenter.org/get-informed/intelligence-report/browse -all-issues/2009/spring/the-year-in-hate.

2. For example, Paul Sniderman's *When Ways of Life Collide*, the subject of a recent symposium in *Perspectives on Politics*, suggests that increasing bigotry toward Muslims is present in the Netherlands. See Paul Sniderman, *When Ways of Life Collide: Multiculturalism and its Discontents in the Netherlands* (Princeton, NJ: Princeton University Press, 2007), and Jeffrey C. Isaac, Robert Rohrschneider, Will Kymlicka, and Jonathan Laurence, "The Challenges of Multiculturalism in Advanced Democracies," *Perspectives on Politics* 6 (2008): 801–10. If such attitudes do indeed become more prevalent, we might expect an increase in organized hate groups.

3. This is a view often ascribed to liberals, such as Bruce A. Ackerman, *Social Justice in the Liberal State* (New Haven, CT: Yale University Press, 1980) and Ronald Dworkin, "A New Map of Censorship," *Index on Censorship* 35, no.1 (February 2006): 130–33. Michael Sandel characterizes liberalism as a neutralist theory and criticizes it on that basis. See Michael J. Sandel, *Democracy's Discontent: America in Search of a Public Philosophy* (Cambridge, MA: Harvard University Press, 1996) and Michael Sandel, *Liberalism and the Limits of Justice, second edition* (New York: Cambridge University Press, 1998): 184–218.

4. Alexander Meiklejohn, *Free Speech and Its Relation to Self-Government* (Clark, NJ: Lawbook Exchange, 2004). This view might be attributed to Meiklejohn. However, I will argue later in chapter 3 that his theory of free speech is more subtle, and relies on an affirmative set of values, not on the state's neutrality towards all values.

5. See Ian Buruma, "Totally Tolerant Up to a Point," *New York Times* (January 29, 2009), A29.

6. *Criminal Code, R.S.C.* 1985, c. C-46, s.319, online: Department of Justice Canada, January 1, 2012, http://laws.justice.gc.ca/eng/acts/ C-46/page-148 .html.

7. *R. v. Keegstra*, [1990] 3 SCR 697, online: Judgments of the Supreme Court of Canada, http://scc.lexum.org/ en/1990/1990scr3-697/1990scr3-697.html.

8. Ibid. For discussion of this case, see Kent Greenawalt, "Free Speech in the United States and Canada," *Law and Contemporary Problems* 55 (1992): 5–33 at 20.

9. *Jones v. Töben*, F.C.A. 1150 (2002). For a description of this case, see Yaman Akdeniz, *Racism on the Internet* (Strasbourg, France: Council of Europe, 2009), 54.

10. "Bardot fined over racial hatred," *BBC News*, June 3, 2008, http://news .bbc.co.uk/2/hi/entertainment/7434193.stm. For a good discussion of the Bardot

case, see Erik Bleich, *The Freedom to be Racist? How the United States and Europe Struggle to Preserve Freedom and Combat Racism* (Oxford: Oxford University Press, 2011), 17–18 and 40.

11. Adam Liptak, "Hate speech or free speech? What much of West bans is protected in U.S." *New York Times*, June 11, 2008, http://www.nytimes.com/2008/06/11/world/americas/11iht-hate.4.13645369.html.

12. Simone Chambers and Jeffrey Kopstein, "Bad Civil Society," *Political Theory* 29, no. 6 (2001): 837–65.

13. Wendy Brown, *States of Injury: Power and Freedom in Late Modernity* (Princeton, NJ: Princeton University Press, 1995).

14. Karl Loewenstein, "Militant Democracy and Fundamental Rights, I," *American Political Science Review* 31 (June 1937): 417–32, and Karl Loewenstein, "Militant Democracy and Fundamental Rights, II," *American Political Science Review* 31 (August 1937): 638–58.

15. Feminist critics of liberalism, such as Wendy Brown, and liberal feminists alike have argued that, in many of its common forms, liberalism fails to recognize deep inequality within the family, because it regards the family as private. See in particular Brown, *States of Injury*.

16. Michael Sandel suggests that liberalism's protection of the rights of civil society groups and its neutrality toward the values present in civil society have rendered it ineffective in fostering a culture of equality. See Michael J. Sandel, *Democracy's Discontent: America in Search of a Public Philosophy* (Cambridge, MA: Harvard University Press, 1996), and Mary Ann Glendon, *Rights Talk: The Impoverishment of Political Discourse* (New York: Free Press, 1993).

17. Consider the example, which I discuss in chapter 1, of the federal government funding the National Center for Bioethics in Research and Health Care at Tuskegee University. President Clinton launched the Center to promote the equal treatment of minorities in health research after apologizing for the United States Public Health Service Study on Syphilis. The study was conducted on African Americans without their informed consent from 1932 to 1972. It purposely withheld treatment for syphilis to study its untreated course from infection to death in African American patients who were not told that they had the disease. President Clinton's apology for the government's conduct, his criticism of the racism underlying the study, and his decision to launch a Center devoted to equal treatment of minorities in health research, were examples of democratic persuasion. See "The Center's Mission and Goals," Tuskegee University National Center for Bioethics in Research and Health Care: http://www.tuskegee.edu/about_us/centers_of_excellence/bioethics_center/the_centers_missions_and_goals.aspx.

18. Erik Bleich, *The Freedom to be Racist?* Bleich highlights the difference between the American approach to free speech and the rest of the world's approach by suggesting that the United States has an "American exceptionalist" view of free speech. He also points out, as I will later, that the doctrine of viewpoint neutrality is a relatively recent development that the U.S. Supreme Court rejected before the early twentieth century.

19. For an argument in favor of privacy and limits to transparency, see Thomas Nagel, *Concealment and Exposure: and Other Essays* (Oxford: Oxford University Press, 2002), 3–26. See also *Griswold v. Connecticut*, 381 U.S. 479 (1965).

20. A similar dystopic vision is arguably at the heart of many conservative attacks on rights. The worry in these accounts, however, is often about the undermining of community or some other value distinct from equality. See, for instance, Glendon, *Rights Talk*.

21. See John Stuart Mill, *Considerations on Representative Government* in *The Collected Works of John Stuart Mill, Volume XIX – Essays on Politics and Society, Part II*, ed. John M. Robson (Toronto: University of Toronto Press, 1977), 371–577, esp. chapters III–IV, where Mill emphasizes the importance of an active citizenry.

22. John Locke, *A Letter Concerning Toleration*, ed. James H. Tully (Indianapolis, IN: Hackett, 1983 [1689]), 27. The idea of persuasion, while clearly present in Locke, is undeveloped. For instance, Locke suggests that the magistrate might promote religion in a way that my "substance based limit," as I later describe it, would prohibit.

23. To give an example of a belief that is implausibly consistent with equality, consider racists who claim that equal treatment for all races requires racial segregation and laws against interracial marriage. These racists do not explicitly say that certain races are inferior, but their viewpoints in favor of segregation and banning interracial marriage are implausibly consistent with equality.

24. On the difference between political and comprehensive doctrines, see John Rawls, *Political Liberalism*, rev. ed. (New York: Columbia University Press, 2005), 13.

25. Alexis de Tocqueville, *Democracy in America* (New York: Library of America, 2004). For a discussion of these multiple meanings of democracy, see Corey Brettschneider, "Tyranny of the Majority," in the *Encyclopedia of Political Science* (Washington, DC: CQ Press, 2010).

26. Corey Brettschneider, *Democratic Rights: The Substance of Self-Government* (Princeton, NJ: Princeton University Press, 2007).

27. I thank Lucas Swaine for discussion of this issue.

28. *Brown v. Board of Education*, 347 U.S. 483 (1954).

29. Nancy L. Rosenblum, *Membership and Morals: The Personal Uses of Pluralism in America* (Princeton, NJ: Princeton University Press, 1998). See in particular chap. 8, pp. 285–318.

30. See Gerald Allan Cohen, *If You're an Egalitarian, How Come You're So Rich?* (Cambridge, MA: Harvard University Press, 2000, and Gerald Allan Cohen, *Rescuing Justice and Equality* (Cambridge, MA: Harvard University Press, 2008).

31. Indeed, it is unclear whether Cohen's view leaves room for any conception of rights at all.

32. See Amy Gutmann, *Democratic Education, with a new preface and epilogue* (Princeton, NJ: Princeton University Press, 1999), Eamonn Callan, *Creating Citizens: Political Education and Liberal Democracy* (Oxford: Oxford University Press, 1997), and Stephen Macedo, *Diversity and Distrust: Civic Education in a Multicultural Democracy* (Cambridge, MA: Harvard University Press, 2000).

33. Unlike Macedo, I focus on the "values" underlying rights rather than a theory of liberal "virtues." See Stephen Macedo, *Liberal Virtues: Citizenship, Virtue, and Community in Liberal Constitutionalism* (Oxford: Oxford University Press, 1990).

34. Joseph Raz, *The Morality of Freedom* (Oxford: Oxford University Press, 1986), and Ronald Dworkin, *Justice for Hedgehogs* (Cambridge, MA: Harvard University Press, 2011). For recent criticisms of comprehensive liberalism, and defenses of political liberalism, see Martha Nussbaum, "Perfectionist Liberalism and Political Liberalism," *Philosophy & Public Affairs* 39 (2011): 3–45, and Jonathan Quong, *Liberalism without Perfection* (New York: Oxford University Press, 2011).

35. See Dworkin, *Justice for Hedgehogs*, 196–97, 242.

CHAPTER ONE
THE PRINCIPLE OF PUBLIC RELEVANCE AND DEMOCRATIC PERSUASION

1. It bears emphasizing that, according to value democracy, if a hate group does commit a crime, such as physically abusing minorities, it should be stopped by the coercive power of the state.

2. *NAACP v. Patterson*, 357 U.S. 449 (1958).

3. On the right to marital privacy, see *Griswold v. Connecticut*, 381 U.S. 479 (1965).

4. John Rawls, "Justice as Fairness: Political Not Metaphysical," *Philosophy & Public Affairs* 14 (1985): 223–51.

5. John Rawls, *Political Liberalism, expanded edition* (New York: Columbia University Press, 2005), 8. See also Corey Brettschneider, *Democratic Rights: The Substance of Self-Government* (Princeton, NJ: Princeton University Press, 2007), 37.

6. See Judith N. Shklar, *American Citizenship: The Quest for Inclusion* (Cambridge, MA: Harvard University Press, 1991).

7. *Romer v. Evans*, 517 U.S. 620 (1996), and *Lawrence v. Texas*, 539 U.S. 558 (2003).

8. *Romer v. Evans*, 517 U.S. 620 (1996).

9. However, animus-based *laws* are not protected by rights, and can be overturned by courts or legislatures.

10. John Rawls, *Political Liberalism*, rev. ed. (New York: Columbia University Press, 2005), 315. Like Rawls, I use "autonomy" in the sense of a political value, and not a comprehensive doctrine that applies to all aspects of life. See Rawls, *Political Liberalism*, 13.

11. Robert D. Putnam and David E. Campbell, *American Grace: How Religion Divides and Unites Us* (New York: Simon & Schuster, 2010).

12. Immanuel Kant, "On a Supposed Right to Lie Because of Philanthropic Concerns," in *Grounding for the Metaphysics of Morals: with, On a Supposed Right to Lie Because of Philanthropic Concerns*, trans. James W. Ellington (Indianapolis, IN: Hackett, 1993), 63–68.

13. I argue elsewhere, however, that democratic rights require a decent minimum of welfare provision for all citizens. See Brettschneider, *Democratic Rights*, chap. 6.

14. On this point, see my exchanges with Thomas Christiano in both the *Journal of Politics* 71 (2009), 1593–97, and the *Journal of Ethics and Social Philosophy* (August 2011): 1–9.

15. Stanley Pignal, "Wilders' Impact Felt As Dutch Coalition Sworn In," *Financial Times* (October 13, 2010).

16. See Rawls, *Political Liberalism, rev. ed.*, xxxvii n. 5, xli, 459.

17. There is, of course, an additional empirical question about whether other kinds of inegalitarian beliefs may also contribute to problematic practices. But for the purpose of this argument, I limit myself to a discussion of beliefs that are inegalitarian in the sense of opposing the ideal of free and equal citizenship.

18. Traditional Values Education and Legal Institute, "Homosexuals Recruit Public School Children," *Traditional Values Special Report* 18, no. 11, http://www .jesus-is-savior.com/Evils%20in%20America/Sodomy/homosexuals_recruit _children.pdf.

19. Margaret Bull Kovera and Eugene Borgida, "Social Psychology and Law," in *Handbook of Social Psychology*, Susan T. Fiske, Daniel T. Gilbert, and Gardner Lindzey, eds. (Hoboken, NJ: John Wiley 2010), 1344.

20. Alice H. Eagly and Linda L. Carli, "Women and the Labyrinth of Leadership," *Harvard Business Review* (September 2007) 62–71 at 64.

21. Ibid.

22. Ibid.

23. It might be objected that there are cases when attitudes are disconnected from actions. However, a meta-analysis of eighty-eight psychological studies shows that attitudes often affect behavior. Moreover, this study suggests that even in instances when attitudes did not affect behavior, general social norms do influence behavior. Therefore, the argument from interconnection suggests that democratic persuasion should be concerned, not only with the discriminatory beliefs of citizens, but also the wider norms of the society at large. See Stephen J. Kraus, "Attitudes and the Prediction of Behavior: A Meta-Analysis of the Empirical Literature," *Personality and Social Psychology Bulletin* 21 (1995): 58–75.

24. President William Jefferson Clinton, "Remarks by the President in Apology for Study Done in Tuskegee," The White House, May 16, 1997, http://clinton4 .nara.gov/New/Remarks/Fri/19970516-898.html.

25. Ibid.

26. Ibid.

27. Ibid.

28. Ibid.

29. Mill recognizes the importance of citizens advancing arguments in the hope of reaching the truth. Indeed, he even admits that when "the acts of an individual may be hurtful to others or wanting in due consideration for their welfare, without going to the length of violating any of their constituted rights . . . the offender may be justly punished by opinion, though not by law." See John Stuart Mill, *On Liberty* in *The Collected Works of John Stuart Mill, Volume XVIII – Essays on Politics and Society, Part I*, ed. John M. Robson (Toronto: University of Toronto Press, 1977), 276. However, unlike value democracy, Mill does not develop a duty either to advance specifically public values or a role for the state in promoting these values.

30. See Rawls, *Political Liberalism*, and Rainer Forst, "The Justification of Human Rights and the Basic Right to Justification: A Reflexive Approach." *Ethics* 120 (2010):711–40.

31. I thank Charles Larmore for this formulation.

32. On reasonable disagreement, see Amy Gutmann and Dennis Thompson, *Democracy and Disagreement* (Cambridge, MA: Harvard University Press, 1996).

33. As I noted earlier, this does *not* mean that the state should refrain from disagreement on any issue of controversy. For instance, the state should engage in democratic persuasion to oppose racist views, even if those views are popular. Reasonable disagreement is not defined by the pervasiveness of disagreement, but by whether it is based on respect for free and equal citizenship. Racist views do not qualify as instances of reasonable disagreement, no matter how pervasive they are.

34. I take this idea of institution-independence to follow from the idea of democratic values as procedure independent. See Brettschneider, *Democratic Rights*, and David Estlund, *Democratic Authority: A Philosophical Framework* (Princeton, NJ: Princeton University Press, 2008).

Chapter Two
Publicly Justifiable Privacy and Reflective Revision by Citizens

1. Bruce Owen, "Swastika children made Crown wards," *National Post* (February 12, 2010): A6. For the court case, see *Director of Child and Family Services v. D.M.P. et al.*, 2010 MBQB 32.

2. I develop this claim in greater detail in the next chapter.

3. In an account of political liberal justification, equal citizenship does not mean that persons must be legal citizens of a particular nation. Rather, the term—with its emphasis on self-rule—is meant to convey an entitlement to a certain kind of political status that recognizes persons who are subject to coercive law as equals.

4. Rawls helpfully distinguishes between empirical and normative understandings of political stability. He differentiates between stability as it exists in a *modus vivendi* and "stability for the right reasons." See Rawls, *Political Liberalism*, rev. ed. (New York: Columbia University Press, 2005), 458–59. In contrast to mere empirical stability, stability "for the right reasons" suggests that a regime is not only peaceful, but legitimate. This has an important implication for the fundamental guarantees of any legitimate regime. In particular, rights in a legitimate society will not only help to achieve peace between potentially conflicting factions, but will be defined and defended in a way that is principled in its treatment of all citizens as free and equal. Such a moral commitment to rights, I argue, has implications that reach deep into the so-called private sphere.

5. Rawls, *Political Liberalism*, 13.

6. Ibid.

7. For a good discussion of the relation between the work of Okin and Rawls, see Sarah Song, "Religious Freedom vs. Sex Equality," *Theory and Research in Education* 4 (2006): 23–40.

8. I do not mean to suggest that race-conscious policies such as affirmative action are therefore never justifiable. I do mean, however, that these policies must be justified on the basis of equal citizenship. For instance, two commonly cited justifications for affirmative action policies are remedying past racial injustices and ensuring future diversity. These justifications are potentially consistent with a respect for all citizens as equals.

9. Susan Okin, "Political Liberalism, Justice, and Gender," *Ethics* 105 (October 1994), 23–43, at 28–29.

10. Ibid., at 29.

11. Nonetheless, I believe that Okin's criticism does help to highlight the failure of much liberal theory to see these broad implications of equal citizenship for how we should think about private beliefs and practices.

12. Rawls, *Political Liberalism*, 31.

13. John Rawls, *The Law of Peoples: with "The Idea of Public Reason Revisited"* (Cambridge, MA: Harvard University Press, 1999), 161.

14. I draw here on Charles Larmore's thought that the domain of the political is not a "prepackaged sector of society, inherently distinct from the other areas of social life." Larmore, "The Moral Basis of Political Liberalism," *Journal of Philosophy* 96 (December 1999): 599–625, 607. Rawls' own view on the role public justification within the role of the family is ambiguous. For an elaboration of the ambiguity in Rawls' texts, see Corey Brettschneider, "The Politics of the Personal: A Liberal Approach," *American Political Science Review* 101, no. 1 (February 2007): 19–31.

15. See Leif Wenar, "Political Liberalism: An Internal Critique," *Ethics* 106 (October 1995): 32–62. Arguably, the transformation of citizens' moral identity cannot and will not happen instantly. Indeed, the dialectical nature of this process can best be gleaned from looking at what Rawls himself says about the transformation from a *modus vivendi* to what he calls an "overlapping consensus." In Rawls' view, a society cannot move immediately through this process, but it evolves through several phases before becoming a fully just polity. Just as a society gradually progresses from a *modus vivendi* to a just overlapping consensus, the individual who internalizes the requirements of the overlapping consensus will progress from an uneasy alliance between liberal public belief and private illiberal belief to a more coherent moral identity that fully accepts democratic values.

16. H.L.A. Hart, *Law, Liberty, and Morality* (Stanford, CA: Stanford University Press, 1963), 52. Hart held that while it was an "acceptable," even "necessary" position to hold that *"some* shared morality is essential to the existence of any society." Devlin's view was wrong to hold that "a society is identical with its morality as that is at any given moment of its history, so that a change in its morality is tantamount to the destruction of a society." *Law, Liberty, and Morality*, 51. For another claim about the insularity of culture, particularly religious culture, see Robert M. Cover, "The Supreme Court, 1982 Term Foreword: Nomos and Narrative," *Harvard Law Review* 97 (1983): 4–68. Cover is particularly concerned about the way that legal rules might change and destroy religious communities, such as the Amish.

17. Nancy Rosenblum, *Membership and Morals: The Personal Uses of Pluralism in America* (Princeton, NJ: Princeton University Press, 1998).

18. Carol Pateman, *The Sexual Contract* (Stanford, CA: Stanford University Press, 1988).

19. Catharine MacKinnon, *Only Words* (Cambridge, MA: Harvard University Press, 1993).

20. For instance, Pateman has famously argued against not just the legitimacy of some contracts, but more generally against the very idea of a contract, label-

ing it a liberal device that invokes autonomy and "individuality" to undermine women's equality.

21. Mill distinguishes between reasoning and coercion when he writes that, faced with a person who is harming himself, we may have "good reasons for remonstrating with him, or reasoning with him, or persuading him, or entreating him, but not for compelling him, or visiting him with any evil, in case he do otherwise." Here Mill is drawing a distinction between coercing on the one hand, and reasoning or persuading on the other. See John Stuart Mill, "On Liberty," in *John Stuart Mill: Three Essays*, intro. Richard Wolheim (Oxford: Oxford University Press, 1975), 15.

22. Habermas describes reasoning as being "free of any internal coercion," and as relying instead on the "unforced force of the better argument." See Jürgen Habermas, *Between Facts and Norms: Contributions to a Discourse Theory of Law and Democracy*, trans. William Rehg (Cambridge, MA: MIT Press, 1996), 305–306.

23. As Gerry Cohen points out, "It is seriously unclear which institutions are supposed to qualify as part of the basic structure." G. A. Cohen, *If You're an Egalitarian, How Come You're So Rich?* (Cambridge, MA: Harvard University Press, 2000), 136. On the one hand, Cohen points out that Rawls defines the basic structure as including "major" institutions, such as the family. On the other hand, the basic structure sometimes seems to refer only to coercive state institutions. The family rests in an uncertain place within this second way of defining the basic structure. The state influences the family through divorce and child custody laws, but many of the decisions within families are made without direct government control. Cohen's critique of political conceptions that apply only to coercive institutions certainly resonates with my own emphasis on the relevance of the values of free and equal citizenship to the family and civil society. I also think Cohen is right to identify some confusion in Rawls' definition of the basic structure.

24. "When the political conception meets these conditions and is also complete, we hope the reasonable comprehensive doctrines affirmed by reasonable citizens in society can support it, and that in fact it will have the capacity to shape those doctrines toward itself." Rawls, *Political Liberalism*, 389.

25. Joshua Cohen, "A Matter of Demolition? Susan Okin on Justice and Gender," in Debra Satz and Rob Reich, eds., *Toward a Humanist Justice: The Political Philosophy of Susan Moller Okin* (New York: Oxford University Press, 2009), 41–54.

26. G. A. Cohen, *If You're an Egalitarian, How Come You're So Rich?* 136.

27. Some thinkers go beyond the account I have given of the obligations of citizenship within the family. Adam Swift and Harry Brighouse suggest a wide variety of obligations to society at large that might trump partial obligations to family members, including children. They argue that a wide range of issues of distributive justice apply in the family and that it would be wrong to advantage our own children financially or educationally at the expense of other children. Exceptions exist, they claim, to the degree that conferring advantage is part of the essential bond between parent and child. Reading to our own children as opposed to other children might confer advantage on them, but it is justifiable because of the emotional bond that it builds. I have aimed in this chapter to lay out a series of fundamental requirements of free and equal citizenship and to show their implications

for reflective revision. By contrast, Swift and Brighouse seem concerned with the distinct question of what decisions might make a person fully just. They are therefore invoking a distinct kind of equality from the one that I develop. In particular, they seem to invoke a notion of equality in which any advantage to one child is a potential disadvantage to another. My view differs in that it is not necessarily the case that an advantage to one child will undermine the free and equal citizenship of other children. In that sense, my concern for free and equal citizenship is not zero-sum. See Adam Swift and Harry Brighouse, "Legitimate Parental Partiality," *Philosophy & Public Affairs* 37 (2009): 43–80.

Chapter Three
When the State Speaks, What Should It Say?

1. See Ian Buruma, "Totally Tolerant Up to a Point," *New York Times*, January 29, 2009, p. A29. Interestingly these laws banning hate speech have been passed through the democratic process, despite what Sniderman sees as rising prejudice against Muslims in the Netherlands. See my introduction, note 2.

2. For a discussion of the meaning of these values, see in particular Rawls' discussion of the "liberal principle of legitimacy" in *Political Liberalism*, rev. ed. (New York: Columbia University Press, 2005), 137.

3. Catharine A. MacKinnon, *Only Words* (Cambridge, MA: Harvard University Press, 1993), 71.

4. Democratic persuasion has some affinities with the idea of "soft power" in international relations. Joseph Nye has argued that nations can pursue objectives by promoting non-profit activities and informal civil society ties between states. I make a related case for the state's domestic persuasive powers. But whereas Nye describes soft power in non-moral terms, instrumentally linking it to national objectives, democratic persuasion is a more moralized ideal with distinct limits drawn from democratic values. See Joseph Nye, *Soft Power: The Means to Success in World Politics* (New York: Public Affairs, 2004). For a distinction between persuasion and soft power, see Robert O. Keohane, "Krasner: Subversive Realist," American Political Science Association 2010 Annual Meeting Paper (Washington, DC), http://papers.ssrn.com/sol3/papers.cfm?abstract_id=1643351.

5. *Virginia v. Black*, 538 U.S. 343 (2003).

6. The Court had protected an act of cross-burning as an instance of free expression under the First Amendment in *R.A.V. v. City of St. Paul*. See *R.A.V. v. City of St. Paul*, 505 U.S. 377 (1992).

7. For a criticism of Scalia's *R.A.V.* opinion, see Steven Shiffrin, "Racist Speech, Outsider Jurisprudence, and the Meaning of America," *Cornell Law Review 80 (1994):* 43–103.

8. In Justice O'Connor's words, "As the history of cross burning indicates, a burning cross is not always intended to intimidate. Rather, sometimes the cross burning is a statement of ideology, a symbol of group solidarity." See *Virginia v. Black* 538 U.S. 343 (2003) at 1551. Although the Court's protection of free speech goes beyond viewpoint neutrality to protect content neutrality with a few exceptions, I focus my inquiry here on viewpoint neutrality, the "core" of First Amendment speech protection.

9. *Brandenburg v. Ohio*, 395 U.S. 444 (1969). In this case, the Supreme Court struck down the Ohio Syndicalism Statute on the grounds that it violated First Amendment protections of free speech. The Court ruled that freedom of expression protects viewpoints that advocate violence against particular groups, but it permitted speech to be banned if it incited imminent violence. *Brandenburg* effectively ended the clear and present danger test, and protected a wide variety of viewpoints against coercive bans, even when those viewpoints oppose the values of liberal democracy.

10. *Schenck v. United States*, 249 U.S. 47 (1919). In this case, Justice Holmes announced the "clear and present danger" test in explaining why the distribution of leaflets opposing the draft during World War I was not protected by the First Amendment. The case upheld the conviction of Schenck, the secretary of the Socialist Party of America, under the Espionage Act of 1917. For almost half a century, the clear and present danger test, or versions of it, was used to uphold the criminalization of certain viewpoints that were largely to the left of center, and believed to be at odds with the interests of the United States. My account of value democracy, like the Court's decision in *Brandenburg*, rejects the clear and present danger test.

11. Rawls, *Political Liberalism*, lecture 8, esp. pp. 302, 332, 334–35.

12. Rawls endorses viewpoint neutrality in *Political Liberalism*, p. 336: "So long as the advocacy of revolutionary and even seditious doctrines is fully protected, as it should be, there is no restriction on the content of political speech, but only regulations as to time and place, and the means used to express it." However, the literature on Rawls is divided over whether viewpoint neutrality extends to hate speech, since he does not address the issue explicitly in his work. See Samuel Freeman, *Rawls* (New York: Routledge, 2007), 72.

I acknowledge that the egalitarian foundation for free speech and other rights that I endorse, and that is found in the work of Rawls, Meiklejohn, and Dworkin, was not necessarily the view of many of the Framers of the Constitution, who drafted the First Amendment well before the Fourteenth Amendment guarantee of equal protection. But my concern is to make an argument in political theory, as opposed to one from an originalist perspective.

13. This view of democratic autonomy corresponds with one of Rawls' moral powers, the capacity for a sense of justice.

14. Dworkin, "A New Map of Censorship," *Index on Censorship*, 35 (February 2006): 131.

15. In *Democratic Rights*, I defend the idea that respect for free and equal status requires a respect not only for democratic rights of participation, but also a respect for other rights protections.

16. See John Stuart Mill, *On Liberty* in *The Collected Works of John Stuart Mill, Volume XVIII – Essays on Politics and Society, Part I*, ed. John M. Robson (Toronto: University of Toronto Press, 1977), 252. As Mill writes: "Such being the partial character of prevailing opinions, even when resting on a true foundation, every opinion which embodies somewhat of the portion of truth which the common opinion omits, ought to be considered precious, with whatever amount of error and confusion that truth may be blended."

17. See Shiffrin, "Racist Speech, Outsider Jurisprudence, and the Meaning of America," 43–103.

18. Mill, *On Liberty*, p. 229: "If the opinion is right, they are deprived of the opportunity of exchanging error for truth: if wrong, they lose, what is almost as great a benefit, the clearer perception and livelier impression of truth, produced by its collision with error."

19. Nancy Rosenblum, especially in *Membership and Morals: The Personal Uses of Pluralism in America* (Princeton, NJ: Princeton University Press, 1998).

20. See in particular the discussion of the founding of the Klan in *Virginia v. Black*.

21. Charles Beitz, *Political Equality* (Princeton, NJ: Princeton University Press, 1989), and T. M. Scanlon, "Freedom of Expression and Categories of Expression," *University of Pittsburgh Law Review* 40 (1979): 519–50.

22. Jeremy Waldron, "Dignity and Defamation: The Visibility of Hate," *Harvard Law Review* 123 (May 2010): 1596–1657, and Jeremy Waldron, "Free Speech and the Menace of Hysteria," *New York Review of Books* 55 (May 29, 2008), http://www.nybooks.com/articles/archives/2008/may/29/free-speech-the -menace-of-hysteria/. Waldron's article is a review of Anthony Lewis, *Freedom for the Thought that We Hate* (New York: Basic Books, 2007).

23. Lon L. Fuller, *The Morality of Law* (New Haven, CT: Yale University Press, 1964), 39.

24. Rawls terms the Supreme Court an "exemplar" of public reason. It is clear he means to do so in my first sense, but it is unclear whether he would agree with my extension of this term to my second sense. In my second sense of the Court acting as an exemplar of public reason, it promulgates the reasons for rights.

25. Elizabeth Anderson and Richard Pildes, "Expressive Theories of Law: A General Restatement," University of Pennsylvania Law Review 148 (2000): 1503–75.

26. My focus is on the right to free speech, but a similar analysis might be given of other negative rights, for instance, to privacy.

27. Charles Lawrence, "If He Hollers Let Him Go: Racist Speech on Campus," in *Words That Wound: Critical Race Theory, Assaultive Speech, and the First Amendment*, eds. Mari J. Matsuda Charles R. Lawrence III, Richard Delgado, and Kimberlè Williams Crenshaw (New York: Westview Press, 1993), 53–88.

28. MacKinnon, *Only Words*. See in particular chapter 3, "Equality and Speech."

29. For instance, the Court relied on the Equal Protection Clause to strike down a male single-sex school in *United States v. Virginia*, and to repeal a Colorado plebiscite that denied the equal rights of gay citizens in *Romer v. Evans*, as I discussed in chapter 1. See *United States v. Virginia*, 518 U.S. 515 (1996). The Court ruled that the Virginia Military Institute's admissions policy, which excluded women, violated the Equal Protection Clause of the Fourteenth Amendment.

30. Robert Nozick, "Coercion," in *Socratic Puzzles* (Cambridge, MA: Harvard University Press, 1997), 15–44.

31. I do not, therefore, rely on a moralized conception of coercion. In a moralized conception, an act counts as coercion only if it is not fully justified. For the moralized conception, see Alan Wertheimer, *Coercion* (Princeton, NJ: Princeton University Press, 1990). However, my definition differs from the moralized conception in that it acknowledges that certain acts can be morally justified and yet coercive. For example, imprisoning murderers is coercive in my definition, but

morally justified. My definition uses the non-moral but normative criterion that acts count as coercion when they attempt to deny a choice. For discussion on this point, I thank Eric Beerbohm and Daniel Viehoff.

32. See Sharon R. Krause, *Civil Passions: Moral Sentiment and Democratic Deliberation* (Princeton, NJ: Princeton University Press, 2008).

33. Susan Moller Okin, "Justice and Gender: An Unfinished Debate," *Fordham Law Review* 72 (2004): 1537–67.

34. I am thinking, for instance, of the case of former Klan Grand Wizard David Duke. His National Association for the Advancement of White People masks clearly inegalitarian views in the language of equality. The Association makes the misleading claim on its website that it "campaigns merely for the equal treatment of all races." See Thomas Jackson, "What is Racism," The Official Website of Representative David Duke, PhD, October 23, 2004, http://www. davidduke.com/general/what-is-racism_32.html.

35. Democratic persuasion allows for certain forms of rhetoric to further the democratic values that underlie rights, provided that the rhetoric is truthful and combined with the promulgation of reasons. My aim, however, is not to provide a road map detailing how such rhetoric might be employed, but to justify and describe the state's role as it engages in democratic persuasion. A model for the rhetoric of democratic persuasion might be found in what Simone Chambers and others have called a "deliberative rhetoric," in which effective communication is tied together with public reasoning, as opposed to a "plebiscitary rhetoric," which tries to change people's minds without explaining the underlying reasons or principles. An account of deliberative rhetoric can help to show that democratic persuasion can effectively promote the ideal of free and equal citizenship. See Chambers, "Rhetoric and the Public Sphere: Has Deliberative Democracy Abandoned Mass Democracy?" *Political Theory* 37, no. 3 (2009): 323–50. For a good discussion for the need for liberal theory to engage in issues of persuasion and rhetoric, see Bryan Garsten, *Saving Persuasion: A Defense of Rhetoric and Judgment* (Cambridge, MA: Harvard University Press, 2006), especially the introduction.

36. *Katzenbach v. McClung*, 379 U.S. 294 (1964).

37. *Roberts v. United States Jaycees*, 468 U.S. 609 (1984).

38. *Boy Scouts of America v. Dale*, 530 U.S. 640 (2000).

39. The previous chapter gave arguments based on democratic congruence, stability, interconnection, and public trust for why citizens should adopt the ideal of free and equal citizenship as their own.

40. Rosenblum, especially in *Membership and Morals*, is widely regarded as a preeminent defender of free association rights for clubs that discriminate. She suggests that the incongruity between a club's private inegalitarian values and the public commitment of citizens to equality is defensible because these clubs present utilitarian benefits to society as a whole. They channel what might be the political violence of extremists, for example, into social organizations where they can be better controlled. In addition, they protect the public realm by providing a psychological outlet for inegalitarian beliefs. I believe, however, that these arguments apply against coercive measures to ban hateful or discriminatory groups. They do not apply to democratic persuasion, or the state's criticism of discriminatory groups in its non-coercive, expressive capacity.

41. John Stuart Mill, "On Liberty" in *John Stuart Mill: Three Essays*, Richard Wollheim introduction (Oxford: Oxford University Press, 1975), 15. At times,

however, Mill conflates these duties to persuade with wholesale attacks on religion. In particular, see his comments on Mormonism in the last paragraph of chapter IV of "On Liberty," p. 112. Mill's approach to Mormonism, however, would clearly violate what I have identified as the substance-based limit on democratic persuasion. For a good account of how to reconcile Mill's liberal and feminist commitments, as well as his views on the family, see Hollie Mann and Jeff Spinner-Halev, "John Stuart Mill's Feminism: On Progress, the State, and the Path to Justice," *Polity* 42 (2010): 244–70.

42. See Richard W. Stevenson and Neil A. Lewis, "Democrats Take Aggressive Tack; Alito Is Unfazed," *New York Times*, January 12, 2006, p. A1, and David D. Kirkpatrick, "From Alito's Past, a Window On Conservatives at Princeton," *New York Times*, November 27, 2005, p. A1. The group, Concerned Alumni of Princeton (CAP), claimed at one point to be merely opposed to affirmative action, but news reports and the Senate inquiry challenged this claim, suggesting that the group aggressively opposed the university's decision to recruit and admit women and minorities. For detailed evidence that CAP was committed to a "homogeneous" male and white student body, quoting the group's own magazine, founder, and members, see Jerome Karabel, *The Chosen: the Hidden History of Admission and Exclusion at Harvard, Yale, and Princeton* (New York: Houghton Mifflin, 2005), 471–78. Importantly, Alito distanced himself from the club's views by stressing his lack of involvement and by never defending its positions, at least implicitly repudiating its views.

43. It is important that the inquiry did not concern affirmative action or preferences in college admissions, but the very presence of African Africans at Princeton. The debate about affirmative action lends itself to multiple plausible interpretations of that practice's implications for equal citizenship and thus should not obligate the state to take a particular position on it. However, on any plausible interpretation of equality, African Americans have a place at an elite educational institution, and the state should defend that claim.

44. This raises the issue of public trust, which I discussed in chapter 2.

45. The same kind of reasoning that made it appropriate for the Alito hearing to inquire into his membership in the Princeton club might also have applied to a Senate inquiry into Senator Edward Kennedy's membership in a networking club that excluded women, if Kennedy had not resigned his membership voluntarily. Such clubs arguably reinforce networks of male power, since they exclude women.

46. Sharon R. Krause, *Liberalism with Honor* (Cambridge, MA: Harvard University, 2002), 164.

47. Children can be coerced into attending school and they do not have the same rights as adults. However, this does not imply that children have no rights at all. As I argue later in this section, once they are in school, children should not be coerced into accepting democratic values. Rather, they should be taught a civics curriculum and exposed to the ideal of free and equal citizenship.

48. *Meyer v. Nebraska*, 262 U.S. 390 (1923).

49. *Pierce v. Society of Sisters*, 268 U.S. 510 (1925).

50. *Mozert v. Hawkins County Board of Education*, 827 F. 2d 1058 (1987).

51. *Wisconsin v. Yoder*, 406 U.S. 205 (1972).

52. It might be argued that the case of the public school teacher with hateful views raises an issue concerning the rights of the schoolchildren to receive a non-discriminatory education, as opposed to an issue concerning democratic

persuasion. The problem with a solely rights-based approach, however, is that it does not specify who has the obligation to provide a non-discriminatory education and to promote the underlying value of free and equal citizenship. This duty, for instance, might be fulfilled by citizens or by parents. By contrast, in this chapter, I have argued that the state has a role and a duty in promoting public values. I thank Steve Macedo for discussion of this point.

53. In *Pickering v. Board of Education*, 391 U.S. 563 (1968), the Supreme Court considered the case of a teacher fired for criticizing the spending priorities of a school on the grounds that it undermined the school's interest in efficiency. Such a neutral analysis, however, would be misplaced in the kind of case I have just described. I go on, in the next section, to elaborate on why neutral evaluations of state speech are mistaken.

54. *R. v. Keegstra*, [1990] 3 S.C.R. 697, http://scc.lexum.org/en/1990/1990 scr3-697/1990scr3-697.html.

55. A fundamental Supreme Court case about the rights of students in schools is *Tinker v. Des Moines School District*, 393 U.S. 503 (1969), in which the Court held that students were wrongly sanctioned for wearing black armbands in protest of military involvement in Vietnam.

56. Onell R. Soto, "Judge says ruling ahead in anti-gay T-shirt," *San Diego Union-Tribune*, September 17, 2004, http://www.signonsandiego.com/news/edu cation/20040917-9999-7m17speech.html.

57. The suit was subsequently dismissed on the grounds that the issue had become moot, because the student had since graduated from the high school.

58. While value democracy accepts the need to coercively ensure that children attend school (not necessarily a public one) and are taught a civics curriculum, it rejects using coercion within the school to force the children to accept democratic values.

59. John Locke, *A Letter Concerning Toleration*, ed. James Tully (Indianapolis, IN: Hackett, 1983 [1689]), 27.

60. Citizens are reasonable when they respect the status of other citizens as free and equal. I describe in detail the ideal of free and equal citizenship in chapter 1.

61. I thank Sam Issacharoff for discussion of this point. See his article, Samuel Issacharoff, "Fragile Democracies," *Harvard Law Review* 120 (April 2007): 1406–67.

CHAPTER FOUR
DEMOCRATIC PERSUASION AND STATE SUBSIDY

1. The Bureau of Economic Analysis of the U.S. Department of Commerce estimated the U.S. gross domestic product (GDP) in 2007 to be $14,028.7 billion, and the portion of GDP contributed by "Government consumption expenditures and gross investment" to be $2,674.2 billion. Government spending thus accounted for 19% of U.S. GDP. See U.S. Department of Commerce, Bureau of Economic Analysis, "National Income and Product Accounts Table: Table 1.1.5. Gross Domestic Product," http://www.bea.gov/national/nipaweb/TableView.asp ?SelectedTable=5&ViewSeries=NO&Java=no&Request3Place=N&3Place=N

&FromView=YES&Freq=Year&FirstYear=2006&LastYear=2007&3Place
=N&Update=Update&JavaBox=no#Mid (accessed February 3, 2012).

2. Value democracy does endorse, however, viewpoint neutrality regarding the right of free speech. No citizen's viewpoint should be coercively banned or punished, as I argued in chapter 3. A coercive ban on certain viewpoints would violate the means-based limit on democratic persuasion.

3. There is an exception for churches, but I argue later that the condition of respect for free and equal citizenship should also apply to them, as it does to other non-profits. For example, a church that says that homosexuals deserve to die should not receive the privileges of tax exemption and tax deductibility.

4. See John Rawls, *A Theory of Justice: Revised Edition* (Cambridge, MA: Harvard University Press, 2001), 179, and John Rawls, *Political Liberalism*, rev. ed. (New York: Columbia University Press, 2005), 325–26.

5. Robert Post, "Subsidized Speech," *Yale Law Journal* 106 (1996): 151–95 at 189. See too his "Meiklejohn's Mistake: Individual Autonomy and the Reform of Public Discourse," *University of Colorado Law Review* 64 (1993): 1109–37. Post defends a strong role for non-viewpoint neutral government speech in these two pieces. He is less specific about what particular viewpoint the state should advance or what the state *should* say as opposed to what it *can* say. This might come from a reluctance to elaborate a set of democratic values in the hope that they will emerge from "public discourse." Much of the distinction for Post about when the state can speak in a viewpoint-based way is dependent on whether the state is occupying a public role or trying to influence "private" public discourse. He therefore maintains more of a traditional public/private distinction than I do in this book. On my view, however, the core values of democracy can be defined and some of their implications elaborated even if they are not recognized in public discourse. I take the rejection of the ideal of free and equal citizenship to mean the rejection of the core values of democracy, regardless of the content of public discourse in any given society. For instance, the Hateful Society might reject these democratic values, but it is precisely such a rejection that value democracy hopes to combat.

6. I agree with Lukes that persuasion might be an aspect of power, but this does not mean that it is tantamount to coercion. Not all forms of power are coercive. See Steven Lukes, *Power: A Radical View*, 2d edition (New York: Palgrave Macmillan, 2005).

7. *Rosenberger v. University of Virginia*, 515 U.S. 819 (1995).

8. A related issue is present in the case of *Bob Jones University v. United States*, 461 U.S. 574 (1983). There, the Internal Revenue Service denied 501(c)3 tax status to the university on the grounds that its policy banning interracial dating was at odds with the public purpose of educational institutions. On my view, the IRS made the right decision, given Bob Jones' explicit opposition to rights of interracial marriage. Opposition to rights of interracial marriage constitutes a viewpoint that is at odds with the ideal of equal citizenship.

9. *Christian Legal Society v. Martinez*, 561 U.S. ___ (2010).

10. Christian Legal Society, "Bylaws of Christian Legal Society," October 8, 2008, http://www.clsnet.org/document.doc?id=2.

11. *Hurley v. Irish-American Gay, Lesbian & Bisexual Group of Boston*, 515 U.S. 557 (1995).

12. For discussion of this point, I thank Rick Garnett, Steven Smith, and other participants in the "Matters of Faith" conference, hosted by the University of Alabama Law School.

13. For a defense of the Court's neutralist approach, which prefigures its Hastings opinion, see Eugene Volokh, "Freedom of Expressive Association in Government Subsidies," *Stanford Law Review* 58 (2006): 1919–68. Although I agree with Volokh that Hastings Law School has an entitlement to deny subsidy to a discriminatory student group, I disagree with him and the Court when he contends that Hastings' all-comers policy is viewpoint neutral. On my view, Hastings' policy was not viewpoint neutral. However, I argue that viewpoint neutrality is the wrong standard for determining state subsidies. Instead, the state should use a non-neutral standard, based on respect for free and equal citizenship, in its decisions to grant funds. The state or a public university should not grant funds to a group that is discriminatory or otherwise fails to respect free and equal citizenship.

14. The notion of allowing limits on discriminatory viewpoints in the limited public forum doctrine might not be palatable to some First Amendment purists. However, Steven Shiffrin argues, rightly in my view, that First Amendment law already uses viewpoint discrimination, such as in content-based exceptions. See Steven Shiffrin, "Racist Speech, Outsider Jurisprudence, and the Meaning of America," *Cornell Law Review 80 (1994):* 43–103. For example, the Court already relies on a type of viewpoint discrimination in justifying limits on commercial speech. Shiffrin finds suspicious the Court's insistence on viewpoint neutrality regarding racist speech, such as Scalia's majority opinion in *R.A.V. v. City of St. Paul,* 505 U.S. 377 (1992).

15. *National Endowment for Arts v. Finley,* 524 U.S. 569 (1998).

16. *Rust v. Sullivan,* 500 U.S. 173 (1991).

17. I would like to thank Micah Schwartzman for discussion about the Establishment Clause.

18. *Pleasant Grove City v. Summum,* 555 U.S. 460 (2009).

19. *Pleasant Grove City v. Summum,* 555 U.S. 460 (2009), http://www.supremecourt.gov/opinions/08pdf/07-665.pdf, p. 2.

20. *Rumsfeld v. Forum for Academic and Institutional Rights, Inc.,* 547 U.S. 47 (2006).

21. I am indebted to Guido Calabresi for discussion on this point. The "don't ask, don't tell" rule has been repealed more recently by the Obama Administration.

22. Michael C. Dorf, "Same-Sex Marriage, Second-Class Citizenship, and Law's Social Meanings," *Virginia Law Review* 97 (2011).

23. I thank Mark Tushnet for valuable comments on this issue.

24. Kathleen M. Sullivan, "Unconstitutional Conditions," *Harvard Law Review* 102 (1989): 1413–1506.

25. It is worth bearing in mind that democratic persuasion, with its substance and means-based limits, requires the promotion only of the values of free and equal citizenship. It does not require the state promotion of particular partisan politics or sectarian views.

26. On this point see *Regan v. Taxation with Representation,* 461 U.S. 540 (1983). In that case, the Court upheld the denial of tax-exempt status to a nonprofit engaged in lobbying. In his discussion of tax exemption, Justice Rehnquist

argued: "Both tax exemptions and tax deductibility are a form of subsidy that is administered through the tax system. A tax exemption has much the same effect as a cash grant to the organization of the amount of tax it would have to pay on its income. Deductible contributions are similar to cash grants of the amount of a portion of the individual's contributions. The system Congress has enacted provides this kind of subsidy to nonprofit civic welfare organizations generally, and an additional subsidy to those charitable organizations that do not engage in substantial lobbying. In short, Congress chose not to subsidize lobbying as extensively as it chose to subsidize other activities that nonprofit organizations undertake to promote the public welfare." For an argument favoring a stricter policy in granting non-profit status, see Rob Reich, "Toward a Political Theory of Philanthropy," in *Giving Well: The Ethics of Philanthropy*, Patricia Illingworth, Thomas Pogge, and Leif Wenar, eds. (Oxford: Oxford University Press, 2010).

27. "Developments in the Law: Nonprofit Corporations," *Harvard Law Review* 105 (May 1992): 1578–1699 at 1646.

28. *Bob Jones University v. United States*, 461 U.S. 574. I discuss the case in greater depth in chapter 5 and in my article, "A Transformative Theory of Religious Freedom: Promoting the Reasons for Rights," *Political Theory* 38 (2010) 187–213.

29. The IRS stipulates that one of the necessary conditions for receiving nonprofit status is that the organization cannot be operated for a private benefit or inurement: "A section 501(c)(3) organization must not be organized or operated for the benefit of private interests, such as the creator or the creator's family, shareholders of the organization, other designated individuals, or persons controlled directly or indirectly by such private interests. No part of the net earnings of a section 501(c)(3) organization may inure to the benefit of any private shareholder or individual. A private shareholder or individual is a person having a personal and private interest in the activities of the organization." See Internal Revenue Service, "Inurement/Private Benefit—Charitable Organizations," (February 6, 2012), http://www.irs.gov/charities/charitable/article/0,,id=123297,00.html.

30. It is important to note that this argument for associative rights applies to organizations in civil society which have an expressive purpose, and not to public accommodations or businesses. The state may rightly prohibit, using coercive law, discrimination in public accommodations and businesses.

31. *Boy Scouts of America et al. v. Dale*, 530 U.S. 640 (2000).

32. One strike against New Jersey's public accommodation law was that it was broader than the federal definition. The Court suggested that, while restaurants, taverns, and hotels could be prohibited from discriminating against gays or other patrons on the basis of race or ethnicity, private clubs were different. The Boy Scouts seemed to qualify as a private club, since it met in a variety of places. Since the Boy Scouts did not seem to qualify as a public accommodation in the traditional sense, the Court ruled that the Boy Scouts could not be forced to accept Dale as a member.

33. Andrew Koppelman with Tobias Barrington Wolff, *A Right to Discriminate? How the Case of Boy Scouts of America v. James Dale Warped the Law of Free Association* (New Haven, CT: Yale University Press, 2009).

34. I describe the ideal of free and equal citizenship, and its inconsistency with second-class status for citizens, in chapter 1 of this book.

35. On the Boy Scouts' relegation of gays to second-class status, see Koppelman, *A Right to Discriminate?* 97. See in particular Koppelman's argument that the Boy Scouts' position toward gays is more extreme than the Catholic Church's position.

36. Internal Revenue Service, *Tax Guide for Churches and Religious Organizations* (Internal Revenue Service: Washington, DC), http://www.irs.gov/pub/irs-pdf/p1828.pdf, p. 3.

37. Westboro Baptist Church, "Westboro Baptist Church Home Page," accessed February 3, 2012, http://www.godhatesfags.com/.

38. *Snyder v. Phelps*, 562 U.S. ___ (2011).

39. One complication in this case is that the issue concerned whether tort damages against the Westboro Church was a form of punishment that would restrict its right of free expression. Westboro was being sued for inflicting "emotional distress" on the father of a dead veteran, because the Church had picketed the veteran's funeral. The Court seemed to assume that the damages for this tort constituted a "punishment" or coercive sanction. See the Court's majority opinion, 562 U.S. ___ (2011) at 3. Although I do not wish to take a stand on the general issue of whether tort damages is equivalent to coercion, it does seem that punitive damages does carry with it the assumption that the behavior in question should in fact be banned.

40. Koppelman, *A Right to Discriminate?* 97.

41. Jeff Spinner-Halev raises civil society objection in his article, "A Restrained View of Transformation," *Political Theory* 39 (2011): 777–84. His piece is a response to my earlier article, Corey Brettschneider, "A Transformative Theory of Religious Freedom: Promoting the Reasons for Rights," *Political Theory* 38 (2010): 187–213. I respond to Spinner-Halev in "Free and Equal Citizenship and Non-Profit Status: A Reply to Spinner-Halev," *Political Theory* 39 (2011): 785–92.

42. Stephen Holmes and Cass Sunstein, *The Cost of Rights* (New York: Norton, 1999).

CHAPTER FIVE
RELIGIOUS FREEDOM AND THE REASONS FOR RIGHTS

1. See Michael McConnell, "Free Exercise Revisionism and the *Smith* Decision," *University of Chicago Law Review* 57 (Fall 1990): 1109–53 at 1109. McConnell does not use the term "accommodationist" explicitly, but he is recognized as a leading advocate of that view. Nussbaum also defends a version of McConnell's jurisprudence in her *Liberty of Conscience: In Defense of America's Tradition of Religious Equality* (New York: Basic Books, 2008). The accommodationist approach was employed by the Supreme Court prior to its decision in *Employment Division, Department of Human Resources of Oregon v. Smith*, 494 U.S. 872 (1990).

2. Martha Nussbaum makes the link most explicit in the final chapter of *Liberty of Conscience*. See also John Tomasi, *Liberalism Beyond Justice: Citizens, Society, and the Boundaries of Political Theory* (Princeton, NJ: Princeton University

Press, 2001), and Lucas Swaine, *The Liberal Conscience: Politics and Principle in a World of Religious Pluralism* (New York: Columbia University Press, 2006).

3. See Nancy Rosenblum, *Membership and Morals: The Personal Uses of Pluralism in America* (Princeton, NJ: Princeton University Press, 1998); Nancy Rosenblum, "Okin's Liberal Feminism as a Radical Political Theory," in *Toward a Humanist Justice: The Political Philosophy of Susan Moller Okin*, Debra Satz and Rob Reich, eds. (New York: Oxford University Press, 2008), 15–40. Rosenblum argues against the "logic of congruence," which suggests we should seek to promote liberal values "all the way down" in citizens' personal morality.

4. Nussbaum has provided a book-length defense of the principle of accommodation. This principle suggests that policies that adversely affect religious belief are limits on religious freedom. She defends this principle, however, by reference to a deeper value of equality. By contrast, I am concerned to highlight tensions between a commitment to equal citizenship and the principle of accommodation. At the same time, our projects are united by an attempt to theorize about religious freedom through the lens of political liberalism. See Nussbaum, *Liberty of Conscience*.

5. *Employment Division v. Smith*, 494 U.S. 872 (1990).

6. *Church of Lukumi Babalu Aye v. City of Hialeah*, 508 U.S. 520 (1993).

7. Ibid.

8. Ibid. at 547.

9. *Romer v. Evans*, 517 U.S. 620 (1996).

10. In the previous chapter on freedom of expression, I introduced the two senses in which the Court is an exemplar of public reason. I extend the analysis in this chapter to freedom of religion.

11. I develop this argument at length in my book, *Democratic Rights*.

12. Peter Singer in correspondence suggests the importance of persuasion on behalf of the interests of animals. My argument in this book, however, is limited to defending a conception of "democratic" persuasion. An argument for persuasion on behalf of the interest of animals might be compelling, but it also would likely go beyond the values I have sketched in this book. I leave it to others to pursue such an inquiry.

13. The amount of transformation the *Lukumi* principle requires is an open question. In societies where the views of the councilmen are widely invoked in public deliberation, there could be a fairly robust role for the state in seeking transformation. In societies where the *Lukumi* principle is widely internalized, such a role might be minimal. I have argued elsewhere about why the ideal of public reason should not necessarily be thought of as a minimal principle. See Corey Brettschneider, "The Politics of the Personal: A Liberal Approach," *American Political Science Review* 101, no. 1 (February 2007): 19–31.

14. Both of these limitations help to clarify why the law targeting the Santeria violated the *Lukumi* principle, while a concern to transform illiberal beliefs, such as the councilmen's, is justified by that principle. The law banning animal sacrifice sought to change a Santeria belief that was not at odds with the ideal of free and equal citizenship. Moreover, the councilmen used outright coercion, not persuasion, to challenge this practice. In contrast, the Court's message to the councilmen did address a belief at odds with free and equal citizenship, as was evidenced by

the statements of the proponents of the law quoted above. Moreover, this message was delivered through expressive, not coercive, means.

15. Rawls, *Political Liberalism*, rev. ed. (New York: Columbia University Press, 2005), 192–93.

16. *Lukumi*, at 541, 542. I assume that the *we* here does not refer to official state actors.

17. See *In re Tax Exemption Application of Westboro Baptist Church*, Kansas Court of Appeals, No. 98,443. The court in his case did not address the non-profit status of the church itself, but only whether it could receive a tax deduction for a truck used during protests. The Court of Appeals held, "Although we accept WBC's contention that its picketing activities represent its sincerely held religious beliefs, we determine that its political activities and secular philosophy, which constitute a significant part of its picketing activities, preclude a tax exemption for its 2002 Ford F-150 truck. In short, we determine that the picketing activities in use of the truck do not fit within the exemption for exclusively religious purposes under K.S.A. 79-201."

18. It is possible, moreover, that this belief in saving one's fellow citizens through law was central to the beliefs of these councilmen. In my analysis, therefore, I do not appeal to a claim that these particular religious beliefs are tangential or marginal in the religions that are subject to democratic persuasion.

19. Arguably, Rawls' use of the word *hope*, despite his attempt to hedge here, implies that religious transformation is normatively desirable. See Rawls, *Political Liberalism*, 192. In another part of *Political Liberalism* (p. 64, n. 19), Rawls writes, "That there are doctrines that reject one or more democratic freedoms is itself a permanent fact of life, or seems so. This gives us the practical task of containing them—like war and disease—so that they do not overturn political justice." However, Rawls does not explain how hateful or discriminatory doctrines (religious or non-religious) can be contained. Value democracy, by contrast, offers an account of how democratic persuasion can counter doctrines that are opposed to the freedom and equality of citizens.

20. For some of the best philosophical work on this topic, which takes seriously concerns about equality and autonomy on all sides of this issue, see Cécile Laborde, "State Paternalism and Religious Dress," *International Journal of Constitutional Law* (forthcoming). For related discussion, also see *Critical Republicanism: The Hijab Controversy and Political Philosophy* (Oxford: Oxford University Press, 2008).

21. Susan Okin et al., *Is Multiculturalism Bad for Women?* (Princeton, NJ: Princeton University Press, 1999), 22. Okin certainly did not mean to say that such extinction should be the intention of any liberal regime—merely that it might be the by-product of promoting certain values in the face of cultures that oppose them.

22. I do not mean to imply, in using the term *dialectical*, that religious reasons will have an equally weighted presence in the resulting synthesis. It is open to question whether this dialectic will play out more by having equality clarified by religious views, as in the case of King, or whether it will result in fundamental transformation of religious views.

23. I thank Charles Larmore and Minh Ly for helpful discussion of this point. Rawls gives a Catholic example of how the transformation of religious beliefs can

occur without religious abandonment in *The Law of Peoples*. There he mentions that in Vatican II, the Church "committed itself to the principle of religious freedom as found in constitutional democracy." See Rawls, *The Law of Peoples*: 21–22 n.15. I differ from Rawls, however, in that I argue that this transformation should be pursued through active democratic persuasion, while Rawls "hopes" that it will occur.

24. Amy Gutmann, *Identity in Democracy* (Princeton, NJ: Princeton University Press, 2004), 160.

25. Christopher Eisgruber and Lawrence Sager note that another downside of insisting on the literal and complete separation of church and state is that such a separation forbids the use of persuasive religious reasons in political arguments for policies. A literal interpretation of the "wall of separation," then, might have precluded King's use of Christian arguments for civil rights. See Eisgruber and Sager, *Religious Freedom and the Constitution* (Cambridge, MA: Harvard University Press, 2007), 49–50.

26. Rob Reich, "Book Review: Amy Gutmann, Identity in Democracy," *Theory and Research in Education* 5 (2007): 241–47, at 247.

27. *Mozert v. Hawkins County Board of Education*, 827 F.2d 1058 (6th Cir. 1987).

28. Stephen Macedo, *Diversity and Distrust: Civic Education in a Multicultural Democracy* (Cambridge, MA: Harvard University Press, 2000), 157–63.

29. See Anne Fadiman, *The Spirit Catches You and You Fall Down: A Hmong Child, Her American Doctors, and the Collision of Two Cultures* (New York: Farrar, Straus and Giroux, 1997). The case is also discussed in Gutmann, *Identity in Democracy*, and in Reich's review of Gutmann's book.

30. See Patrick Devlin, *The Enforcement of Morals* (Oxford, UK: Oxford University Press, 1965).

31. *Bob Jones University v. United States*, 461 U.S. 574 (1983).

32. Provision 2 of the policy read: "Students who are members of or affiliated with any group or organization which holds as one of its goals or advocates interracial marriage will be expelled." See *Bob Jones University v. United States*, 461 U.S. 574 at 582.

33. *Loving v. Virginia*, 388 U.S. 1 (1967).

34. Bob Jones University, "Statement about Race at BJU," http://www.bju .edu/welcome/who-we-are/race-statement.php (accessed June 17, 2009). Despite this change, Bob Jones has not applied to reclaim its tax-exempt status.

35. For a worry that decisions like *Bob Jones* might destroy the character of communities like Bob Jones University or the Amish, see Robert M. Cover, "The Supreme Court, 1982 Term Foreword: Nomos and Narrative," *Harvard Law Review* 97 (1983): 4–68. But as I noted before, citing H.L.A. Hart, communities can change without necessarily being destroyed. Hart held that while "*some* shared morality is essential to the existence of any society," it was wrong to hold that "a society is identical with its morality as that is at any given moment of its history, so that a change in its morality is tantamount to the destruction of a society." See H.L.A. Hart, *Law, Liberty, and Morality*, 51.

36. Archon Fung, "Loosening the Constraints on Public Reason" (unpublished). Fung's view differs from my own in that he seeks to make public reason less demanding on religion. Fung bases much of his analysis of the mother's own

views on quotations reported in Stephen Bates, *Battleground: One Mother's Crusade, the Religious Right, and the Struggle for Our Schools* (New York: Poseidon Press, 1993).

37. Another example of the role religious belief can play in educating the wider culture about the requirements of public values can be drawn from an amicus curiae brief filed by the Mennonites in the *Bob Jones* case. Ultimately, the brief suggests that the Court should support the university's free exercise claim. Yet the brief is also clear in its condemnation of the practice of racial discrimination. Indeed, the brief's point is that, overall, there has been more promotion of the values of justice from groups that have been "let alone" by the state than from those that have faced state interference.

The flaw in the brief's argument, however, is that it fails to distinguish between instances when private religious groups promote public values and instances when they undermine them. The Mennonites clearly distinguish, on substantive grounds, the examples they cite from the case of Bob Jones's discriminatory policies. Yet they fail to see that this distinction should be the basis of policy. In this sense, their stance is a static one that takes an excessively monolithic view of religion. State efforts to change specific illiberal religious beliefs need not deprive religion of its power to work for justice and change.

38. For example, consider the acceptance of religious toleration in the Catholic Church that was brought about by the Vatican II conference, partially in response to interaction with wider liberal society. Although some conservative factions within Catholicism have lamented Vatican II's changes, these changes have largely met with approval by both laypeople and clergy within the Catholic faith.

39. *NAACP v. Alabama*, 357 U.S. 449 (1958).

40. See, e.g., *Roberts v. United States Jaycees*, 468 U.S. 609 (1984), in which the Court found that the Jaycees did not have an expressive purpose in excluding women, as opposed to *Boy Scouts of America v. Dale*, 530 U.S. 640 (2000), in which the Court found the Boy Scouts had an expressive purpose in excluding gays. The first question, according to my account, is whether excluding gays went beyond an internal policy and indeed rejected free and equal citizenship. But even if the latter were the case, my means-based limit would suggest that the organization might still have a right to exclude gays. It would be a different matter, in my analysis, whether those groups that received public subsidies could have them revoked. Still another question would be raised if such groups claimed a right to meet in public facilities.

41. One of the only universities that relinquished federal funding rather than comply with such legislation is Hillsdale College, a small, nondenominational liberal arts school in rural Michigan. Hillsdale's administration justifies its decision on the grounds that federal guidelines that require the college to count students by race would violate the college's commitment to nondiscrimination.

42. Originally, the board members of Catholic Charities had agreed that, as a state licensee, Catholic Charities should comply with state policy on the right of gays to adopt. The policy of the lay-dominated board came into conflict with Vatican doctrine, however, which opposes gay adoption. Following the failure of Boston bishops to obtain an exception to the law, the organization stopped facilitating adoptions. For an important discussion of this and related issues, see Martha L. Minow, "Should Religious Groups Ever Be Exempt from Civil Rights Laws?"

Boston College Law Review 48 (September 2007) 781–849. I read Minow's general argument to suggest caution about the state's means of transformation. Even if my account of transformation is correct as a matter of political legitimacy and at the level of principle, I take Minow's account to offer a warning about how imprudent means of transformation might at times backfire.

43. The issue is complicated by the fact that Massachusetts, unlike the large majority of states, requires the use of a state-licensed adoption agency for a child to be legally adopted. If Massachusetts allowed unlicensed adoptions, it could discontinue state funds to Catholic Charities; having discontinued funding, the state would have to allow Catholic Charities to continue operating. The fact that Massachusetts state law combines the licensing and subsidy-provision process makes the question more difficult. Should the state be allowed to forbid Catholic Charities from operating because that operation would automatically entail public funding, or should the state be forced to continue financing an organization that refuses to comply with anti-discrimination laws? In the particular case of Massachusetts, the state's action may well qualify as action in its role as coercer rather than as spender, and as a result, may be illegitimate.

44. Even in the Massachusetts example, the Church remains free to find potential foster families for children. Its lack of a license to facilitate adoption merely forces it to refer such families to other adoption agencies to perform the legal adoption process.

45. There is thus a contrast between my view and those that seek merely to show that a commitment to transformation—for instance, through education—does not entail a limit on rights. My account does not just posit compatibility but argues for a necessary moral connection between the protection of religious freedom and transformation. For a narrow account of compatibility that admits to being open to the charge of ethical liberalism, see Stephen Macedo, "Liberal Civic Education and Religious Fundamentalism: The Case of God v. John Rawls?" *Ethics* 105 (April 1995): 468–96.

CONCLUSION
VALUE DEMOCRACY AT HOME AND ABROAD

1. Tanya Hernandez, "Hate Speech and the Language of Racism in Latin America: A Lens for Reconsidering Global Hate Speech Restrictions and Legislation Models," *University of Pennsylvania Journal of International Law* 32 (2011): 805–41.

2. "President Obama's Press Briefing," *New York Times*, June 23, 2009, http://www.nytimes.com/2009/06/23/us/politics/23text-obama.html.

3. The treaty defines discrimination as "any distinction, exclusion or restriction made on the basis of sex which has the effect or purpose of impairing or nullifying the recognition, enjoyment or exercise by women, irrespective of their marital status, on a basis of equality of men and women, of human rights and fundamental freedoms in the political, economic, social, cultural, civil or any other field." See United Nations, Division for the Advancement of Women, "Convention on the Elimination of All Forms of Discrimination against Women," http://www.un.org/womenwatch/daw/cedaw/cedaw.htm.

4. The United States has signed, but not ratified, the Treaty. See *United Nations Treaty Collection*, "Chapter IV: Human Rights: Convention on the Elimination of All Forms of Discrimination against Women," http://treaties.un.org/Pages/ViewDetails.aspx?src=TREATY&mtdsg_no=IV-8&chapter=4&lang=en.

5. United Nations, Division for the Advancement of Women, "Convention on the Elimination of All Forms of Discrimination against Women," http://www.un.org/womenwatch/daw/cedaw/cedaw.htm.

Bibliography

· · · · · · · · · · · · · · · ·

BOOKS AND ARTICLES

Ackerman, Bruce A. *Social Justice in the Liberal State*. New Haven, CT: Yale University Press, 1980.

Akdeniz, Yaman. *Racism on the Internet*. Strasbourg, France: Council of Europe, 2009.

Alt, James E., Simone Chambers, Geoffrey Garrett, Margaret Levi, and Paula D. McClain, eds. *The Encyclopedia of Political Science*. Washington, DC: CQ Press, 2010.

Anderson, Elizabeth and Richard Pildes. "Expressive Theories of Law: A General Restatement." *University of Pennsylvania Law Review* 148 (2000): 1503–75.

Bates, Stephen. *Battleground: One Mother's Crusade, the Religious Right, and the Struggle for Our Schools*. New York: Poseidon Press, 1993.

Beitz, Charles. *Political Equality*. Princeton, NJ: Princeton University Press, 1989.

Bleich, Erik. *The Freedom to be Racist? How the United States and Europe Struggle to Preserve Freedom and Combat Racism*. Oxford: Oxford University Press, 2011.

Brettschneider, Corey. "Free and Equal Citizenship and Non-Profit Status: A Reply to Spinner-Halev." *Political Theory* 39 (2011): 785–92.

———. "Judicial Review and Democratic Authority: Absolute v. Balancing Conceptions." *Journal of Ethics and Social Philosophy* (August 2011): 1–9.

———. "A Transformative Theory of Religious Freedom: Promoting the Reasons for Rights." *Political Theory* 38 (2010): 187–213.

———. "Tyranny of the Majority." In *The Encyclopedia of Political Science*, James E. Alt, Simone Chambers, Geoffrey Garrett, Margaret Levi, and Paula D. McClain, eds. Washington, DC: CQ Press, 2010.

———. "Review of T. Christiano, The Constitution of Equality: Democratic Authority and Its Limits." *Journal of Politics* 71 (2009): 1593–94.

———. "Response to Christiano." *Journal of Politics* 71 (2009): 1596–97.

———. *Democratic Rights: The Substance of Self-Government*. Princeton, NJ: Princeton University Press, 2007.

———. "The Politics of the Personal: A Liberal Approach." *American Political Science Review* 101, no. 1 (February 2007): 19–31.

Brown, Wendy. *States of Injury: Power and Freedom in Late Modernity*. Princeton, NJ: Princeton University Press, 1995.

Callan, Eamonn. *Creating Citizens: Political Education and Liberal Democracy*. Oxford: Oxford University Press, 1997

CEDAW 29th Session 30 June to 25 July 2003. *Welcome to the United Nations: It's Your World*. June 3, 2010. http://www.un.org/womenwatch/daw/cedaw/text/econvention.htm.

Chambers, Simone. "Rhetoric and the Public Sphere: Has Deliberative Democracy Abandoned Mass Democracy?" *Political Theory* 37, no. 3 (2009): 323–50.

Chambers, Simone, and Jeffrey Kopstein. "Bad Civil Society." *Political Theory* 29, no. 6 (December 2001): 837–65.

Christian Legal Society. "Bylaws of Christian Legal Society" (October 8, 2008), www.clsnet.org/document.doc?id=2.

Christiano, Thomas. "Response to Brettschneider." *Journal of Politics* 71 (2009): 1594–95.

———. "Review of C. Brettschneider, Democratic Rights: The Substance of Self-Government." *Journal of Politics* 71 (2009): 1595–96.

Cohen, G. A. *Rescuing Justice and Equality.* Cambridge, MA: Harvard University Press, 2008.

———. *If You're an Egalitarian, How Come You're So Rich?* Cambridge, MA: Harvard University Press, 2000.

Cohen, Joshua. "A Matter of Demolition? Susan Okin on Justice and Gender." In *Toward a Humanist Justice: The Political Philosophy of Susan Moller Okin.* Debra Satz and Rob Reich, eds. New York: Oxford University Press, 2009.

"Convention on the Elimination of All Forms of Discrimination against Women New York, 18 December 1979." OHCHR Homepage. June 3, 2010. http://www2.ohchr.org/english/law/cedaw.htm.

Cover, Robert M. "The Supreme Court, 1982 Term Foreword: Nomos and Narrative." *Harvard Law Review* 97 (1983): 4–68.

Department of Justice, Canada. Canadian Criminal Code, Section 319 (2). http://laws-lois.justice.gc.ca/eng/acts/C-46/page-148.html.

"Developments in the Law: Nonprofit Corporations." *Harvard Law Review* 105 (May 1992): 1578–1699 at 1646.

Devlin, Patrick. *The Enforcement of Morals.* Oxford: Oxford University Press, 1965.

Dorf, Michael C. "Same-sex Marriage, Second-Class Citizenship, and Law's Social Meanings." *Virginia Law Review* 97 (2011).

Dworkin, Ronald. *Justice for Hedgehogs.* Cambridge, MA: Harvard University Press, 2011.

———. "A New Map of Censorship." *Index on Censorship* 35, no. 1 (2006).

Eagly, Alice H., and Linda L. Carli. "Women and the Labyrinth of Leadership." *Harvard Business Review*, September 2007, 62–71.

Eisgruber, Christopher L., and Lawrence G. Sager. *Religious Freedom and the Constitution.* Cambridge, MA: Harvard University Press, 2007.

Estlund, David M. *Democratic Authority: A Philosophical Framework.* Princeton, NJ: Princeton University Press, 2008.

Fadiman, Anne. *The Spirit Catches You and You Fall Down: A Hmong Child, Her American Doctors, and the Collision of Two Cultures.* New York: Farrar, Straus, and Giroux, 1997.

Forst, Rainer. "The Justification of Human Rights and the Basic Right to Justification: A Reflexive Approach." *Ethics* 120 (2010): 711–40.

Freeman, Samuel. *Rawls.* New York: Routledge, 2007.

Fuller, Lon L. *The Morality of Law.* New Haven, CT: Yale University Press, 1964.

Garsten, Bryan. *Saving Persuasion: A Defense of Rhetoric and Judgment.* Cambridge, MA: Harvard University Press, 2006.

Glendon, Mary Ann. *Rights Talk: The Impoverishment of Political Discourse.* New York: Free Press, 1993.

Greenawalt, Kent. "Free Speech in the United States and Canada." *Law and Contemporary Problems* 55 (1992): 5–33.

Gutmann, Amy. *Identity in Democracy*. Princeton, NJ: Princeton University Press, 2004.

———. *Democratic Education*. Princeton, NJ: Princeton University Press, 1999.

Gutmann, Amy, and Michael Ignatieff. *Human Rights as Politics and Idolatry*. Princeton, NJ: Princeton University Press, 2003.

Gutmann, Amy, and Dennis F. Thompson. *Democracy and Disagreement*. Cambridge, MA: Belknap Press of Harvard University Press, 1996.

Habermas, Jürgen. *Between Facts and Norms: Contributions to a Discourse Theory of Law and Democracy*, trans. William Rehg. Cambridge, MA: MIT Press, 1996.

Hart, H.L.A. *Law, Liberty, and Morality*. Stanford, CA: Stanford University Press, 1963.

Hernandez, Tanya. "Hate Speech and the Language of Racism in Latin America: A Lens for Reconsidering Global Hate Speech Restrictions and Legislation Models." *University of Pennsylvania Journal of International Law* 32 (2011): 805–41.

Holmes, Stephen, and Cass Sunstein. *The Cost of Rights*. New York: Norton, 1999.

Internal Revenue Service. *Tax Guide for Churches and Religious Organizations* (Washington DC: Internal Revenue Service), http://www.irs.gov/pub/irs-pdf/p1828.pdf.

Isaac, Jeffrey C., Robert Rohrschneider, Will Kymlicka, and Jonathan Laurence. "The Challenges of Multiculturalism in Advanced Democracies." *Perspectives on Politics* 6, no. 4 (December 2008): 801–10.

Issacharoff, Samuel. "Fragile Democracies." *Harvard Law Review* 120 (April 2007): 1406–67.

Jackson, Thomas. "What is Racism." The Official Website of Representative David Duke, PhD, October 23, 2004, http:// www.davidduke.com/general/what-is-racism_32.html.

Kant, Immanuel. "On a Supposed Right to Lie Because of Philanthropic Concerns." In *Grounding for the Metaphysics of Morals: With, On a Supposed Right to Lie Because of Philanthropic Concerns*, trans. James W. Ellington. Indianapolis, IN: Hackett, 1993.

Karabel, Jerome. *The Chosen: the Hidden History of Admission and Exclusion at Harvard, Yale, and Princeton*. New York: Houghton Mifflin, 2005.

Keohane, Robert O. "Krasner: Subversive Realist." *American Political Science Association* 2010 Annual Meeting Paper (Washington, DC). http://papers.ssrn.com/sol3/papers.cfm?abstract_id=1643351.

Kirkpatrick, David D. "From Alito's Past, a Window on Conservatives at Princeton." *New York Times*, November 27, 2005: A1.

Koppelman, Andrew, with Tobias Barrington Wolff. *A Right to Discriminate? How the Case of Boy Scouts of America v. James Dale Warped the Law of Free Association*. New Haven, CT: Yale University Press, 2009.

Kovera, Margaret Bull, and Eugene Borgida. "Social Psychology and Law." In *Handbook of Social Psychology*, Susan T. Fiske, Daniel T. Gilbert, and Gardner Lindzey, eds. Hoboken, NJ: John Wiley, 2010, 1344.

Kraus, Stephen J. "Attitudes and the Prediction of Behavior: A Meta-Analysis of the Empirical Literature." *Personality and Social Psychology Bulletin* 21 (1995): 58–75.

Krause, Sharon R. *Civil Passions: Moral Sentiment and Democratic Deliberation.* Princeton, NJ: Princeton University Press, 2008.

———. Liberalism with Honor. Cambridge, MA: Harvard University, 2002.

Laborde, Cécile. "State Paternalism and Religious Dress." *International Journal of Constitutional Law* (forthcoming).

———. *Critical Republicanism: The Hijab Controversy and Political Philosophy.* Oxford: Oxford University Press, 2008.

Larmore, Charles. "The Moral Basis of Political Liberalism." *Journal of Philosophy* 96 (December 1999): 599–625.

Lawrence III, Charles R. "If He Hollers Let Him Go: Racist Speech on Campus." In *Words That Wound: Critical Race Theory, Assaultive Speech, and the First Amendment*, Mari J. Matsuda, Charles R. Lawrence III, Richard Delgado, and Kimberlé Williams Crenshaw, eds. New York: Westview Press, 1993.

Liptak, Adam Liptak. "Hate Speech or Free Speech? What Much of West Bans Is Protected in U.S." *New York Times*, June 11, 2008, http://www.nytimes.com/2008/06/11/world/americas/11iht-hate.4.13645369.html.

Locke, John. *A Letter Concerning Toleration*, ed. James Tully. Indianapolis, IN: Hackett, 1983 [1689].

Loewenstein, Karl. "Militant Democracy and Fundamental Rights, I." *American Political Science Review* 31 (June 1937): 417–32.

———. "Militant Democracy and Fundamental Rights, II." *American Political Science Review* 31 (August 1937): 638–58.

Lukes, Steven. *Power: A Radical View*, 2nd edition. New York: Palgrave Macmillan, 2005.

Macedo, Stephen. *Diversity and Distrust: Civic Education in a Multicultural Democracy.* Cambridge, MA: Harvard University Press, 2000.

———. "Liberal Civic Education and Religious Fundamentalism: The Case of God v. John Rawls?" *Ethics* 105 (April 1995): 468–96.

———. *Liberal Virtues: Citizenship, Virtue, and Community in Liberal Constitutionalism.* Oxford: Oxford University Press, 1990.

MacKinnon, Catharine A. *Only Words.* Cambridge, MA: Harvard University Press, 1993.

Mann, Hollie, and Jeff Spinner-Halev. "John Stuart Mill's Feminism: On Progress, the State, and the Path to Justice." *Polity* 42 (2010): 244–70.

Matsuda, Mari J., and Charles R. Lawrence, III. *Words That Wound: Critical Race Theory, Assaultive Speech, and the First Amendment.* New York: Westview, 1993.

McConnell, Michael. "Free Exercise Revisionism and the *Smith* Decision." *University of Chicago Law Review* 57 (Fall 1990): 1109–53.

Meiklejohn, Alexander. *Free Speech and Its Relation to Self-Government.* Clark, NJ: Lawbook Exchange, 2004.

Mill, John Stuart. *On Liberty* in The Collected Works of John Stuart Mill, Volume XVIII – Essays on Politics and Society, Part I. ed. John M. Robson. Toronto: University of Toronto Press, 1977.

———. *Considerations on Representative Government* in The Collected Works of John Stuart Mill, Volume XIX – Essays on Politics and Society, Part II. ed. John M. Robson. Toronto: University of Toronto Press, 1977.

———. John Stuart Mill: *Three Essays*. Richard Wollheim, introduction. Oxford: Oxford University Press, 1975.

Minow, Martha L. "Should Religious Groups Ever Be Exempt from Civil Rights Laws?" *Boston College Law Review* 48 (September 2007): 781–849.

Nagel, Thomas. *Concealment and Exposure: and Other Essays*. Oxford: Oxford University Press, 2002.

"Neo-Nazi Group Resurfaces, Citing Obama." *New York Times*, (April 26, 2009): A19.

Nozick, Robert. *Socratic Puzzles*. Cambridge, MA: Harvard University Press, 1997.

Nussbaum, Martha. "Perfectionist Liberalism and Political Liberalism," *Philosophy & Public Affairs* 39 (2011): 3–45.

———. *Liberty of Conscience: in Defense of America's Tradition of Religious Equality*. New York: Basic, 2008.

Nye, Joseph. *Soft Power: The Means to Success in World Politics*. New York: Public Affairs, 2004.

Okin, Susan M. "Justice and Gender: An Unfinished Debate." *Fordham Law Review* 72 (2004): 1537–67.

———. "Political Liberalism, Justice, and Gender." *Ethics* 105 (October 1994): 23–43.

Okin, Susan Moller, Joshua Cohen, Matthew Howard, and Martha Craven Nussbaum. *Is Multiculturalism Bad for Women?* Princeton, NJ: Princeton University Press, 1999.

Owen, Bruce. "Swastika children made Crown wards." *National Post* (February 12, 2010): A6.

Pateman, Carole. *The Sexual Contract*. Stanford, CA: Stanford University Press, 1988.

Post, Robert. "Subsidized Speech," *Yale Law Journal* 106 (1996): 151–95.

———. "Meiklejohn's Mistake: Individual Autonomy and the Reform of Public Discourse." *University of Colorado Law Review* 64 (1993): 1109–37.

Putnam, Robert D., and David E. Campbell. *American Grace: How Religion Divides and Unites Us*. New York: Simon & Schuster, 2010.

Quong, John. *Liberalism without Perfection*. Oxford: Oxford University Press, 2011.

Rawls, John. *Political Liberalism*, rev. ed. New York: Columbia University Press, 2005.

———. *A Theory of Justice: Revised Edition*. Cambridge, MA: Belknap Press of Harvard University Press, 2001.

———. The Law of Peoples; With, *The Idea of Public Reason Revisited*. Cambridge, MA: Harvard University Press, 1999.

———. "Justice as Fairness: Political Not Metaphysical." *Philosophy & Public Affairs* 14 (1985): 223–51.

Raz, Joseph. *The Morality of Freedom*. Oxford: Oxford University Press, 1986.

Reich, Rob. "Toward a Political Theory of Philanthropy." In *Giving Well: The Ethics of Philanthropy*. Patricia Illingworth, Thomas Pogge, and Leif Wenar, eds. Oxford: Oxford University Press, 2010.

———. "Book Review: Amy Gutmann, Identity in Democracy." *Theory and Research in Education* 5 (2007): 241–47.

Rosenblum, Nancy L. *Membership and Morals: the Personal Uses of Pluralism in America*. Princeton, NJ: Princeton University Press, 1998.

Rosenblum, Nancy L., and Robert Post. *Civil Society and Government*. Princeton, NJ: Princeton University Press, 2002.

Sandel, Michael J. *Democracy's Discontent: America in Search of a Public Philosophy*. Cambridge, MA: Belknap Press of Harvard University Press, 1996.

———. *Liberalism and the Limits of Justice, second edition*. New York: Cambridge University Press, 1998.

Satz, Debra, and Rob Reich. *Toward a Humanist Justice: The Political Philosophy of Susan Moller Okin*. Oxford: Oxford University Press, 2009.

Scanlon, T. M. "Freedom of Expression and Categories of Expression." *University of Pittsburgh Law Review* 40 (1979): 519–50.

Shiffrin, Steven. "Racist Speech, Outsider Jurisprudence, and the Meaning of America." *Cornell Law Review* 80 (1994): 43–103.

Shklar, Judith N. *American Citizenship: The Quest for Inclusion*. Cambridge, MA: Harvard University Press, 1991.

Sniderman, Paul M. *When Ways of Life Collide: Multiculturalism and Its Discontents in the Netherlands*. Princeton, NJ: Princeton University Press, 2007.

Song, Sarah. "Religious Freedom vs. Sex Equality." *Theory and Research in Education* 4 (2006): 23–40.

Soto, Onell R. "Judge Says Ruling Ahead in Anti-gay T-shirt." *San Diego Union-Tribune*, September 17, 2004. http://www.signonsandiego.com/news/education/20040917-9999-7m17speech.html.

Spinner-Halev, Jeff. "A Restrained View of Transformation." *Political Theory* 39 (2011): 777–84.

"Statement about Race at BJU." Bob Jones University. 17 June 2010. http://www.bju.edu/welcome/who-we-are/race-statement.php.

Stevenson, Richard W., and Neil A. Lewis. "Democrats Take Aggressive Tack; Alito Is Unfazed." *New York Times*, January 12, 2006: A1.

Sullivan, Kathleen. "Unconstitutional Conditions." *Harvard Law Review* 102 (1989): 1413–1506.

Swaine, Lucas. *The Liberal Conscience: Politics and Principle in a World of Religious Pluralism*. New York: Columbia University Press, 2006.

Swift, Adam, and Harry Brighouse. "Legitimate Parental Partiality." *Philosophy & Public Affairs* 37 (2009): 43–80.

Tocqueville, Alexis de, and Arthur Goldhammer. *Democracy in America*. New York: Library of America, 2004.

Tomasi, John. *Liberalism Beyond Justice: Citizens, Society, and the Boundaries of Political Theory*. Princeton, NJ: Princeton University Press, 2001.

U.S. Department of Commerce. Bureau of Economic Analysis. National Income and Product Accounts Table: Table 1.1.5 Gross Domestic Product. 2007.

Volokh, Eugene. "Freedom of Expressive Association in Government Subsidies." *Stanford Law Review* 58 (2006): 1919–68.

Waldron, Jeremy. "Dignity and Defamation: The Visibility of Hate." *Harvard Law Review* 123 (May 2010): 1596–1657.

————. "Free Speech and the Menace of Hysteria." *New York Review of Books* 55, May 29, 2008. http://www.nybooks.com/articles/archives/2008/may/29/free-speech-the-menace-of-hysteria/.

Walzer, Michael. "The Moral Standing of States: A Response to Four Critics." *Philosophy & Public Affairs* 9 (2003): 209–29.

Wenar, Leif. "Property Rights and the Resource Curse." *Philosophy & Public Affairs* 36 (Winter 2008): 2–32.

————. "Political Liberalism: An Internal Critique." *Ethics* 106 (October 1995): 32–62.

Wertheimer, Alan. *Coercion*. Princeton, NJ: Princeton University Press, 1990.

Yudof, Mark G. *When Government Speaks: Politics, Law, and Government Expression in America*. Berkeley: University of California Press, 1983.

LEGAL CASES

Bob Jones University v. United States, 461 U.S. 574 (1983)

Boy Scouts of America v. Dale, 530 U.S. 640 (2000)

Brandenburg v. Ohio, 395 U.S. 444 (1969)

Brown v. Board of Education, 347 U.S. 483 (1954)

Christian Legal Society v. Martinez, 561 U.S. ___ (2010)

Church of the Lukumi Babalu Aye v. City of Hialeah, 508 U.S. 520 (1993)

Director of Child and Family Services v. D.M.P. et al., 2010 MBQB 32

Employment Division, Department of Human Resources of Oregon v. Smith, 494 U.S. 872 (1990)

Griswold v. Connecticut, 381 U.S. 479 (1965)

Hurley v. Irish-American Gay, Lesbian & Bisexual Group of Boston, 515 U.S. 557 (1995)

In re Tax Exemption Application of Westboro Baptist Church, Kansas Court of Appeals, No. 98,443

Jones v. Töben, F.C.A. 1150 (2002)

Katzenbach v. McClung, 379 U.S. 294 (1964)

Lawrence v. Texas, 539 U.S. 558 (2003)

Loving v. Virginia, 388 U.S. 1 (1967)

Meyer v. Nebraska, 262 U.S. 390 (1923)

Mozert v. Hawkins County Board of Education, 827 F.2d 1058 (6th Cir. 1987)

NAACP v. Alabama, 357 U.S. 449 (1958)

NAACP v. Patterson, 357 U.S. 449 (1958)

National Endowment for Arts v. Finley, 524 U.S. 569 (1998)

Pierce v. Society of Sisters, 268 U.S. 510 (1925)

Pickering v. Board of Education, 391 U.S. 563 (1968)

Pleasant Grove City v. Summum, 555 U.S. 460 (2009)

R. v. Keegstra, [1990] 3 S.C.R. 697

R.A.V. v. City of St. Paul, 505 U.S. 377 (1992)

Regan v. Taxation with Representation, 461 U.S. 540 (1983)

Roberts v. United States Jaycees, 468 U.S. 609 (1984)

Romer v. Evans, 517 U.S. 620 (1996)

Rosenberger v. University of Virginia, 515 U.S. 819 (1995)
Rumsfeld v. Forum for Academic and Institutional Rights, Inc., 547 U.S. 47 (2006)
Rust v. Sullivan, 500 U.S. 173 (1991)
Schenck v. United States, 249 U.S. 47 (1919)
Snyder v. Phelps, 562 U.S. ___ (2011)
Tinker v. Des Moines School District, 393 U.S. 503 (1969)
United States v. Virginia, 518 U.S. 515 (1996)
Virginia v. Black, 538 U.S. 343 (2003)
Wisconsin v. Yoder, 406 U.S. 205 (1972)

Index

· · · · · · ·